Baseball c

Baseball on the Brink

The Crisis of 1968

WILLIAM J. RYCZEK

McFarland & Company, Inc., Publishers
Jefferson, North Carolina

Photographs are courtesy National Baseball Hall of Fame.

ISBN (print) 978-1-4766-6848-2 ∞
ISBN (ebook) 978-1-4766-2803-5

LIBRARY OF CONGRESS CATALOGUING DATA ARE AVAILABLE

BRITISH LIBRARY CATALOGUING DATA ARE AVAILABLE

Front cover images © 2017 iStock

Printed in the United States of America

*McFarland & Company, Inc., Publishers
Box 611, Jefferson, North Carolina 28640
www.mcfarlandpub.com*

Acknowledgments

Many people were helpful in the preparation of this book, but the first person I would like to thank is historian, writer, and friend Doron (Duke) Goldman, who read the entire manuscript and made many, many improvements to the text. His suggestions included matters of style, phrasing, fact-checking, and overall approach. I am extremely grateful to him for being honest enough to provide criticism where warranted and encouragement when needed.

In previous books, my thanks included a number of librarians, but as the years go on, more of my research is done online. Thanking Hewlett-Packard for my sturdy desktop or Al Gore for inventing the Internet seems too generic and impersonal, so I will pass in that regard. Libraries still play a role in modern research, and I want to thank Jim Gates and the staff at the Giamatti Research Center at the Baseball Hall of Fame, who are always knowledgeable, helpful, and accommodating.

Once again, my friend Fred Dauch read the entire manuscript and offered a number of helpful suggestions.

Last, and certainly not least, I want to thank my wife Susan. Her deep-seated aversion to clutter notwithstanding, she has made minimal comment on the stacks of notebooks piled around my desk chair like sandbags guarding against The Great Flood. Now that this book is finished, another batch of files will move to the basement, and a mild semblance of order will prevail until the next project takes shape. Thank you for your patience.

Table of Contents

Introduction

In my Introduction to *The Yankees in the Early 1960s*, I noted that I had written far more than was possible to include in an intended single volume history of the Yankees and Mets in the 1960s, and that the final product was enough for almost three books. "My publisher and I," I wrote, "decided to divide the work into one book about the Yankees through 1966 and one on the Mets through 1969, with about 50,000 words left over for an undetermined future project."[1]

This, with further additions and embellishments, is that future project, for during my original research, I became fascinated not just by the story of the Yankees and Mets, but by baseball's crisis of the late 1960s. The game was in decline; many thought it was no longer America's "national pastime," while others believed that by the 1970s baseball would no longer be a major sport. There were numerous problems, and they began at the top. In 1965, in their quest to find a compliant commissioner, the owners had chosen an inept one. While America experienced a decade marked by violence, divisiveness, and rapid change, baseball seemed mired in the 1950s, and William Eckert was not the man to move it forward. He stood by and watched while the American and National Leagues bickered. They all watched as attendance stagnated. They stood by while the labor situation deteriorated and while professional football gained in popularity.

In addition to all of its problems off the field, baseball faced a crisis on the diamond, where pitching had become dominant, resulting in a succession of dull, low-scoring games. This book summarizes the 1968 season, which saw offense become an almost lost art, while pitching marks that had stood for decades were shattered one after the other. The American League had just one .300 hitter, Carl Yastrzemski, who closed with a rush to poke his nose over the magic number after hitting just .270 by mid–August, sparing his league an ignominious fate that had never occurred in the history of major league baseball.

1

In order to boost attendance, baseball shifted franchises, built attractive new stadiums and, in 1969, added four new teams. The expansion was nearly bungled, as two of the new additions, Seattle and San Diego, drew poorly during their first year while a third, Montreal, was selected without sufficient due diligence and nearly failed to leave the starting gate.

Youth was rebellious during the 1960s, battling with the "establishment" and protesting the war in Vietnam. Baseball players were young, and while most were not political radicals, large numbers of them were eligible for the military draft. Very few went to Vietnam, but many served in reserve units and had their seasons disrupted by military obligations.

Baseball sought new heroes to replace aging stars like Mickey Mantle and Willie Mays, but it was a non-conformist age, and the sport needed a different kind of hero to catch the fancy of young fans. Jim Bouton's groundbreaking 1970 book *Ball Four* scared the owners, who thought that Bouton had damaged the game's image, failing to understand that it appealed to people who had not been fans of their staid old game but might follow one more in step with the times. They didn't realize that neither Bouton nor Marvin Miller, the aggressive head of the Players Association, could destroy the essence of a game that had captured the American imagination for more than a century. They simply made it different and, in many ways, more appealing.

Somehow, baseball survived. The owners rid themselves of their bumbling commissioner and hired Bowie Kuhn, who, despite the criticism he drew during his lengthy tenure, was clearly an improvement. Despite its problems, baseball not only survived; it prospered. Helped along by a couple of rule changes, batters regained their ability to hit and the game on the field became more appealing. In 1969, the New York Mets won the World Series, a seemingly miraculous achievement that enraptured America's largest city.

Baseball was on the brink in 1968, seemingly ready to be toppled by football, but nearly 50 years later, attendance is at record levels and franchises sell for astronomical amounts. The sport pulled itself, or was pulled in spite of itself, back from the brink, and moved forward into the 1970s. This is the tale of the sorry state of baseball in the late 1960s, its challenges—many self-inflicted—the way the game was played, and how it crawled back from the abyss.

1

Gentlemen, Please Be Seated, We Have Some Other Business to Discuss

Baseball's winter meetings had followed the same script for decades. General managers met in hotel rooms, restaurants, and lobbies, talked about trading players, and occasionally consummated a blockbuster deal. Job-seekers roamed the corridors, hoping to make connections. Each league's owners met among themselves and then got together to announce that nothing would be done because the two leagues couldn't agree on anything. Meanwhile, reporters swarmed everywhere, following up on rumors and looking for scoops about potential trades. It was all harmless fun and generated good mid-winter publicity for baseball.

The meetings that took place in San Francisco during the first week of December 1968 seemed no different from any others until suddenly, on the final day of the session, Baltimore Orioles owner Jerry Hoffberger launched a revolution that led to the ouster of Commissioner William Eckert. Hoffberger, 49, was a dynamic man, not exactly self-made, but he had taken a moderately successful family business and turned it into one of the best in its field. After serving in World War II, Hoffberger, then in his 20s, took over the National Brewing Company from his father and grew it almost tenfold, increasing sales from 230,000 barrels in 1946 to more than two million in 1966. In 1953, the company became a major sponsor of the Washington Senators, and Hoffberger found that he liked associating with baseball people. In 1965 he purchased 40 percent of the Orioles, which gave him effective control of the club.

Hoffberger became influential in American League circles and a leader of a group of owners who were known as the "Young Turks" or "Young Lords," men in their 40s and 50s who were relatively new to baseball. For years, most owners of baseball teams were men like the Griffiths in Washington, Charles

Comiskey in Chicago, Connie Mack in Philadelphia, and Bill Veeck in St. Louis and Chicago. These men had either played baseball or grown up in the game. The Young Turks made their money in other businesses and bought baseball teams as toys. They were used to getting their own way and were not happy when someone tried to tell them how to play with their toy.

In San Francisco, Hoffberger gathered the Turks together to discuss the future of baseball. There was a great deal of criticism of the commissioner, and on the evening before the final combined meeting of the two leagues, a number of executives met in Pirates owner John Galbreath's room and decided that Eckert had to go. Hoffberger was chosen to orchestrate the commissioner's dismissal.

The next day, the commissioner, as uninspiring as ever, conducted a lackluster session. When the meeting ended, he left the room to meet with the press and give them a report of what had taken place, news that would very shortly become irrelevant. As the others also started to leave the room, Hoffberger stood up and said, "Gentlemen, please be seated. We have some other business to discuss. Everyone but the owners should leave the room."[1]

Hoffberger summarized the prior evening's discussion and asked for a vote to remove Eckert. It was done quickly, and 22 of the 24 owners supported Hoffberger. Only Calvin Griffith of Minnesota stood by Eckert. The new Seattle owners said they didn't know enough about the situation and abstained.

In the midst of his press conference, Eckert received a message that he was wanted by the owners. It was typical of baseball's structure that the commissioner, who was nominally in charge, would be summoned by those of whom he was in charge. Eckert was brought into a meeting with Hoffberger, Bob Reynolds of the Angels, Galbreath, Walter O'Malley of the Dodgers, and Gabe Paul of the Indians. The latter three were not part of Hoffberger's clique; they were Old Turks who'd become fed up with Eckert's inertia. Paul, on one occasion, had said to Eckert in frustration, "Do something. Fine me."[2]

The owners did not have the right to fire Eckert, who had four years remaining on his contract. All they could do was offer him the choice of resigning with a full settlement or presiding over a group of men who almost unanimously wanted him gone. Eckert decided to leave, and was told to go back downstairs and announce his resignation to the press.

Eckert's tenure had been an embarrassment, and his dismissal was a fiasco. The commissioner was not good with impromptu remarks, preferring to rely upon index cards. He didn't have any index cards containing notes for a resignation speech, and he was lost. Eckert took the podium, began awkwardly, and hesitated. He was quickly whisked away and Francis Dale, president of the Reds, strode to the podium to announce that Eckert had offered his resignation and that the owners had accepted.

The timing of Eckert's departure, and the manner in which it was

Commissioner William Eckert appears stunned, while his predecessor Ford C. Frick seems to be pushing the media away. Eckert, probably the worst commissioner of all time, was ousted in December 1968.

orchestrated, came as a shock. There were few people, however, who disagreed with the notion that William Eckert was the wrong man for the job of baseball commissioner. "You can't blame Eckert," said longtime baseball executive Frank Lane. "He tried hard but he is involved in a game he doesn't know a damn thing about. If you sent a watch to a lumber yard for repairs and it still didn't work you could find one of the biggest reasons why just by looking in the mirror."[3]

Eckert's abrupt exit was less shocking than his selection three years earlier. When Ford Frick announced that he would retire as commissioner at the end of 1965, a number of prominent Americans, including Supreme Court Justice and former football star Byron "Whizzer" White, General Curtis LeMay, who ran as George Wallace's vice presidential candidate in 1968 ("Bombs Away with Curtis LeMay"), and New York Mayor Robert Wagner were mentioned as possible successors. Baseball's first and most powerful commissioner, Judge Kenesaw Mountain Landis, had been an outsider, as had his successor, Happy Chandler. Frick, who'd previously served as National League President, had been the first inside man ever selected for baseball's top job.

On November 17, 1965, the owners announced they had unanimously

selected 56-year-old retired Air Force General William D. "Spike" Eckert as
the fourth commissioner of baseball. Eckert, a compact, 5'8", 160-pounder,
was a graduate of the West Point Class of 1930, where he established a knack
for mediocrity by graduating 128th in a class of 240. "A less flamboyant man
you could hardly imagine," recalled a classmate. "He was very quiet, dignified
and orderly. A man of moderation."[4]

Eckert earned a Master's degree in Business Administration from Harvard in 1940 and served in a number of Air Force posts during the Second
World War, including commander of the 452nd Bomb Group in Europe. For
the most part, however, Eckert handled logistics and supply. After suffering
a heart attack in 1961, he retired from the service as a three-star general and
entered the business world.

No one seemed to know why Eckert had been selected, and he was not
sure how his name had been included among the initial 150 candidates. The
general had never been mentioned among the front-runners, and reaction
to the announcement of his selection was one of surprise. "Who's he?" asked
Willie Mays. When told who Eckert was, Willie replied, "I'll be darned. They
get all kinds of guys."[5]

Eckert was forever damned by Larry Fox of the *New York World-
Telegram,* who uttered the memorable phrase, "Good God, they've elected
the Unknown Soldier."[6] The new commissioner was indeed an unlikely
choice. "He does not seem," wrote veteran columnist Arthur Daley, "to have
the dynamism of Judge Kenesaw Mountain Landis, the effusiveness of Albert
Benjamin [Happy] Chandler or the warmth of Frick."[7]

Amazingly, the owners never interviewed Eckert. The primary reason
for his selection was his experience in management and administration and
his contacts in Washington. The business of baseball had become increasingly
complex, with television contracts, pensions, and franchise shifts. It seemed
there was more business than baseball, and if Eckert could move planes,
ammunition, and flight crews, he could probably bring coherent structure to
the arcane world of baseball. Although he knew virtually nothing of the sport,
in the business world of the mid-'60s there was a strong belief that any activity
could be analyzed by dispassionate experts and structured to create efficiency.
While Eckert was administering the sport, the owners could go about their
business as usual and, perhaps most important, move their teams whenever
they pleased, like farmers who deplete the soil in one location and leave for
a more fertile field.

What baseball needed in 1965, however, was a marketing and public
relations man, not a logistics and supply expert, for it was a sport in crisis,
its long-time supremacy challenged by professional football and other sports.
Eckert was no marketer. He spoke mechanically of his duty to serve his three
constituencies: the fans, the players, and the owners. The sticky part of his

mission was, of course, that the agendas of the three parties were frequently in conflict, and Eckert had neither the power base nor the personal charisma to reconcile them. Further, he was employed by the owners, who had certain ideas about the pecking order of the three constituencies.

The general quickly discovered that baseball was nothing like the Air Force. In the military, the general gave orders and the colonels obeyed. In baseball, it was the colonels, the 20 owners, who gave the orders, while the general pretended he was in charge. "I've got everything I own invested in this business," said Walter O'Malley in 1960. "We pay [Ford Frick] a salary of $65,000 a year. Why should Frick tell us what we can do?"[8]

Eckert was stiff in public, rarely smiled, and spoke mostly in clichés and platitudes, usually delivered from cue cards provided by his assistant, Joe Reichler. He was not quick with a joke and did not make conversation easily. His emotions, *Sports Illustrated* noted, "ran the gamut from stoicism to constraint."[9] Frick had not been possessed of a dazzling personality, but at least he was affable. And he was a baseball man. Although Eckert played baseball in high school, he rarely attended or even saw many games. "No stretch of the imagination," said *SI*, "would allow you to conclude that William Eckert knows baseball."[10]

Eckert tried. He read the rulebook, tried to familiarize himself with the game, and read one baseball book after another. He made public appearances. In 1966, his first year as commissioner, he went to spring training and had his picture taken posing stiffly with a group of Florida beauty queens, holding a wicker basket filled with oranges as if it were a canister of grenades. He toured the training sites and spoke to the players, who listened politely.

Eckert's first public appearance was a fiasco. Speaking to a group of writers and baseball people at a luncheon shortly after he'd been named commissioner, Eckert pulled his ever-present index cards[11] from his pocket and proceeded to speak glowingly of the airline industry and the great technical advances in aviation. He was scheduled to deliver a speech at a United Airlines cocktail party that evening and had pulled the wrong set of cards from his pocket.[12]

The new commissioner was an easy target for reporters. "The press was unkind but not unfair to him," wrote his successor, Bowie Kuhn. "The press cannot necessarily break a commissioner, but it can play a key role in breaking him. It did in Spike's case."[13] Frick had been a journalist, knew the business, and knew the men who covered baseball. Eckert did not. Once, three months after the *New York World Journal Tribune* folded, he encountered one of its unemployed former writers and commended him on the great piece he'd produced that day. "You've really been writing some fine stuff lately," Eckert said.[14]

"Every time I'd see the commissioner," wrote Detroit columnist Joe Falls, "either wandering through the lobbies at the baseball conventions, a confused man, a faceless man, or see him sitting in his private box at one of the World Series games, sitting there stone-faced and serious, I'd always think of Winston Churchill's old line: 'An empty cab drove up and Clement Atlee got out.'" Falls recounted the story of Eckert posing for pictures at the 1967 World Series. As the photographer was about to shoot, one of Eckert's assistants leaned over and said, "Smile."[15] The commissioner smiled. If only it were so easy to have an assistant lean over and say, "Get the American and National Leagues to work together, make the game of baseball more exciting, and bring it into the 20th century."

Knowing of Eckert's shortcomings, the owners assigned veteran baseball man Joe Reichler to accompany him wherever he went and coach him on the duties of the commissioner. Reichler was as gregarious as Eckert was reticent and had great rapport with sportswriters. "I will be surprised," he told them, "if this man does not become an excellent commissioner." He said Eckert was the kind of man who "grows on you."[16]

Eckert did not grow on too many people during the next three years, and as the public image of baseball continued to suffer, the owners grew weary of him. They couldn't profess to be surprised, for Eckert delivered exactly what he appeared capable of providing when he was hired. In three years under the logistics and supply expert, the major leagues never ran out of baseballs—or bats. Eventually, however, the owners ran out of patience. They had wanted someone who wouldn't cramp their individual styles, but they also wanted someone to save them from themselves and each other. Eckert was not the cause of baseball's problems, but he was not the man to solve them.

Eckert's successor would face a very difficult task, for baseball was on the brink in 1968. It was on the brink of being eclipsed by professional football—many thought football was already America's favorite sport—and it was on the brink of becoming irrelevant, for it seemed to have lost the pulse of America. The United States was a violent country in 1968, deeply divided by race and the Vietnam War, while Eckert, commander of a World War II bomber group, led baseball. Baseball was two wars and a generation behind.

American society was being redefined, and the change was reflected in baseball. Two decades after the arrival of Jackie Robinson, major league rosters had an increasing numbers of blacks and Latinos. And the white players weren't like their counterparts of the 1950s. American youth was in a rebellious mood, and most ballplayers were young men in their twenties. Managers worried about long sideburns, probably should have been concerned about drug use, and found their authority questioned more than ever before.

The players' newly-discovered assertiveness was due in large part to the arrival of Marvin Miller in 1966. Before Miller became Executive Director of the Major League Baseball Players' Association, baseball's owners had successfully thwarted every effort to form a strong union. There weren't a lot of major league jobs, and most players were loath to risk one by antagonizing their employers. Miller had tread lightly in his first couple of years on the job, but he was a formidable personality and the owners were afraid of him.

Even the umpires were restive, looking for a bigger piece of what, thanks to television revenue, appeared to be a growing pie. In mid–September 1968, umpires Al Salerno and Bill Valentine were fired, allegedly for attempting to unionize American League arbiters. Rather than frighten the remaining umpires, as AL president Joe Cronin intended, the dismissals served as a rallying cry, turning Salerno and Valentine into the Sacco and Vanzetti of baseball.

The new commissioner would also be faced with the task of integrating four new franchises into the major leagues, for baseball had just expanded and for the first time would have a team outside of the United States. Nineteen-sixty-nine would also be the first year in which each league was divided into two divisions, with the division winners meeting in a League Championship Series to determine which would go to the World Series.

More pennant races would seemingly generate greater fan interest, but many baseball men worried that, in a five-game playoff, an inferior team could get to the World Series with a couple of lucky breaks. But making certain that the two best teams reached the World Series was not necessarily in the best economic interest of the sport. Few claim that the NCAA basketball tournament is the best way to determine the top team in the country. A decent team can get hot or lucky and sweep through the tournament, which purists may view as unfair. But if the goal is to create excitement and revenue, few sporting events capture the interest of America like the NCAA tournament.

Baseball had developed a greater symbiosis with television, which would eventually dictate the schedule. Most television viewers prefer a 30-day sprint to a six-month, 162-game marathon that unfolds at a snail's pace. Audiences want the dazzle and tempo of "American Idol" rather than the gradual unfolding of "Masterpiece Theater." The possibility that an underdog can catch fire creates the excitement needed to attract casual fans and boost ratings. With the merger of the National and American Football leagues slated for 1970, pro football was again ahead of baseball, with a multi-tiered playoff system and a wild-card team.

Eckert's successor would also have to address a decline in offense that had made the game tedious and boring. The 1968 season saw a continuance of the downward trend in offense that began in 1963. Eighty-two games ended in a score of 1–0, including one that lasted 24 innings. Fittingly, the All-Star Game was a 1–0 affair in which the two teams combined for just eight hits and the only run scored on a double play. The Cardinals' Bob Gibson threw

13 shutouts and ended the year with a microscopic 1.12 ERA. Gibson and Detroit's Denny McLain, who won 31 games, won the MVP awards in their respective leagues. The Dodgers' Don Drysdale established a record consecutive scoreless innings pitched streak. Pitching was so dominant that only one hitter in the American League and just five in the National topped the .300 mark. The American League batting average was a dismal .230, and the National League wasn't much better at .243.

Nearly every American institution was impacted by the dramatic social events of 1968, and baseball had not responded well. In the days following the assassination of Robert Kennedy, the weak, ineffective leadership of major league baseball was pitilessly exposed, and the sport was embarrassed by its inability to orchestrate a coherent tribute to the fallen senator.

Baseball reached a crossroads in 1968, forced to choose between breaking with decades of revered tradition to move into the modern era, or foundering its way into the 1970s in the wake of professional football. By the 1960s, most fans experienced sports through television, and football was much better adapted to the visual medium than the spacious, slower-moving game of baseball.

"Baseball is a game," said ABC's Roone Arledge, "that was designed to be played on a Sunday afternoon at Wrigley Field in the 1920s, not on a 21-inch screen. It is a game of sporadic action interspersed with long lulls."[17] "It's really becoming clear," said Robert Thompson of Syracuse University, "that baseball may be America's pastime, but football is television's sport."[18]

America was changing, and if baseball was going to be an integral part of the new America, it must change as well. But the national pastime was not good at evolving and adapting. It was blessed but also burdened by a history that other sports like football and basketball did not have. Baseball had a dull, unimaginative commissioner, while professional football was governed by Pete Rozelle, perhaps the best league executive in the history of professional sports. Baseball had long been woven into the fabric of American society, but by the end of the 1960s, the fabric was torn and society was moving in new directions. Would baseball be able to react and keep pace?

2

Baseball Is Essentially a Nonviolent Sport in a Violent Time

Whenever baseball defended the sanctity of the reserve clause, one of its principal arguments was that without it, the wealthiest teams would sign all the best players and destroy baseball's competitive balance. Yet, from 1921 through 1964, during the heyday of the reserve clause, the Yankees dominated the American League, and at various times the National League was under the dominion of the Cardinals, Dodgers, or Giants. Other than occasional flashes of glory, the Senators, Athletics, Cubs, Phillies, and St. Louis Browns spent the majority of their time in the second division. The Cubs had money, but they couldn't use it to hire the star players who might help boost them out of the basement. All they could do was sign teenage prospects and attempt the difficult proposition of trading players from their second division teams for better talent. Rapid upward mobility was rare, as building a winner from scratch took time. Teams embarked on five-year plans, but generally at the end of five years there was no pennant.

By the early 1960s, many baseball men began to worry that the Yankees' stranglehold on the American League pennant was bad for baseball. In 1963, William Leggett wrote an article in *Sports Illustrated* called *A Success Is Killing the American League.*[1] Teams could only draw well, Leggett pointed out, when they played the Yankees, citing numerous crowds of less than 5,000 for games between other teams. The televised *Game of the Week* nearly always featured the Yankees. It seemed as though the New York dynasty was nearly impregnable, for despite being without injured stars Mickey Mantle and Roger Maris that summer, the Yankees had made a shambles of the pennant race.

Perhaps Leggett was needlessly alarmed, for baseball had reached some of its greatest heights, in the 1920s and the years after World War II, during periods of Yankees dominance. In any event, the question of whether the situation was good for baseball became academic in 1965 when the Yankees collapsed, suddenly and without warning.

Before the season, AL President Joe Cronin predicted, "There is one thing I guarantee. The Yankees will not run away with the race in 1965. There is no possibility whatsoever of them running away with it."[2] Cronin was never more prescient. The Yankees finished sixth in 1965 and last the following year, and no one knew why. Later some said the amateur free agent draft leveled the playing field, but the draft wasn't instituted until 1965, and its effects would not be felt for several years.

Some said the Yankees stars all got old at once and the farm system failed to produce replacements, but the Yankees' roster of the mid–'60s included talented youngsters like Jim Bouton, Al Downing, Tom Tresh, Mel Stottlemyre, and Joe Pepitone, all products of the farm system, and young veterans like Bobby Richardson, Tony Kubek, and Clete Boyer.

Whatever the reason, the Yankees' collapse gave other American League teams a chance to win the pennant. But for the first two years of the Yankees' eclipse, the pennant races were duller than they'd been when the Yankees were winning. The Twins won by seven games in 1965 and the Orioles by nine the next year.

While American League seasons ended anti-climactically, the National League had one exciting race after another. The 1962 Giants beat the Dodgers in a playoff, the Cardinals took a three-team race on the final day of the 1964 season, and the Dodgers nosed out the Giants on the final weekend in both 1965 and 1966.

In 1967, the tables were turned, as the Cardinals won a dreary NL race while the American League had one of its most exciting pennant battles in years. Rookie manager Dick Williams led the Red Sox from ninth place to first in a wild, four-team scramble that wasn't decided until the final Sunday evening of the season. The Red Sox story was great for baseball, and for the first time in many years gave a town crazy about its team something to cheer about. They rooted passionately for the Sox and their star, outfielder Carl Yastrzemski, the AL MVP and Triple Crown winner. During the stretch run, it seemed as though every time Boston needed a key hit, Yaz was at the plate, and he almost always delivered.

Despite the Red Sox's thrilling win and an exciting seven-game World Series, attendance was down from 1966. There was no way to guarantee an exciting finish, and baseball executives couldn't help but wonder what attendance would be if both leagues had uncompetitive pennant races.

The most troubling problem with baseball of the mid–1960s was an imbalance created by a persistent decline in offensive production that had been creeping up for several years. In 1961, when the American League expanded, and the following year, when the National League followed suit, there had been some impressive offensive performances. Maris and Mantle led the way in 1961, and in 1962 Tommy Davis of the Dodgers led the National League with a .346 mark and drove in 153 runs. Three other National Leaguers drove in more than 125 runs. To help baseball's beleaguered pitchers, the strike zone was enlarged in 1963, and averages dropped. The National League staged a brief recovery, but in the American, the league average exhibited a continual decline, as shown below:

	American League	*National League*
1961	.256	.262
1962	.255	.261
1963	.247	.245
1964	.247	.254
1965	.242	.249
1966	.240	.256
1967	.236	.249

As a result of the diminishing averages, the number of runs scored in the American League declined from 7,342 in 1961 to 5,992 in 1967. In 1961, American Leaguers, led by the Yankees with a record 240, hit 1,534 home runs. In 1967, they hit just 1,197, a 22 percent decline. There were more runs scored per game in 1915 than there were in 1967. In the Deadball Era, teams made up for a lack of power with speed, but American League teams weren't running any better than they were hitting. The Athletics, with Bert Campaneris, and the White Sox, once again in a "go-go" mode, paced the league in 1967 with 132 and 124 steals, respectively, but the Red Sox were a distant third with 68, and were caught 59 times.

Individual statistics were equally unimpressive. Yastrzemski had a phenomenal year at the bat while leading Boston to the 1967 pennant, but he was one of only four .300 hitters in the league. That was an improvement from 1966, when only two AL batters, Frank Robinson and Tony Oliva, cracked the .300 barrier and Harmon Killebrew was the league's fifth-leading hitter at 281.

For lovers of tight pitching duels, it was a good time to be a baseball fan. American League pitchers posted a composite 3.23 ERA in 1967, while their NL counterparts weren't far behind at 3.38. Unfortunately, and much to the dismay of baseball "purists," fans stubbornly preferred the home run and higher-scoring game to a string of 3–1 contests. Most fans enjoy a well-pitched shutout from time to time, but when it becomes commonplace, it becomes boring. If fans liked low-scoring games, they would flock to fast-pitch softball, where making contact with the ball is a triumph.

The men who ran professional football understood that fans liked offense. Back in the 1930s, football games were low-scoring, defensive battles, and the popularity of the pro game reached its nadir. The NFL amended its rules to encourage passing and scoring, and attendance increased. Baseball, which discovered offense and Babe Ruth in the 1920s and featured prodigious offense in the 1930s, had moved in the opposite direction.

Admirers of any sport, art, or craft are most impressed by what is rare and seemingly more difficult to achieve. When baseball began and fielders were bare-handed, good fielding was valued over batting because catching a ball without a glove and executing a play in the field were not easy tasks. As the use of gloves became prevalent and error totals declined, fielding became more routine and thus less exciting. Low-scoring games, the standard of excellence in the 1870s, became tedious by the 1960s, and there were far too many of them.

In 1961, there were 100 shutouts pitched in the American League; six years later, the total increased to 153. One of the shortcomings of defensive baseball is that the opportunity for a late-inning rally is diminished, and a 4–1 lead becomes almost insurmountable, removing suspense and excitement from the game.

Fans express their preferences in polls, but ratify them by their decision to come to the park or stay home. National League attendance had risen from 11,360,159 in 1962, the first year it operated with ten clubs, to 12,971,430 in 1967.[3] The 1967 total was down more than two million, however, from the peak of 15,015,471 in 1966. American League turnstiles admitted 10,163,016 fans in the first year of the league's expanded format (1961) and 11,336,923 six years later, hardly a substantial increase, given the fact that the U.S. population had increased 8.1 percent from 1961 to 1967.

Attendance problems were even more severe in the minor leagues. Not only was television broadcasting major league games into minor league territory, but other television programming was an alternative to a night at the ball park. Many minor leagues shut down during World War II due to a lack of playing talent, but they revived and boomed after the war. Attendance peaked at almost 40 million in 1949 before dropping precipitously to 24 million in 1952 and 10 million in 1963, a decline attributed to television.

During the early part of the 1960s, the minor leagues struggled to find an identity. They wanted to be independent and competitive, but they had to rely on subsidies and players on option to survive. They chafed when star players were recalled in mid-season, but by the late 1960s most minor league franchises had become resigned to the fact that, if they were to survive, they had to function solely as a feeder system for the major leagues.

Even though major league attendance was up during the 1960s, the majority of the increase was due to the construction of new stadiums. The Astrodome, which opened in 1965, drew nearly 2.2 million fans its first season, compared to the 725,000 the team had drawn the previous year at Colt Stadium. The Astrodome factor accounted for nearly all of the five-year NL increase, even without considering the fact that Cardinals attendance increased by nearly 500,000 when Busch Stadium opened in 1966 or that the

Mets' attendance soared by more than 600,000 when they moved into Shea Stadium in 1964. In ten consecutive dates at their new stadium in 1967, the Cardinals drew more fans than the 1934 championship club had drawn all season. They led the league in attendance for the first time in 66 years.[4]

The Braves, who drew just over half a million fans as lame ducks in Milwaukee in 1965, attracted more than 1.5 million in their first season in Atlanta, and about the same the next year. While these totals were much improved over the last years in Milwaukee, the Braves had done much better during their first years in Wisconsin, drawing a total of nearly four million in 1953 and 1954. Perhaps a second relocation was not the same magic elixir it was the first time around.

In 1967, attendance in Pittsburgh declined by about 300,000, as the disappointing Pirates averaged just 7,300 fans in their last 26 dates, and that included a crowd of 28,000 on a day when the club gave away $10,000 in prizes.[5] In their first season without Sandy Koufax, the Dodgers' attendance had plummeted by a million customers, from 2,617,029 to 1,664,362.

American League figures told a similar story, as the Angels' 1966 move to their new stadium in Anaheim resulted in an attendance gain of over 800,000. "Eventually," said Angels VP Cedric Tallis, "we will outdraw the Dodgers. I don't believe it will happen next year, but eventually we will pass them."[6] Tallis projected that the three million people who lived within 20 miles of Anaheim Stadium would increase to eight million by 1980.

The 1967 American League attendance figures were heavily impacted by the fact that the Red Sox, in their "Impossible Dream" season, despite playing in the smallest park in the league, showed an increase from 811,172 to 1,727,832.[7]

Major league teams that remained in the same ballpark, especially those that performed poorly on the field, suffered at the gate. Cleveland drew only 662,980 spectators in 1967, its lowest total in three years. Yankees attendance was in a steady decline from 1,747,725 in 1961, dropping each year through 1966, before bouncing back slightly to 1,259,514 in 1967. Generally, a team experiences a sharp gain in attendance after a World Championship, but Baltimore's turnstile count dropped 250,000 in 1967. Even the Mets, renowned for their large, enthusiastic crowds, showed a decline of nearly 400,000 from 1966 to 1967. Of the six National League teams that remained in one park, four experienced attendance declines from 1961 to 1967. In the American League, which was much less mobile, the total was four of nine. If the Boston and California gains were removed from the 1967 AL figures, the other eight teams, in aggregate, showed a net decline in attendance over the six-year period of approximately 400,000.

Sports Illustrated pointed out a disturbing long-term trend. In 1948, the peak of the postwar boom, average attendance was 17,010 per game for a 154-

game schedule. Twenty years later, with four additional teams and an expanded schedule, average attendance was 14,270, despite the fact that the population of league cities had increased by 43 percent. Following the integration of major league baseball in 1947, black attendance surged, but it declined after 1950.

One solution to the attendance woes would seemingly be to build a series of new stadiums. Since public financing was becoming more available, that was a tempting strategy, neatly addressing the problem with someone else's money. A second strategy would be to emulate the Braves and relocate. Charley Finley wanted desperately to move his Kansas City Athletics and attempted to bolt to Louisville, Dallas, Oakland, or any place that promised to build him a stadium; he had finally been given permission to move to Oakland for the 1968 season.

Relocation was a curious business. In earlier days, teams had moved to larger population centers where they thought they could attract more fans. By the 1960s, live attendance had become just one part of the package. The Braves moved from Boston, which had a population of 801,000 in 1950, to Milwaukee, with just 657,000 people. By 1960, the population of Milwaukee had increased to 741,000, but the Braves moved to Atlanta, with its population of 487,000. Finley left Kansas City's 507,000 people for Oakland's 339,000.[8] It was not the size of the city that mattered; it was the package, the major facets of which were a stadium deal and a broadcasting contract. Atlanta and Oakland had come through on both counts.

The Chicago White Sox didn't think they could obtain permission to relocate and took a partial step, scheduling nine 1968 regular season games and one exhibition in Milwaukee. A 1967 exhibition between the White Sox and Twins had drawn well, and a determined Milwaukee group led by auto dealer Bud Selig, which wanted major league baseball back in their city, had approached the Cubs about the possibility of moving some of their games. When Phil Wrigley declined, stating that it would be unfair to Cubs fans, Selig approached the struggling White Sox, who readily accepted.[9] If the experiment was successful, the White Sox indicated they might increase the number of games in future seasons.

Many social commentators explained baseball's sluggish attendance by linking the sport to the staid "establishment" and its conservative and unchanging values. Football—fast, violent and relatively new—was the sport of the '60s, they claimed, for it was compatible with the rapid, violent changes taking place in American society. "If I have been a self-starting Cassandra shouting 'Doom,' said maverick former owner Bill Veeck, "it is because [baseball] has become too slow for the modern pace of life."[10]

"Baseball essentially is a nonviolent sport," said Yankees President Mike Burke, "in a violent time."[11] This theory was intellectually comforting, but ignored, among other things, the fact that people seemed to like the staid, nonviolent, uninspiring sport when it was played in new stadiums, or when it was played in an exciting fashion, as by the Red Sox in 1967. The lure of violence may have been exaggerated, for in a much-cited poll showing the declining popularity of baseball, twice as many Americans expressed a preference for the rough-and-tumble sport of bowling over hockey.

One of baseball's problems was that its older stadiums were located in urban areas, most of which had declined during the rush to suburbia in the 1940s and 1950s. The new stadium in St. Louis was, along with the Gateway Arch, the centerpiece of an ambitious urban development project, and other new stadia were built in the growing suburbs. But many of the older parks were stuck in deteriorating central cities. Comiskey Park was located in a neighborhood many considered dangerous, as were Yankee Stadium and Tiger Stadium. "Detroit's Tiger Stadium seems to belong in another time," noted *The Saturday Evening Post.* "It resembles an aging federal penitentiary."[12] If fans wanted to see violence, all they had to do was go to night games.

Football, it was said, appealed to the young because of its youthful, rebellious heroes like Joe Namath ... and well, Joe Namath. The Jets quarterback's name was the one that was always mentioned when speaking of football's appeal to youth, yet it is hard to think of any other football stars who resembled Namath. Quarterback is the sport's glamour position, and Namath's cross-town rival, Fran Tarkenton of the Giants, was a conservative Southerner and an ambitious entrepreneur who pursued a number of capitalist ventures. The Colts were champions of the NFL and featured two quarterbacks, Johnny Unitas and Earl Morrall, whose crewcut hair totaled about an inch in combined length and who favored high-top shoes rather than the pantyhose Namath wore in a controversial 1974 commercial. Pro football's top rushers, Leroy Kelly and Gale Sayers, were as unexciting off the field as they were thrilling between the hash marks. Packers coach Vince Lombardi, who was perhaps more famous than any player, was a disciplinarian who exemplified the 1950s much more than the free-wheeling 1960s.

There were a few rebellious counterculture football players like Dave Meggyesy and Chip Oliver, but they were marginal players whose views led them to leave the game. No other football stars had the youth appeal of Namath, and baseball, with Ken Harrelson, Joe Pepitone, and Denny McLain, had a number of young, charismatic players.

Perhaps the most dynamic sporting figure of the mid-'60s was Muhammad Ali, still known to conservative commentators as Cassius Clay. With his braggadocio, poetry, good looks, and remarkable skill, Ali captured the imagination of American youth, dispatching the "good Negro," Floyd Patterson, the hulking, dangerous criminal Sonny Liston, and a host of faceless challengers to become the heavyweight champion of the world.

Ali's conversion to the Muslim religion and his refusal to submit to the military draft had alienated many who'd liked him as a black, modern version of Dizzy Dean, but whether the public liked him or not, they paid attention to him. By 1968, Ali was not fighting, banned from the ring and stripped of his heavyweight crown. While he created increased interest in boxing, the sport had too many flaws to challenge baseball as the national pastime. It was too violent, it lacked cerebral attributes, and its integrity was always suspect. After Ali defended his crown against Liston in Lewiston, Maine, there were strong rumors that Liston had taken a dive.

While boxing was not a threat to baseball, football was clearly nipping at its heels. In January 1967, football staged the first Super Bowl, and while it was nowhere near the spectacle it would become—the game wasn't even sold out—it would eventually upstage the World Series. In December of that year, the Packers and Cowboys played the famed Ice Bowl on a frigid Sunday in Green Bay, a game filled with the drama too often lacking in baseball.

In May 1968, a much-publicized Harris poll indicated that baseball was losing the young and affluent markets to football. Among the under-35 demographic, football was favored by 46 percent, with baseball being the favorite sport of only 24 percent. Upper-income individuals preferred football by the even greater margin of 52 percent to 22 percent. The older and less affluent preferred baseball, giving the sport a number one ranking at 39 percent. Football was second with 32 percent and basketball third with 12 percent.

Sociologist John Robinson found that middle class people were more apt to prefer football, while those in the lower class were more likely to be baseball fans.[13] Advertisers follow demographics, and therefore football had networks fighting over its weekly schedule, while baseball could only sell its "Game of the Week" offering by packaging it with the World Series and the All-Star Game, the only events the networks really wanted.

Perhaps the most alarming facet of the Harris poll was that just three years earlier, only 25 percent of those surveyed listed football as their favorite sport. Was baseball slipping, or were the others gaining? *The Sporting News* warned of oversaturation, given the expansion of all sports leagues and the lengthening of their schedules. Basketball now stretched into May, and the Super Bowl was played in mid–January. Soon baseball, with an additional round of post-season play, would extend its season by another week. Did Americans have too many choices?

As usual, baseball's upper echelon was in a state of denial. Lee MacPhail, assistant to the commissioner, was tired of hearing about football. "When they ask if football is gaining on baseball," he said, "the answer is no." He pointed out that the Dodgers drew nearly as many fans at home and away as the entire NFL, ignoring the fact that the Dodgers played 162 games while NFL teams played just 14 each.[14]

The same month the Harris poll was released, Commissioner Eckert addressed 300 members of the Economic Club in Detroit. "Baseball has never been healthier," he said. "Attendance is up, television ratings are higher and our owner-player relations are exceptionally good."[15]

Things also looked rosy in Cooperstown, from the vantage point of Hall of Fame historian Lee Allen.

> [E]very time the imminent death of baseball is predicted by some partisan of another sport, along comes a Mickey Mantle or a Willie Mays, a Sandy Koufax or a Frank Howard to provide some sensational burst of the spectacular to capture public imagination and restore the old game to its position of glory. In other words, *rigor mortis* has not set in yet, or if it has, the symptoms are not visible in this sylvan village which is the game's home.[16]

The signs may not have been visible in Cooperstown, but they were obvious everywhere else, even to the 1967 AL Cy Young Award winner. As Jim Lonborg recuperated from knee surgery, he told a reporter, "I can't stand to watch a baseball game. There is just no action. It's dull. I do enjoy playing baseball, but I'd rather watch basketball or hockey."[17]

Joe Iglehart, the Baltimore Orioles' largest stockholder, thought baseball should copy other sports. When the Orioles' Curt Blefary was called out for interference after upending California shortstop Jim Fregosi, Iglehart said, "Baseball is criticized for not having enough action, and Blefary's play was certainly action. In hockey, for instance, people don't come out just for the game. They come to see fights, action."[18]

On the other side of the fence was Rheingold Brewery, sponsor of Mets games, which ran a full-page ad in *The New York Times* touting baseball as representative of solid old American values. "Why do you suppose some people say baseball is a dull spectacle?" was the large print opening. The text continued with:

> No shoot-em-up
> No stabbing
> No sex
> No torture
> No sock-thud
> No robbery (except stolen bases)
> **Baseball is just clean, wholesome fun**

The problem was that a significant segment of the American people wanted their entertainment to contain some shoot-em-up, sex, and sock-thud. Joe Namath and professional football contained all three. *The Sporting News* reproduced the Rheingold ad and, after noting race riots, Vietnam, rebellious youth, and assassinations, editor C.C. Johnson Spink wrote,

We know that some critics sneer at baseball as an infantile means of escapism from
life's realities. We see it in a different light. Baseball, in its way, shows that we still
hold to our fundamental values of fair play, sportsmanship and teamwork.... If you
believe that working in harmony with your fellow man is dull stuff, if your kicks are
psychedelic, if Bonnie and Clyde are your heroes, then baseball and Willie Mays and
Mickey Mantle will be dull.[19]

Clearly, Spink was not living in the world of most Americans, or even
that of *Sports Illustrated,* which gave extensive coverage to the Olympic boycott movement and the racial divide between black athletes and sports admin-
istrators. A series on "The Black Athlete" was provocative and impartial
enough to be lambasted by readers on both sides in the highest volume of
letters ever received by the magazine in response to an article.

Occasionally, *The Sporting News* sounded the warning that fair play,
sportsmanship, and teamwork were not striking a chord with the American
public, which saw little of those qualities in contemporary political life. By
the latter stages of the lackluster 1968 season, even *TSN* saw trouble on the
horizon. In October, it referred to a *United Press International* study in which
the favorite "sports" of the average American family were: "Professional and
college football, hunting, fishing, and tinkering with automobile engines."

Baseball, Spink concluded, needed to tinker with its own engine. "[Base-
ball] no longer can afford to let selfish interests block the legitimate direction
of expansion," he wrote. "It no longer can afford to create rules and then
ignore them. It no longer can afford to let the daily games proceed at a lackluster, low-scoring pace. It no longer can afford to squabble when a united
front is needed to revitalize public interest."[20] It appeared that sportsmanship,
fair play and teamwork were needed off the field.

In 1964, Commissioner Frick said that the major problems facing the
game were public relations—exacerbated by the actions of the owners and
management—television, which was threatening to take over the game, and
shortsightedness and self-interest on the part of the owners. They needed,
he said, to work for a common good.

In January 1969, Leonard Koppett, the intellectual and thoughtful writer
for *The New York Times,* composed a lengthy article on the problems facing
baseball.[21] Number one on the list, Koppett declared, was the contentious
relationship among the owners, who were unable to put aside perceived self-
interest for the common cause. This attitude had to be changed, Koppett said,
before anything meaningful could be achieved. Greater trust had to be man-
ifested by deciding key issues by majority vote, rather than allowing tenacious
minorities to thwart progress, and by taking many items that had been designated as "league matters" and making them issues for discussion by all owners.

Having stated the problem with his typical clarity and incisiveness, Koppett
did not propose the obvious solution—a strong commissioner, one answerable

to all of baseball's constituencies rather than just the owners. Koppett recommended as commissioner a man of persuasive talents who could convince the owners to act in a way that benefited baseball as a whole. Persuasiveness absent authority, however, is generally a losing hand.

Koppett also advocated a blurring of the divisions between the two leagues, with a unified staff and league presidents who reported to the commissioner rather than being responsible to the owners of each league. He endorsed the planned reorganization of baseball, which was to encompass all aspects of the sport, including the minor leagues, television contracts, racial diversity in management, and many other topics.

Koppett pointed out a number of changes in the game, the most prominent being an increase in teams from the 16 that had been the status quo for 60 years to 24 over an eight-year span. The greater number of teams and players made the game more difficult to follow closely, a deficit that could be remedied with better and more coherent television coverage. That, of course, would require coordinated action, something the owners had yet to achieve.

The magnates of baseball could not control what was happening in society, but they *could* make the game on the field more appealing. There were a number of suggestions, the most radical of which was a batter who would hit for the pitcher, either for the entire game or twice at selected intervals. No far-reaching experiments were initiated in the spring of 1968, for the situation was not yet desperate. It wouldn't become desperate until after the season, for in 1968 offensive baseball plunged to depths not seen since the Deadball Era.

3

The Division Between the "Haves" and the "Have Nots" Has Been Narrowing

There was every reason to expect that 1968 would bring another exciting American League pennant race. The Red Sox had barely won in 1967, with the lowest winning percentage ever for an AL champion, in a year when so many things had gone right for them. It didn't seem possible that Carl Yastrzemski could be that good again, for prior to hitting 44 home runs in 1967, he'd never hit more than 20. Nor had he ever driven in more than 100 runs.

While Yastrzemski carried the Boston offense, Cy Young Award winner Jim Lonborg had been the standout among an otherwise weak pitching staff. Lonborg had blossomed suddenly, winning 22 games after going 19–27 his first two seasons, and there was doubt whether he could repeat his sterling 1967 performance.

In the December 23 issue of *The Sporting News*, there was a picture of Lonborg skiing the slopes of Vail, and shortly thereafter, an ad appeared in a Boston paper inviting Red Sox fans to join him on a ski trip to New Hampshire. Two weeks later, shortly after Lonborg signed a 1968 contract that included a hefty raise, *The Sporting News* published another picture of him. This time he was being wheeled to an x-ray room after tearing two ligaments in his knee at Lake Tahoe. While recuperating from surgery, Lonborg said that, despite his injury, skiing was the greatest thing he'd ever done, and gave him more pleasure than winning a World Series game.[1] Manager Dick Williams was less thrilled and more concerned with replacing his star pitcher, who was expected to be out at least until May.

If the Lonborg-less Red Sox couldn't repeat, the White Sox, Tigers, and Twins, each of which had come so close the previous year, were poised to overtake them. For the White Sox, as always, the challenge was to find enough hitting to support their splendid pitching. In 1967, right-hander Joe Horlen won 19 games and led the league with a 2.06 ERA. Lefty Gary Peters was second with a 2.28 ERA, and Tommy John, still throwing with his original elbow, was fourth at 2.46. Overall, the White Sox led the league with a 2.45 mark, the lowest team ERA since 1919. In addition to their fine starters, Chicago had a strong, deep bullpen, with ageless, 44-year-old knuckleballer Hoyt Wilhelm, fellow flutterballer Wilbur Wood, and veterans Don McMahon and Bob Locker.

With any kind of hitting, the White Sox would have waltzed to the 1967 pennant, but Chicago didn't *have* hitting of any kind, tying the Yankees for last with a .225 average and managing just 89 home runs, good for ninth in a ten-team league. Only one player batted over .250, and that was veteran Ken Boyer, who hit .261 in just 180 at-bats. In order to beef up their offense, the White Sox obtained former National League batting champion Tommy Davis and reacquired All-Star shortstop Luis Aparicio, a hero of the 1959 Chicago pennant winners.

In addition to their popgun offense, the White Sox had another liability—volatile manager Eddie Stanky. When things got tough, Stanky got weird. He had a perpetually testy relationship with the press, the umpires, his players, and the fans. When the Sox lost, it was never Stanky's fault, and he took losses very hard. His teams were tense and nervous, and it showed in their play under pressure.

Stanky had been a scrappy player without much talent, and he wanted his team to play like he did. "A good professional," he said, "adjusts to where he is and any manager. A manager doesn't adjust to a ballplayer."[2] Stanky was from the old school, wedded to an era when players were at the manager's mercy. In the brave new world of 1968, managers had to adjust to the players, especially if they had talent.

The Twins and Tigers had plenty of hitting, at least by 1967 standards. Minnesota had sluggers Harmon Killebrew, who'd tied Yastrzemski for the home run title with 44, and Tony Oliva, the batting champion in 1964 and 1965. Dean Chance, a former Cy Young Award winner who'd captured "Comeback of the Year" honors for his 20–14 mark in 1967, led the pitching staff. Lefty Jim Kaat, a 25-game winner in 1966, had injured his elbow in his final 1967 start in Boston, possibly costing the Twins the pennant, and his physical condition entering the 1968 season was questionable.

During the off-season, the Twins traded shortstop Zoilo Versalles, the 1965 MVP, along with pitcher Jim "Mudcat" Grant to the Dodgers for catcher John Roseboro and relief pitchers Ron Perranoski and Bob Miller. The temperamental and erratic Versalles had worn out his welcome in Minnesota, where he hadn't gotten along particularly well with his managers. When asked about his team's prospects before the 1967 season, manager Sam Mele said, "If Versalles feels like playing, we've got a shot at it."[3] Versalles batted just

.200 in 1967, and although he was only 28, he had some physical problems, and the Twins were ready to part with him.

The Tigers hadn't won a pennant since 1945 but they, like the Twins, had a number of good hitters, including Al Kaline, Bill Freehan, Willie Horton, Norm Cash, Jim Northrup, and Dick McAuliffe. Horton was one of the keys to the Tigers' success. When he played, he had always hit, but the problem was that he spent too much time on the injury list. Following ankle surgery, Horton reported for spring training in 1968 with a limp, but insisted he would be ready by Opening Day.

Another Detroit question-mark was shortstop, where Ray Oyler could field as well as any infielder in baseball, but couldn't hit as well as many pitchers. He hit .207 in 1967, which was by far the best average of his big league career. The previous two seasons, he'd batted .186 and .171.

Earl Wilson was the best Tigers pitcher in 1967 with a 22–11 record. A big, 6'3", 216-pound right-hander, Wilson was obtained from the Red Sox in the middle of the 1966 season and had gone 35–17 in a year and a half with Detroit. He could also hit much better than Ray Oyler, and already had 26 career home runs. Left-hander Mickey Lolich had been consistent in aggregate, winning 18, 15, 14, and 14 games the past four years, but he'd gotten there in very inconsistent fashion, going long stretches without a win. Lolich also had military reserve obligations that would take him from the Tigers at various times during the summer.

Right hander Joe Sparma went 16–9 in 1967, but Denny McLain, a 20-game winner in 1966, slipped to 17–16, with a relatively high ERA of 3.79. McLain was just 24, with great stuff, but needed to harness his eccentric personality and concentrate on pitching. Pitching guru Johnny Sain joined the Tigers' staff in 1967, and Sain had a knack for producing 20-game winners. He taught McLain a tight slider and talked with him about pitching strategy and the mental approach to pitching, subjects Sain probably knew better than anyone in baseball.

The rest of the American League teams were unlikely to contend for the pennant. Any optimism on their part was based upon the fact that the Red Sox had come from ninth place in 1966 to win the pennant the following year, so why couldn't they? The team with perhaps the best chance to leap forward was the Baltimore Orioles, who'd won the 1966 World Series. The young pitchers who shut down the Dodgers that year had all come down with sore arms in 1967. If the pitchers came back, the Orioles had an excellent chance to win the pennant. If they didn't, manager Hank Bauer had an excellent chance to be fired.

The Yankees, only three years removed from the World Series, had a pathetic offense and a leaky defense. Mickey Mantle was literally on his last legs, and by 1967 the Bronx Bombers had become the Bronx Bumblers, batting just .225 with 100 home runs. Right-hander Mel Stottlemyre was one of the steadiest, most reliable pitchers in the league, but the Yankees had little behind him and a weak bullpen. After listening to perennially optimistic manager Ralph Houk gush about his team, columnist Francis Stann wrote, "Houk has to be deluding himself. He has no real ball club. The outfield is weak and the Yankees really need infield help at third base and shortstop."[4]

Washington's main attraction was mammoth Frank Howard, who occasionally interrupted Senators losses by hitting balls incredible distances. The Athletics, who finished last in 1967, had moved to Oakland and had a new manager, Bob Kennedy. Kennedy had a young pitching staff with great potential and some good hitters, especially promising rookie outfielder Reggie Jackson.

While the American League was experiencing an exciting 1967 finish, the National League race had been decided early, as the Cardinals cruised home a comfortable 10½ games ahead of the Giants. They were expected to repeat in 1968, since they had strengthened themselves during the winter in their one weak area—the bench.

The Cardinals were good and they were relatively young, for during the past three years, they had turned over much of the roster. Three of the four members of the 1964 World Championship infield—Bill White, Dick Groat, and Ken Boyer—were gone. In their places were first baseman Orlando Cepeda,[5] light-hitting, slick-fielding shortstop Dal Maxvill, and Mike Shannon, who was shifted from right field to third base.

Shannon's replacement in right field was Roger Maris, who had appeared to be at the end of the line when he arrived from the Yankees before the 1967 season. Maris had been injured, and New York fans and the press made his life so miserable that he planned to retire rather than spend another season with the Yankees. The Cardinals got him for journeyman third baseman Charley Smith. Maris had been accustomed to aiming at the inviting right field fence of Yankee Stadium, but when he saw spacious Busch Stadium, he changed his batting style and stopped concentrating on home runs.

Of the three top starting pitchers on the 1964 Cardinals, only Bob Gibson remained. In place of Ray Sadecki and Curt Simmons were young Nelson Briles, who, given a chance to start when Gibson had suffered a broken leg, won his last nine decisions in 1967, Dick Hughes, who was 16–6 as a 29-year-old rookie, and 23-year-old lefty Steve Carlton. In 1966, Hughes, Carlton, and Briles went a combined 9–19. In 1967, they were 44–20.

The biggest surprises of the 1967 season were the Cubs and Dodgers. Chicago, after two decades of wallowing in the second division, won 87 games and finished third. In his second season as manager, Leo Durocher had lifted the team up from the cellar, a feat almost as miraculous as Dick Williams leading the Red Sox from ninth to first.

The Dodgers, pennant winners in 1963, 1965, and 1966, went into a complete collapse, finishing eighth, with only 73 wins, after posting 97 and 95 victories the two previous seasons. They were only the second team (the 1915 Athletics were the other) to go from first to eighth in one season. Sandy Koufax had retired due to his arthritic elbow, and the subtraction of his 27 wins almost equaled the decline in Dodgers victories. It was the franchise's smallest victory total since the war year of 1944, and the club had not finished that low in the standings since 1905.

Prior to the 1967 season, the Dodgers traded star shortstop Maury Wills, who had left the club with an injury during a post-season tour of Japan in 1966. When owner Walter O'Malley learned that Wills had returned to the United States and was touring with his musical group, he was livid and demanded that Wills be traded. It was supposedly the only time O'Malley ever interfered with personnel decisions. Unfortunately, the Dodgers were unable to fill the hole at shortstop and, therefore, during the winter, acquired the malcontent Versalles from Minnesota.[6]

One thing the Dodgers always had in abundance, even without Koufax, was pitching. Don Drysdale returned as the ace of the staff, supported by Claude Osteen and Don Sutton. The Dodgers traded their two top relievers to the Twins in the Versalles deal, but they had a number of young arms in the farm system with which they planned to re-populate the bullpen.

The Cubs, who made such great strides in 1967, believed they had shored up the club's biggest weakness when they acquired veteran right fielder Lou Johnson from the Dodgers. With sluggers Ernie Banks, Billy Williams, and Ron Santo, plus ironman catcher Randy Hundley and future All-Star infielders Don Kessinger and Glenn Beckert, it appeared that Chicago had the offensive firepower to challenge the Cardinals.

Twenty-four-year-old Ferguson Jenkins, a 6'5", Canadian right-hander, had the first of six consecutive 20-win seasons in 1967, and 22-year-old lefty Ken Holtzman, despite shuttling between college and military commitments, was 9–0. He would be available full-time in 1968, and many were predicting he would be the next Koufax—after all, he was left-handed and Jewish. The biggest Cubs weakness was a very thin bullpen.

The Giants' Willie Mays had the worst season of his career in 1967, batting just .263 with 22 home runs and 70 RBI. He would turn 37 early in the 1968 season, had begun to slow down in the field, and was no longer one of the best players in baseball. The other Willie, Willie McCovey, was at the peak of his career, and while never the all-around player Mays was, McCovey was possibly the most-feared batter in the league.

Where the Giants truly shone, however, was in their starting rotation. Mike McCormick, the 1967 Cy Young Award winner, was probably the third-best pitcher on the San Francisco staff, behind Juan Marichal and Gaylord

Perry. Marichal, after winning 20 games each season from 1963–1966, had an injury-plagued 1967 during which he won only 14 games.

Perry slumped from 21–8 in 1966 to 15–17 in 1967, despite the fact that his ERA declined from 2.99 to 2.61. At one point, he put together a string of 41 consecutive scoreless innings and, as always, the burly pitcher was a indefatigable workhorse, once pitching 16 scoreless innings in a 21-inning game and logging 293 innings overall.

The fourth member of the rotation, left-hander Ray Sadecki, had been obtained from the Cardinals in 1966 in a trade for first baseman Orlando Cepeda. Cepeda led the Cardinals to the 1967 pennant and won the MVP Award, while Sadecki was a disappointment in San Francisco. He had been just 3–7 for the Giants in 1966 and started slowly the following year. Just when it appeared that the trade was one of the worst the Giants had ever made, Sadecki regained his form and finished strong. Restored to the starting rotation at the end of June, he won nine of his last 12 decisions to finish 12–6 with a 2.78 ERA. He was 6–0 in September.

While the Giants had pitching, the Reds and Pirates had hitting. Cincinnati's Pete Rose batted over .300 each year from 1965–1967, and young sluggers Tony Perez and Lee May, the latter the 1967 Rookie of the Year, seemed poised on the verge of stardom. During the winter, the Reds acquired a moody young outfielder named Alex Johnson, who had been found wanting by the Cardinals. Johnson had averaged around .300 for the Phillies, but in two seasons in St. Louis hit just .186 and .223 in limited action. Worse yet, he had rejected the help of the Cardinals' coaches and refused to follow their advice. Reds manager Dave Bristol planned to platoon Johnson in left field.

The Reds, like so many teams in this era of little scoring, had pitchers with impressive statistics, headed by 27-year-old veteran Jim Maloney, who won 23 games in 1963 and 20 in 1965. He'd pitched two no-hitters the latter year,[7] and struck out over 200 hitters four years in a row. Nineteen-year-old Gary Nolan had emerged from the low minors in 1967 and won 14 games while striking out 206. Converted outfielder Mel Queen and veteran Milt Pappas gave the Reds four solid starters. Thirty-five-year-old submariner Ted Abernathy was the mainstay of the Cincinnati bullpen, having led the league with 70 appearances and 28 saves, in addition to posting a sterling 1.27 ERA.

The Pirates, who were in the 1966 pennant race until the final weekend, floundered in 1967, coming in sixth. Playing in Forbes Field, with its rock-hard infield and distant fences, they led the league with a .277 average but hit just 91 home runs, eighth in the league. Roberto Clemente won the batting title with a .357 mark, and 1966 champ Matty Alou was third at .338. Willie Stargell, Donn Clendenon, and Maury Wills provided power and speed, but the Pirates had little pitching. Big lefty Bob Veale was the ace of the staff, but

Veale's record had not yet equaled his potential. Roy Face was the best reliever, but he was 40 years old.

In order to improve their pitching, the Pirates traded left-hander Woodie Fryman and young shortstop prospect Don Money to the Phillies for star pitcher Jim Bunning. Bunning, 36, was one of the best pitchers in the National League; since going to Philadelphia in 1964, he'd won 19, 19, 19, and 17 games. In 1967, despite posting his lowest win total in four years, he led the league in innings pitched and strikeouts and posted a 2.29 ERA (second only to Phil Niekro of the Braves). His record would have been better than 17–15 except that he lost five 1–0 decisions. Bunning was a workhorse, having averaged more than 300 innings over the past three years, and appeared to be just what the Pirates needed to complement their strong hitting. And the Pittsburgh hitting was expected to make Bunning a big winner. New Pirates manager Larry Shepard said, "I think Bunning will win at least 20 games, and I'm emphasizing the words—at least."[8]

Bunning was excited at the change of scenery. "I couldn't have picked a better team than the Pirates," he said, "if the Phils had allowed me to make the trade.... This is great, simply great. I presume they'll expect big things from me. Well, I expect to start 40 games and win at least half of them.... I don't think I've reached my peak yet."[9]

"I was in Mexico City for the baseball meetings," said Clemente, "and I told some of the Pirate officials if we had a pitcher like Bunning we could win the pennant."[10] "We'll win the pennant this year with Bunning," said Wills. "Bunning could be to the Pirates what Koufax was to the Dodgers."[11] In Chicago they were saying the same types of things about Lou Johnson, and in Los Angeles it was Zoilo Versalles who was going to lead the Dodgers to the Promised Land.

Versalles had been the AL MVP in 1965, but his performance had fallen off dramatically the past two years and he had a bad back. Early in his career, he had been moody and difficult, but when Billy Martin became a Twins coach in 1965, Martin cajoled, coddled, and inspired Versalles and got the best out of the erratic young shortstop. The Dodgers planned to assign coach Preston Gomez to try to duplicate what Martin had done, but based upon his recent performances, Gomez would need to work a miracle to get a second MVP performance out of Versalles.

The Cubs' optimism over the acquisition of Lou Johnson was even more difficult to explain. After signing with the Yankees organization in 1953, Johnson played with 15 minor league teams in 13 leagues before landing a permanent place in the majors at the age of 30. When former batting champion Tommy Davis broke his ankle in 1965, Johnson had been a life-saver in the Dodgers' drive to the World Series title, but he'd played in just 104 games in 1967. He was 33 years old, and the Dodgers were willing to let him go in return for utility man Paul Popovich.

The four remaining teams, the Phillies, Astros, Mets, and Braves, didn't have much hope of winning the pennant. The Phillies finished two games over .500 in 1967, but the trade of Bunning was a signal that they were rebuilding. The future of All-Star third baseman Richie Allen was in doubt, for he had been pushing his disabled car late in the summer of 1967 when the headlight shattered and damaged tendons in his hand.

Since he was the controversial Richie Allen, many doubted his story about the car. One rumor had him getting knifed in a bar fight, while another said he cut his hand climbing out of a bedroom window after being caught with a teammate's wife. When spring training

When the Pirates obtained veteran right hander Jim Bunning from the Phillies, they thought they had assured themselves of the 1968 pennant. Bunning, hampered by a series of injuries, finished 4–14, and the Pirates wound up sixth.

began, Allen's hand was still weak, and it was uncertain how much or where he would play. He couldn't throw well enough to play third, and would probably play either first base or left field.

In 1967 the Braves, in their second season in Atlanta, had been a disappointment, finishing seventh, 24½ games out of first. The club was plagued by dissension, and third baseman Clete Boyer spent the off-season blasting the lackadaisical attitude of some of his teammates. At a Chattanooga banquet in February 1968, Boyer said that many of his teammates didn't hustle and didn't care about winning. Even worse, he mentioned the alleged offenders by name and took a particularly hard swipe at outfielder Rico Carty.

Carty was an interesting character. In 1959, he signed his first professional contract—in fact, he signed with nine major league clubs and three in the Dominican. "I just wanted to play baseball," he said, "and since I had no idea how serious those offers really were, I said yes to everyone that gave me one, just in case the others didn't work out."[12]

"He loafs," Boyer said bluntly of Carty.[13] He said that if he were manager of the Braves, he'd put Felipe Alou in left-center, Hank Aaron in right-center, and station Carty in the right field bullpen to catch foul balls. The Braves had tried to trade Carty, Boyer added, but found they couldn't give him away. For good measure, he said fellow infielders Denis Menke and Woody Woodward lacked baseball knowledge, the Braves' pitching stank, and the club didn't have enough talent to contend for the pennant.

The Chattanooga fans loved the juicy gossip and peppered Boyer with questions for an hour and a half. Some called him "refreshing", and a local radio reporter said he was thrilled to hear a player who didn't insult his audience's intelligence with sugar-coated platitudes. Atlanta general manager Paul Richards was not so thrilled, for this was not the first time Boyer had made injudicious remarks in public. "I would think playing third base was a big enough job for him," Richards said.[14]

Letter writers to *The Sporting News* took both sides. One praised Boyer for his forthright, courageous statements, while another felt that the third baseman had best look to his own performance. "If he's so great," wrote Minos G. Rigopoulis of Maywood, New Jersey, who probably remembered Boyer's often anemic hitting with the Yankees, "the record books sure are misleading."[15]

Boyer was not the only Brave who doubted his teammates' work ethic, for after the final game of the 1967 season, Aaron hinted that several players had slacked off once the Braves were eliminated from contention. Aaron and Carty also had a much-publicized fight on an airplane. It was apparent that the Braves needed to get their own house in order before they could take on the rest of the National League.

The Astros, in their six years in the league, had never won more than 72 games nor finished higher than eighth. Owner Roy Hofheinz's greatest accomplishment was building the Astrodome, but he proclaimed that the time had come to start winning baseball games. Given the team's dearth of talent, however, Houston fans seemed destined for another season of admiring the Astrodome.

The Mets had climbed to ninth in 1966, for the first time in their history, but slipped back to tenth the following year, posting more than 100 losses for the fifth time in six years. They had a new manager, Gil Hodges, and 1967 Rookie of the Year Tom Seaver, but possessed a pitiful offense that had produced just 483 runs, by far the lowest total in the league. Moreover, they had traded their best hitter, Tommy Davis, to the White Sox.

The general consensus was that there would be another dogfight in the American League and that the Cardinals would probably repeat in the National. *The Sporting News* writers' poll yielded the following predictions:

American League	National League
Minnesota	St. Louis
Detroit	Pittsburgh
Chicago	Cincinnati
Boston	San Francisco
Baltimore	Chicago
California	Atlanta
Cleveland	Los Angeles
New York	Philadelphia
Washington	Houston
Oakland	New York

Sporting News readers also picked the Twins and Cardinals, while *TSN*, as always, predicted the greatest pennant races in history. "The division between the 'haves' and the 'have nots' has been narrowing," it opined in April, "and 1968 should see more clubs contending in the pennant race than ever before."[16] C.C. Johnson Spink picked the White Sox to win the American League title, due principally to the managerial talent of Eddie Stanky, but said the Tigers had their best chance at a flag in 23 years. He picked the Cardinals to repeat in the NL.

It was not the pennant races, however, that would make 1968 a season to remember. It would be a year where baseball continued to lose ground to professional football. It would be a year when current events impacted baseball to an extent unprecedented except for the war years. But what everyone would recall most about 1968 was that it was the year when everyone forgot how to hit.

4

Almost Any Strong and Passably Coordinated Young Man Can Learn to Pitch

If major league executives were worried about the lack of offense before the 1968 season began, they were in an advanced state of panic by October. During what became known as "The Year of the Pitcher," it seemed as though new standards of offensive futility were established nearly every week. The All-Star Game, a 1–0 victory for the National League, typified the season, as the winning run was unearned and scored on a double play grounder. At one point, National League pitchers retired 20 men in a row. By the end of the game, the American League had scored just one run its last 32 innings of All-Star competition.

For the first time in history, pitchers captured the MVP Award in both leagues. Denny McLain of the Tigers won 31 games, the first pitcher to win 30 since Dizzy Dean in 1934 and the first American Leaguer since Lefty Grove in 1931. Juan Marichal had a shot at 30, but fell off the pace and finished with a mere 26 victories. Bob Gibson of the Cardinals posted a 1.12 ERA, the lowest since Mordecai "Three Finger" Brown in 1906. He won 15 straight games and at one point allowed only two earned runs in 92 innings.

Don Drysdale threw six consecutive shutouts, breaking a record set in 1908, and hurled 58⅔ straight scoreless innings, besting the mark Walter Johnson established in 1913. Five American League pitchers who threw 162 or more innings (the number required to qualify for the ERA title) had earned run averages below 2.00, the first time that had happened since 1917. American League teams had a combined 2.98 ERA, while their counterparts in the National had an almost identical 2.99.

Even some journeyman pitchers were nearly unhittable in 1968. Bob Bolin of the Giants, who had a solid but unremarkable career as a reliever and spot starter from 1961–1973, and a career ERA of 3.40, posted a 1.99 mark in 176⅔ innings in 1968. Cleveland's Vicente Romo had a 1.63 ERA, and Ron Kline of the Pirates 1.67.

In late April, the Mets and Astros played 24 innings before either team could score a run. It was the longest National League game ever played to a decision, and of course the longest two teams had ever gone without scoring. The end of the 23rd inning marked 38 consecutive shutout innings for the talented young Mets staff.

A lot of teams had difficulty hitting in 1968, but none fell farther than the once-mighty Yankees, their offense a puny shadow of the offensive juggernaut that had terrorized the American League just a few years earlier. They scored five earned runs in their first 40 innings. By the end of April, nine of the 15 non-pitchers on the Yankees' roster were batting less than .200, with two hitting below .100. The team average was an anemic .186. On May 5, the Yankees got as many as nine hits in a game for the first time all season.

In 1961, Roger Maris and Mickey Mantle set batting records almost every week. In 1968, Yankees heroics were of more modest dimensions. On May 12, Joe Pepitone became the first Yankee to get two extra-base hits in a game. On the 21st, the club pulled its aggregate batting average above .200 for the first time. Second baseman Horace Clarke, in his 165th at-bat, got his first extra-base hit. There was so little to celebrate that the Yankees made a big deal about the fact that Dick Howser reached base six straight times as a pinch-hitter. Five of those were due to walks, but in 1968 even that was a reason for celebration.

Other teams were almost as impotent as the Yankees. The Cubs set a record by going 48 innings without scoring a run. In 1967, they had been shut out six times, but in 1968, they were blanked seven times in their first 37 games. On May 24, the Red Sox led the American League with a batting average of .239. The Twins were second at .233, while New York brought up the rear at .203. Only the Athletics, with 18, had fewer home runs than the 19 hit by the Yankees. The White Sox had scored the fewest runs, just 92 in 36 games, an average of just 2.6 per outing.

The facts were staggering. During the season's first 290 games, teams were held to three hits or fewer 40 times. Cleveland pitchers threw 12 shutouts in their first 36 games. By mid–May, 32 major league pitchers had ERAs of less than 2.00. By late May, there had already been 22 1–0 games. The offensive woes affected superstars like Frank Robinson, who was hitting just .192 in early June, and even retired players. On Old Timers' Day in New York, the Yankees veterans managed only one hit, by Joe DiMaggio, of course, during their two-inning exhibition.

The future didn't look too bright, either, for minor league statistics were just as discouraging. The AA Eastern League posted an aggregate batting average of .218, and the individual leader was Tony Torchia at .294. Of EL players with 400 or more at-bats, the next-best hitter was Carmen Fanzone at .270, and Larry Bowa was tenth at .242.

What was the cause of these woeful statistics? Some of the blame was placed on the new stadiums that had done so much to boost attendance. Cozy old parks like the Polo Grounds and Ebbets Fields had been replaced by cavernous facilities like Dodger Stadium, the Astrodome, and Busch Stadium. Playing in the old Busch Stadium in 1965, the Cardinals averaged 4.61 runs per game. In the new park the following year, they averaged just 3.37 runs a game. The number of shutouts increased from seven in the old park to 15 in the new one. The Cards' roster had not changed dramatically, and the decline in offense was attributed principally to the more distant fences in the new facility.

When designing their new stadium, St. Louis had engaged the services of Robert Kingsley, a former Pentagon mapmaker who described himself as a "home run expert." Kingsley had consulted with the Dodgers during the construction of Chavez Ravine and accurately predicted the number of home runs that would be hit in the park the first year.[1] Given the lack of home runs in Los Angeles and St. Louis by 1968, it appeared that Kingsley had not anticipated some of the changes in baseball, and that he had never tried to hit against Bob Gibson.

"You got at least two parks in our league," said the Cardinals' Curt Flood, "that ought to be outlawed. In San Francisco, the wind blows 90 m.p.h. in your face. In Los Angeles, the park is so big you got to play golf—hit the ball, go get it, and hit it again."[2]

"At Dodger Stadium," said Don Cardwell, "there were two different mounds, one for Drysdale and one for Koufax. They had different motions and the mound was changed to fit their pitching style. After the game, after you showered, you could see the grounds keepers out there working on the mound."[3]

Even in some of the older parks, conditions were not conducive to hitting. Cleveland moved its fences back for the 1968 season. The White Sox didn't need to. The fences were already distant, and the infield was a rain forest. "I'd estimate that playing in Comiskey Park costs any hitter from 20 to 25 points in his batting average from what he'd hit normally anywhere else," said Ken Boyer, who'd joined the White Sox a year earlier. "They wet down the infield in front of the plate," Boyer complained, "and also let the grass grow long. You need a cannon to drive a ground ball through that infield— and nobody can hit enough line drives to hit .300."[4]

Everyone had a theory to explain the mystery of the disappearing offense. Many blamed the slider. Willie Mays thought the umpires had enlarged the strike zone. Brooks Robinson believed that pitching coaches were better than hitting coaches. Mets executive Johnny Murphy thought the

Despite an aching shoulder and a propensity for trouble, Denny McLain won 31 games in 1968, capturing the AL Cy Young and Most Valuable Player Award.

shortage of runs was due to poor lighting and too many night games. Houston manager Harry Walker blamed Little League. "When I was a kid," Walker said, "I'd have a bat in my hand and I'd be by myself, hitting a ball against the side of a house like that, or the garage. In Little League, there's so much emphasis on winning that managers won't let some of the kids hit. They tell the boys the pitcher is wild, and he'll walk 'em, so DON'T SWING."[5]

Pitcher Dave Baldwin offered an unusual explanation; perhaps the poor batting was due to the extensive use of amphetamines during the 1960s. Baldwin said that, contrary to rumor, trainers and managers did not encourage the use of "greenies," but many players got them from their wives, who used them to lose weight. More batters than pitchers indulged, and many of them came to the plate in a state of high anxiety. "Some of them looked like Don Knotts on overdrive," Baldwin recalled. An over-anxious batter was likely to chase bad pitches; pitchers knew it and took advantage of it.[6]

Roger Angell had a more conventional theory. "Almost any strong and passably coordinated young man can learn to pitch," he wrote, "but batting is not generally teachable; even after a lifetime in the game, most pitchers still swing like their old aunties."[7]

Both league presidents weighed in with their opinions. There were 43 shutouts in the first 192 National League games, said NL President Giles, and that was far too many, almost double the 1967 total. After identifying the problem, however, Giles said he didn't believe any dramatic changes should be made to correct it.

American League President Joe Cronin didn't think there *was* a problem. "After all," he said, "It's only Memorial Day—when it gets warmer, the hitters are going to catch up with the pitchers."[8] A 2–0 game, Cronin insisted, was much more exciting than a 9–2 contest.

Caustic New York writer Dick Young disagreed. Responding to a letter he received praising the wonderful pitching of 1968, Young replied, "If that's the way baseball ought to be played, then they should bottle it and sell it as the ideal sedative."[9]

A number of baseball people proposed solutions. Braves manager Luman Harris suggested making the ball bigger. Yankees executive Lee MacPhail recommended that pitchers no longer hit; a regular player should bat in their place. Broadcaster and former Yankees shortstop Tony Kubek proposed limiting pitching staffs to eight per team, which would prevent managers from throwing in a fresh pitcher every few innings.

Another former Yankees shortstop, Phil Rizzuto, put the onus on the hitters. "[T]he main reason for the decline in batting averages," Rizzuto said, "is the decline in smart hitters, who try to do more with a bat than swing it trying for homers."[10] Angels manager Bill Rigney concurred, urging batters to choke up and try for singles. Sacrificing home runs for singles, of course, was unlikely to lead to an increase in scoring, and older fans recalled that neither Rizzuto nor Rigney could hit home runs during their playing days even if they tried.

The Pirates tried an unconventional solution. After going scoreless for 25 innings, they threw 50 of their bats on the outfield grass, poured gasoline on them, and lit them on fire.[11]

One of the few men who wasn't worried about the dearth of hitting was perennially optimistic Yankees manager Ralph Houk. "Just wait until the weather gets hot," he said in early June. "Then the hitting will pick up and all the complaints about low scoring will be forgotten."[12]

The weather got hot, but Houk's club didn't. In a three-game stretch they "drove in" six runs with bases-loaded walks. The Yankees' futility was leaving their pitchers without much support. Fred Talbot began the season 0–8 and wondered why. "All the other pitchers have had days when the club doesn't score," he said, "but any time I pitch there's no runs." In the 54 innings he had pitched, the Yankees had scored a grand total of *four runs.* "Sometimes I feel that if I had a hand grenade," Talbot said, "I'd put it in my mouth and pull the pin."[13]

When two weak-hitting clubs like the Yankees and White Sox met, it seemed a distinct possibility that every game would end a scoreless tie. On May 24, New York beat Chicago, 1–0, in 13 innings, part of a streak in which the Yankees scored two or fewer runs in nine straight games. Leonard Koppett wrote, "It took the New York Yankees and Chicago White Sox only 3½ hours and 13 innings of play to produce a run at Yankee Stadium last night. Then the Yankees scored it with the aid of an intentional pass, a good bunt and a wild throw by Sandy Alomar. The simplest method—hitting the ball squarely a few times in the same inning, seems simply beyond them."[14]

There were many dominating pitchers in 1968, but the two best were Gibson and McLain, whose 31 wins are unlikely to be matched unless modern pitching practices are dramatically altered. In 2014, no major league pitcher made more than 34 starts—no one has made as many as 37 starts since Greg Maddux in 1991—and it is nearly impossible to win 30 games in 34 starts, especially when complete games are rare.

McLain was a 24-year-old right-hander with an insatiable need for attention who always seemed to find himself on the wayward side of authority. The product of a father who drank and died of a heart attack at 36 and a mother who showed him no affection, McLain had a knack for turning triumph into disaster. In his first professional game, he pitched a no-hitter and struck out 16, then went AWOL because he missed his girlfriend. "If I want to do something," he said, "and the pope lays down a law saying I can't do it, I'll still go ahead."[15]

McLain kept getting in trouble in the minor leagues, always assuming that as long as he won, he would be forgiven. And he was. "When you can do it out there between the white lines," he said later, "then you can live any way you want."[16]

McLain came up to the major leagues in 1963 and hit a home run in his first major league game, the only homer he would hit in his career. He began the 1966 season 13–4 and started the All-Star Game, but slumped in the second half and finished with a record of 20–14, and his ERA that year and the next was nearly four runs a game, well above the league average. He was 17–16 during a 1967 campaign in which the Tigers lost the pennant on the final day and McLain missed his last few starts with a back ailment and a mysterious toe injury. He didn't have a single victory in the final month. McLain said his foot fell asleep while he was lying on his couch and he injured it when he got up too quickly. According to *Sports Illustrated*, an alleged gambling debt of $46,000 may have been the cause.

Like he did with nearly everything else, McLain made a joke of the toe injury. He shrugged it off, discarded his horn-rimmed glasses for contact lenses, and predicted a pennant for the Tigers and a great year for himself in 1968. He said the Tigers would win the pennant "by six or seven games if we get off to a good start and nobody falls off any couch."[17] He'd had both physical and mental problems in 1967, McLain said. "I had two tons of problems."[18]

McLain's biggest physical problem was a shoulder that had been bothering him off and on since 1964. Pitch limits were almost non-existent, and McLain had thrown as many as 229 pitches in a single game. As the pain increased, McLain began taking cortisone shots. He had the first one in 1965, took four more the next year, and had at least ten in 1967. In 1968, McLain said he took a dozen cortisone shots, in addition to Xylocaine and amphetamines, the latter of which mostly helped him maintain his hectic lifestyle.[19]

McLain had more than physical problems. In 1965, when he had his first big season, columnist Joe Falls expressed an opinion that would not stand the test of time. "But what he has," Falls wrote, "more than anything else— is an innate honesty that sets him apart from any athlete I've ever met."[20] Almost before the ink was dry on Falls' column, McLain became involved in gambling—in a big way. Virtually every athlete who has gotten in trouble for gambling, from Pete Rose to Art Schlichter, has lost heavily. Knowing the game, and being good at it, is not enough to beat odds that are stacked in the bookies' favor, but McLain thought he had a solution to that dilemma. Since it was the bookies who made the money, he would become a bookmaker. Somehow, McLain managed to lose money on that end of the game, and Tigers GM Jim Campbell found out that McLain was $15,000 behind.

McLain always had problems with money, even when it was earned legally. "Money impresses me," he said. "Big business impresses me…. I'm a mercenary. I admit it. I want to be a billionaire."[21] But he had no sense of economy or of the need to honor financial obligations. Money came, money went, and there always seemed to be more going than coming. As McLain said, as long as he could pitch, people would forgive him.[22]

Womanizing was another of McLain's problems, one that led to ongoing marital troubles with his wife, Sharon, daughter of former star shortstop Lou Boudreau. McLain liked to drink alcohol, but his primary liquid vice was

Pepsi, and he drank more than ten bottles per day,[23] so many that he had serious dental problems as well as a tendency to gain weight. By 1968, half of his teeth were capped, and the other half would be soon. "I'm down to about 60 or 70 bottles a week," he said, "but now I cheat a bit and get the king-sized 16-ounce bottles.... And I don't drink any of that diet stuff either."[24]

McLain had some unusual training methods. He believed that bowling was an excellent way to strengthen his right arm, and during the winter it was not unusual for him to bowl ten games a day. McLain was a pretty good bowler, with an average of nearly 200, and the game not only gave him a way to exercise his arm, it also afforded him an opportunity to gamble. Bowling for money in the winter gave the adventurous young right-hander the thrills he experienced on the mound during the summer. "My advantage," he wrote, "came when the crowd gathered for the last few frames and the other guy would succumb to the pressure. I loved the tenth frame like I loved the ninth inning."[25]

When the 1968 season began, Detroit newspapers were in the midst of a 277-day strike that wouldn't end until early August, but McLain managed to get himself in trouble by spouting off to out-of-town writers. When asked what he thought about Tigers fans who booed the team when they had a losing streak, McLain said, "If they think we're stupid for playing this game, how stupid are they for watching us?" He criticized the fans for getting on Tigers star Al Kaline, and his final line was the memorable, "But the fans in this town are the worst in the league." As the writers left, McLain said to Tom Loomis of the *Toledo Blade,* "I only meant 1 percent of the fans." But the other writers had stopped listening at that point, and the only thing their readers gleaned from the story was the fact that McLain said the Tigers fans were the worst in the league.

"I was right about the two-faced nature of fans," he wrote later. "But you never win when you rip your fans. I'd say what I thought, embellish it to make good copy, and then absorb whatever pain came with it. I lacked the maturity to think out of the moment and handle all the angles."[26]

Shortly afterward, McLain found a smoke bomb attached to the undercarriage of his car. The first time he pitched at home in front of the "worst fans in the league," he looked like the worst pitcher in the league. He gave up a three-run homer to Boog Powell of the Orioles in the first inning and left after two innings to a rousing chorus of boos and catcalls.

When the 1968 season began, McLain was the number three starter on the Tigers club. Veteran Earl Wilson earned the Opening Day assignment, and Mickey Lolich was number two. McLain had no decisions in his first two starts, but by early June, he'd won nine of ten and, with Wilson nagged by minor injuries and Lolich shuttling between the Tigers and his Army Reserve unit, McLain became the ace of the staff.

He wasn't racking up shutouts like Drysdale and Gibson, but with the lusty (by 1968 standards) Tigers attack, McLain was winning almost every time out; after his first two starts, there was only one more no-decision game prior to the season finale. By the end of June McLain was 14–2, and when the next month was over he was 21–3, at which point it was clear that he had a shot at 30 wins.

McLain was named to the All-Star squad and decided to go from Detroit to Houston by way of Las Vegas. He chartered a jet and flew west with Tigers catcher Bill Freehan and their wives. The Tigers played on Sunday, and the All-Star Game was on Tuesday, which didn't leave much time in Las Vegas, but the McLains and Freehans made the most of it. "We were wined and dined 24 hours a day at the Riviera Hotel," McLain wrote, "given chips and lavished with booze. All I was asked to do was be visible, talk to people, and give autographs."[27] About the only thing McLain didn't do in Vegas was sleep, but after a side trip to Disneyland, he got to Houston in time for the game and, fueled by a few Pepsis, pitched two scoreless innings.

After the game, Freehan went back to Detroit, while the McLains returned to Vegas for another day of fun before the season resumed on Thursday. McLain said he didn't sleep more than four or five hours in three days. "You've got to take care of your body,"[28] he'd said in 1966, but he wasn't doing that by 1968.

En route to Minneapolis, where the Tigers opened the second half of the season, the door of McLain's jet popped open at 18,000 feet, and he and the pilot had to put on their oxygen masks. They descended to 10,000 feet and limped to Minneapolis without incident. "The adrenaline rush was incredible," McLain wrote. "When we landed I thought, 'How could anything possibly go wrong for me in 1968?'"[29]

Not much went wrong for McLain and the Tigers during the second half of the season. After losing to the Yankees on August 24 to drop to 25–5, he ripped off four consecutive wins, although he was hurting more than ever. His best pitch was a hard slider, which put tremendous strain on his shoulder. Tigers physician Russell Wright diagnosed a "tired" arm, caused by an irritation of the trapezoid muscle. He didn't think it would cause McLain to miss any starts. Like Hoss Radbourn when he won 59 games in 1884, McLain endured almost constant pain. Radbourn, however, didn't have the miracle of cortisone at his disposal.[30]

Manager Mayo Smith talked about taking McLain out of games earlier and letting the bullpen finish, but between July 27 and August 16, he pitched six complete games in a row. On September 1, the start of a game against the Orioles was delayed 43 minutes due to rain. After McLain gave up two runs in the top of the first, the game was delayed another 51 minutes while the Tigers batted in the bottom half of the inning. McLain got in the shower to let the hot water keep his arm loose and went back out to the mound when the game resumed. He wasn't particularly sharp, but bailed himself out by starting a triple play on a Boog Powell line drive that nearly put an end to his womanizing. He threw his final pitch and notched his 27th win four hours and 11 minutes after the scheduled starting time.

"I was running a marathon," he wrote, "trying to get to 30 before my arm fell off. The pain after the games was overwhelming. I'd ice it, swallow aspirin, and have a few drinks the next day to alleviate the pain."[31] Despite the physical discomfort, McLain was enjoying himself immensely, soaking up the attention so many athletes dreaded. Chasing Babe Ruth in 1961 had nearly driven the introverted Roger Maris to a nervous breakdown, but for McLain the attention was intoxicating. Maris hated the writers; McLain wanted to be in the papers every day. "It was heaven," he wrote of the chase for 30.[32] When he went to Los Angeles to try for win #29, he visited Tom and Dick Smothers at Tom's house, Glen Campbell at his house, and taped an organ segment for the *Steve Allen Show.* Then he beat the Angels, 7–2, and struck out 12.

McLain's first opportunity for his 30th win came on September 14 in Detroit against the Athletics in a Saturday afternoon, nationally televised game. Before a start, most pitchers like to be alone with their thoughts, but McLain spent the time before his quest for #30 holding court with the writers in the clubhouse. On the field, he pitched as he had all season, just good enough. While Gibson and Drysdale were throwing shutouts, McLain was just winning games. Against the Athletics, he gave up two home runs to rookie Reggie Jackson, the second giving Oakland a one-run lead that held up into the bottom of the ninth.

Al Kaline led off the ninth as a pinch-hitter for McLain and walked. He eventually scored the tying run, and the Tigers won the game on Willie Horton's single. McLain leapt out of the dugout, a 30-game winner and holder of the Tigers' record for most victories in a season, which had been 29 by Hal Newhouser. Dean, the last 30-game winner, was on hand to offer congratulations and said McLain might win 35 games in 1969.

It was appropriate that McLain succeeded Dean as the most recent 30-game winner, for the two men had a number of similarities. Both were very good pitchers with great faith in their ability. Both broke rules they thought didn't apply to them because of their skills, and each had his career ended prematurely due to arm trouble.

McLain was called from the locker room for a curtain call and, emerging from the Tigers dugout, waved and blew kisses to the cheering fans. As he had prophesied, a few wins had converted the people he'd called the worst fans in the world into *his* fans.

No one else came close to winning 30 games in 1968, but it looked for a while as though Juan Marichal had a chance. Like McLain, Marichal was coming off a 1967 season that ended prematurely because of a suspect injury, pitching only once after pulling a hamstring muscle against the Mets on August 4. Many in the Giants' organization wondered how a pulled hamstring could sideline a pitcher for so long, and Marichal greatly resented the insinuations. He had a history of unusual injuries, and after nearly every one his courage was questioned. During the 1962 World Series, Marichal injured a finger while attempting a bunt and had to leave the game. In 1966, teammate Manny Mota accidently slammed a car door on his hand. When he failed to bounce back as quickly as his managers thought he should, Marichal was unfairly branded a malingerer.

After all the success he'd had for the Giants, Marichal felt unappreciated and hinted that he might like to be traded. After the 1967 season, columnist Bob Addie opined, "[T]here seems to be little doubt that Juan's days are numbered with the Giants."[33]

The Giants might have been upset with Marichal, but they were smart enough not to trade one of the best pitchers in the game. They needed an infielder or two, but who could replace Marichal in the rotation? He returned to San Francisco for the 1968 season, pitched consistently well all year, and captured his 20th win on August 1, just five days after McLain won his 20th.

Marichal made 12 more starts and might have been able to squeeze in another if he'd been close to 30 or if the Giants had a chance to win the pennant. He didn't reach the 30-win plateau, but finished 26–9, with a remarkable 30 complete games in 38 starts. In four other starts, he went at least eight innings, and left only three times before the end of the seventh. Three times he pitched into extra innings. Over a period of 19 consecutive starts from May 24 through August 13, Marichal worked an incredible 176 innings, or about 9⅓ per start. He was 15–3 over that stretch, getting one no-decision in an extra-inning game.

While McLain may have been the biggest winner, Bob Gibson of the Cardinals was the most dominant pitcher in a season in which so many hurlers were dominant. Gibson had tough luck early in the season, which foreclosed any chance of winning 30 games, and had just a 3–5 record at the end of May, despite a 1.52 ERA. He then commenced a 15-game winning streak that featured some of the most remarkable pitching of all time. He threw five straight shutouts and eight in ten starts (during which he gave up only two runs total). Like Marichal, Gibson had an iron-man stretch, 19 straight starts in which he pitched at least nine innings. By the end of the season, Gibson had a record of 22–9, 13 shutouts, and an ERA of 1.12.

Bill Deane analyzed Gibson's season and pointed out that had the Cardinals scored the league average of 3.43 runs per game when Gibson started, his record would have been 30–4. Even had they scored just one run per game, he would have been 13–10.[34]

Don Drysdale did not sustain his excellence over the entire season, but from May 14 through June 8, he threw a greater number of consecutive scoreless innings than anyone had done in major league history. Like Gibson, Drysdale had a losing record early in the season (1–3), but after shutting out the Cubs on May 14, he proceeded to blank the Astros, Cardinals, and Astros again. Despite all the shutouts, Drysdale was barely winning, his first three victories being 1–0, 1–0, and 2–0. One more whitewash (which would coincidentally be Drysdale's 200th major league win) would tie Doc White's major league record, set in 1904.

On May 31, Drysdale was three outs away from history, leading the Giants, 3–0, when he loaded the bases with none out in the ninth inning. He grazed Giants catcher Dick Dietz on the left elbow with a 2–2 pitch. Before he'd come to the plate, Dietz told Marichal that if Drysdale threw anything other than a fastball, he'd make sure he got hit in order to end the streak,[35] and it looked as though he'd succeeded. Before Dietz could take first, however, plate umpire Harry Wendelstedt ruled that he had not made an effort to avoid the pitch and called it ball three.

Giants manager Herman Franks charged out of the dugout as if his pants were on fire. Although the rule requiring a batter to make a legitimate attempt to avoid being hit had been on the books for some time, it was rarely enforced. After the game, Dodgers manager Walt Alston said it was the first time in his 34 years of professional baseball he'd seen it called.

Dietz's teammate, Ron Hunt, was somewhat of an expert at getting hit by pitches—he was once hit 50 times in a season and was plunked 243 times in his career. Hunt was the 20th century record-holder in both categories when he retired in 1974, and he thought Dietz had something to learn about the art. "He stood there like a post," Hunt said. "It was a high slider and he didn't make an attempt."[36] Franks and Giants coach Peanuts Lowrey carried on the argument for, according to some sources, 25 minutes, while Drysdale stood on the mound and tossed the ball to catcher Jeff Torborg, trying to stay loose.

Wendelstedt finally ejected Franks, and Dietz returned to home plate with a 3–2 count and a place in baseball history. The Giants' catcher was a good ballplayer who hit a home run in the 1970 All-Star Game, but when he died in 2005, his *Associated Press* obituary was titled, "Dick Dietz, 63, Hit by Drysdale Pitch in Famed 1968 Dispute."[37] Reprieved, Drysdale retired Dietz on a short fly ball and the next two hitters on a grounder and pop-up to tie the record.

Drysdale's next and final shutout was much less eventful, a 5–0 victory over Pittsburgh, which put him in the record books by himself. In his six shutouts, Drysdale, in 54 innings of work, gave up just 27 hits and nine walks, while striking out 42. Four days later, he broke Walter Johnson's record with 58⅔ scoreless innings before finally allowing a run to the Phillies in the fifth inning. The rest of the big Dodgers righty's year was not so spectacular; he lost six of his last eight decisions and finished with a 14–12 mark and a sore shoulder that ended his season in late August.

The best ERA in the American League belonged to Luis Tiant of Cleveland. Tiant, who left Cuba before Castro bolted the gate, had pitched with the Indians since 1964, with mixed results. In his debut, he pitched a 3–0 shutout, striking out 11, to beat Whitey Ford and the pennant-winning Yankees, and there had been other sparkling performances, but the overall results had been mediocre. During the past three seasons, he had won 35 games and lost 31, and there was frequent talk that he needed to lose weight to be effective. He was also the victim of some tough luck, having lost seven games by one run in 1967.

In 1968, like Gibson and Drysdale, Tiant's early appearances gave little indication of what was to come. He appeared in relief and lost, then split two decisions. Four consecutive shutouts followed, leaving Tiant with a 5–2 record and a 1.03 ERA by mid–May.

For the rest of the summer, other than a short stretch in mid–September when he missed a couple of starts due to arm trouble, Tiant was spectacular. He finished the season with a 21–9 record, nine shutouts and a 1.60 ERA, which broke the Cleveland record of 1.82 set by Stan Coveleski in 1917. Nine times he struck out more than ten batters in a game, including 16 Twins in September and 19 Twins in a ten-inning game in July.

Although Tiant was superlative, he was barely better than teammate Sam McDowell, a left-hander who had signed with the Indians in 1960 for a $75,000 bonus. In his senior year at Central Catholic High School in Pittsburgh, McDowell was 8–1, did not allow an earned run in 63 innings, and struck out 123 batters. He said that between Little League, high school, and sandlot games, he'd thrown 40 no-hitters.

Through 1967, however, McDowell was an enigma, a big man (6'5") who could throw unbelievably hard and had flashes of brilliance, but not a consistently good major league pitcher.

McDowell pitched his first major league game before he turned 19, but at 25, the Indians were still waiting for him to fulfill his immense potential. He had a career record of only 56–52, but led the American League in earned run average with a 2.18 mark in 1965, and twice paced the circuit in strikeouts, with a high of 325 in 1965. His 17–11 record that year was by far his best, but McDowell had gone just 22–23 during the succeeding two campaigns. He'd had some arm trouble and always had difficulty controlling his blazing fastball; he was in the midst of an eight-year streak in which he walked at least 100 batters each year.

Rather than just rely on his strong left arm, McDowell was always trying to prove that he was a smart pitcher. One day, Jim Gosger of the Athletics was batting and Gosger's good friend, Duke Sims, was the Cleveland catcher. McDowell's first pitch was a breaking ball over Gosger's head, and after Sims caught it, he laughed. "What are you laughing about?" Gosger asked. "Just wait," Sims replied. McDowell's second pitch was a fastball and the third a knuckleball. "I put down a sign," he said to Gosger, "and he throws whatever he wants." "Then he hung a slider," said Gosger, "and I got a base hit and we won the game. He was screaming at me and I said, 'You stupid SOB. All you've got to do is throw it over the plate.' But that's the way Sam was. He had a million dollar arm and all he had to do was throw the heater, but he wanted to fool them. "[38]

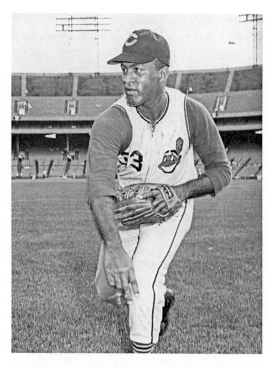

Luis Tiant joined the Indians with a big splash in 1964, shutting out the Yankees and Whitey Ford in his debut. He was steady but unspectacular until posting a 21–9 record, a 1.60 ERA, and 9 shutouts in 1968.

During the winter following the 1967 season, McDowell said he wanted to be traded to a team that had a chance to win the pennant, but he later explained to reporter Russ Schneider that he didn't mean it. "You know me," he said, and told Schneider how enthusiastic he was about the Indians and the trades they'd made. He wasn't too enthused about the salary he'd been offered, but understood that a team that drew fewer than 700,000 fans wasn't giving raises to pitchers with losing records. He signed for a slight pay reduction and vowed to win 20 games. "I've had trouble concentrating," he said, "because I've been lazy."[39]

When the regular season began, McDowell looked like he might have conquered his demons. He broke a record held by Walter Johnson and Bob Feller by striking out 40 batters in three consecutive games. In one of those games, he struck out 16 and, for the first time in his big league career, went nine innings without issuing a single walk. In a July game against the Athletics, he struck out the first five batters to face him. Against the White Sox, he threw over 200 pitches in eight innings. "When you're as big and strong and dumb as I am," he said after the game, "you can throw all night."[40]

McDowell continued his dominating performance throughout 1968, finishing with a 1.81 ERA and a league-leading 283 strikeouts, while yielding only 181 hits in 269 innings. Yet he didn't come close to his goal of 20 wins, and his 15–14 record was barely over .500. He was called "the best 20-game winner who never won 20 games."[41] In 13 of his starts, the Indians were either shut out or scored just a single run. Perhaps McDowell *should* have been traded to a club that could score a little more than the Indians. Four times, he left a start winless despite not having yielded an earned run.

None of the pitchers whose achievements are chronicled above pitched a no-hitter in 1968, although Tiant threw a one-hitter in his final start and the hard-luck Gibson managed to lose a game in which he surrendered only one hit. In a season where pitching dominated the hitters, however, it was inevitable that someone would hold the opposition hitless. It didn't take long; Baltimore right-hander Tom Phoebus set down the Red Sox without a hit on April 27.

Less than two weeks later, Jim "Catfish" Hunter of Oakland did even better than Phoebus, retiring 27 Twins in a row for just the 11th perfect game in major league history, the third in the past four years. It was the first regular season perfect game in the American League, however, since Charley Robertson of the White Sox accomplished the feat in 1922.

Hunter had just turned 22 in April, but he was in his fourth full season with the Athletics after signing for a $75,000 bonus in 1964. He sat out the 1964 season while recovering from the effects of a hunting incident in which his brother accidentally shot off one of the pitcher's toes and left 30 pellets in his right foot. The Athletics gambled that the injury wouldn't prevent him from pitching, and they were right.

Hunter won 30 games in his first three seasons with a very bad Kansas City team. His first appearance on the national stage had come the previous July, when he pitched very well in a losing cause in the 15-inning All-Star Game. Hunter, like most members of the Athletics, had a strained relationship with Charley Finley, but said during the off-season, "[A]s long as Finley pays me, I'll play for him."[42]

Although 1968 was the Year of the Pitcher, it was not a particularly good year for a pitcher named Catfish Hunter, who finished with a 13–13 record and a 3.35 ERA that was well above the major league average. Hunter had pitched five no-hitters in high school, but had none in professional ball when he took the mound against the Twins on May 8.

After 97 pitches and 26 straight outs (including ten strikeouts) Hunter faced pinch-hitter Rich Reese, the only man standing between him and immortality. The count reached 2–2, after which Reese fouled off four straight pitches. On the next pitch, Hunter and catcher Jim Pagliaroni thought they had a third strike, but plate umpire Jerry Neudecker thought otherwise, and Hunter had a three-ball count on a Minnesota hitter for the seventh time in

Big lefty Sam McDowell was a bonus baby who had a blazing fastball and lots of strikeouts but never achieved consistency. He had a 1.81 ERA in 1968 but his record was a mediocre 15–14.

the game. Hunter reared back and threw a fastball over the plate, which Reese swung at and missed for the 27th straight out.[43] A few days later, Finley presented the young pitcher with a $5,000 check in a ceremony at home plate.

George Culver of the Reds threw an unusual no-hitter against the Phillies in July, winning 6–1 and surrendering a run on a two-base error, an infield out and a sacrifice fly. Before the game, Culver was suffering from an upset stomach and took a shot of Novocain for a painful ingrown toenail. His physical maladies made the prospect of a sterling performance highly unlikely, for if Hunter was in the midst of a mediocre season, Culver was in the midst of a mediocre career, which saw him post a lifetime mark of 48–49 over nine seasons. He had the best season of his career in 1968 (11–16) but was better known for his flashy wardrobe and as the boyfriend of professional golfer Donna Caponi.

Other years had seen multiple no-hitters, but the season of 1968 provided an additional thrill in September. On the 17th, Gaylord Perry of the Giants beat Bob Gibson, about the only way Gibson could be beaten in 1968, by pitching a no-hitter. Ron Hunt hit a home run off Gibson in the first inning, one of just four hits off the Cardinals right-hander, or the game might have gone on all night. The win was Perry's 15 against 14 losses, a record that was the product of many tough defeats, for his ERA for the year was 2.44.[44]

The Giants pitcher had just turned 30 two days earlier and had been a highly paid disappointment in his early years. After receiving a $90,000 bonus, he beat a path between Tacoma and San Francisco before winning 12 games in 1964 after veteran pitcher Bob Shaw taught him how to throw a spitball. Two years later, he was a 21-game winner, but he had a mediocre 73–69 career mark before throwing his masterpiece against the Cardinals.

On September 17, 1968, Gaylord Perry of the Giants pitched a no-hitter against the Cardinals. The following night, Ray Washburn of the Cardinals duplicated Perry's feat against the Giants.

Perry had thrown, by his own account, six or seven no-hitters in high school, and his battery mate, Dick Dietz, had caught three in the minors, but neither had ever been part of such a feat in the majors. Dietz accepted a kiss from Perry after the game and praised his fastball, slider and "sinking slider."

The following day, the Giants faced another 30-year-old right-hander, Ray Washburn of the Cardinals, whose career had been as uneven as Perry's. Like the Giants' pitcher, Washburn had signed for a large bonus ($45,000), based upon the blazing fastball he had shown as a prep phenom. Washburn won 12 games in 1962 and his first five in 1963 before tearing a muscle in his shoulder that nearly ended his career. In 1967, he broke the thumb on his pitching hand. But in 1968, the slow curve he'd developed started working for him. With his new pitch, he won seven straight games and was 12–7 when he took the mound on September 18. Through six innings, Washburn and Bob Bolin of the Giants were locked in a scoreless duel. Finally, the Cards scored a run in the seventh and another in the eighth. Washburn set down Hunt, Willie Mays, and Willie McCovey in the ninth to complete a second successive no-hitter. The Cardinals' hurler, who walked five, threw 138 pitches but allowed only two balls to be hit out of the infield.

Not many San Franciscans witnessed the historic events. Attendance was 9,546 for Perry's no-hitter, and the locals were so enthused that 4,703 turned out the following afternoon to see Washburn match the feat. The small crowds pointed out the problem associated with the lack of offense in major league baseball. Shutouts were commonplace, and in 1968 not even a no-hitter was rare. A second problem was that 1968 was the first season the Bay area had two teams. The Athletics had relocated from Kansas City, and neither they nor the Giants were drawing fans, especially after both were eliminated from pennant contention and the fall cold crept in.

There has not been a 30-game winner in the major leagues since McLain's 31 wins in 1968. No one has come close to Gibson's 1.12 ERA or his 13 shutouts. It was 20 years before Orel Hershiser broke Drysdale's record for consecutive scoreless innings. Baseball executives had finally realized they needed to do something to reverse the trend of pitching dominance that threatened to render baseball a tedious succession of low-hit, low-scoring games that kept fans away from major league stadiums. Pitchers were happy in 1968, although, like the Yankees' luckless Fred Talbot, they would have preferred that their own team score a few more runs. But happy pitchers did not lead to profits at the box office. The game had to change.

5

You Handsome Sonofagun,
Don't You Ever Die

In its January 5, 1963, issue, *The Sporting News* ran an article titled, "Bo's Hijinks Pale Beside Old Reveler Antics."[1] The essence of the story was that there were no longer any colorful performers in baseball, and modern players like Angels pitcher Bo Belinsky, the so-called characters of the 1960s, were frauds. Belinsky, *TSN* said, "had some comparatively innocuous adventures bordering on escapades. But compared with [Rube] Waddell and [Bugs] Raymond, Bo was just a tyro." "Where," they lamented, "are the screwballs, oddballs and other freakish characters of yesteryear among the players of the major leagues? ... Possibly there isn't enough fun in the game."

Pictured above the text were Waddell, Raymond, Rabbit Maranville, and Casey Stengel, the "characters of yesteryear." It was an unusual group. Waddell may have suffered from mental illness, Raymond was a pathetic drunk who died a year after leaving baseball, Maranville was also known for his drinking and Stengel, in case the journal hadn't noticed, was still in the game as manager of the Mets.

Alcohol seemed to be a critical component of "color," and *TSN* noted wistfully that with more women and youngsters following baseball, owners and managers were less tolerant of those who had a "serious addiction to John Barleycorn's company.... The days of the pixie and the Barleycorn pal are gone, never to return." Bill Veeck felt the same way. "My nostalgia for the drunks," he wrote, "probably goes back to the Chicago Cubs, with whom I was raised. Three of my Cubs are in the Hall of Fame. Two of them [Grover Cleveland] Alexander and Maranville, were drunks."[2]

There was no need to worry, for while Veeck and baseball's bible lamented the passing of alcoholism from the game, Mickey Mantle, several of his Yankees teammates, and numerous other major leaguers were upholding the tradition as well as ever. Management had simply become more adept at keeping knowledge of the players' private lives from the public.

During the 1960s, *The Sporting News* was far from alone in thinking that baseball lacked color; many said it was dull and out of step with a riotous decade. But those lamenting the absence of characters just didn't look hard enough.

Any discussion of baseball eccentrics of the 1960s must begin with Athletics owner Charles O. Finley, who came on the scene in 1961 with more original ideas than his fellow owners combined. Some of Finley's schemes were ingenious, like playing World Series games at night, while others were hare-brained, but he advocated for all of them with a fervor that was never dampened when no one else agreed with him and everyone ridiculed him. "If anyone had kept count," wrote Marvin Miller, "he would probably find that Finley came up with as many crackpot ideas as good ones. But I'll grant him this: He never stopped trying to think up ways to improve the game and bring out more fans."[3]

Bo Belinsky (right) enjoys a cocktail with Mamie Van Doren and American fitness pioneer Gypsy Boots. After pitching a no hitter in his rookie season, Belinsky took full advantage of his limited fame and carved out a reputation as one of baseball's foremost playboys. He eventually married and divorced Playboy Playmate of the Year Jo Collins.

Finley never attended college, but he was an entrepreneur during his teenage years, always cooking up some money-making scheme. After he finished high school, he unloaded boxcars for U.S. Steel Corporation while selling insurance part-time. He eventually became a full-time salesman, and then hit upon the idea of selling group medical policies to doctors, which is where he earned his fortune.

No one cared about insurance moguls, however, and Charles Finley desperately wanted to be noticed. Owners of baseball teams were public figures, and that's what Finley set out to be. He offered $3 million to Connie Mack for the Philadelphia Athletics in 1954 but didn't get the team, tried to buy the Tigers two years later, and attempted by purchase the White Sox in 1958. In 1960, he tried to get one of the American League expansion franchises, but was unsuccessful once more.

Finley finally bought the Athletics from the estate of Arnold Johnson in 1961 for $3 million and, seemingly from the moment he acquired the team, tried to move it out of Kansas City. There was talk of moving to Oakland as early as 1963, for Finley said he had lost $1 million in his first three years. The Kansas City lease expired at the end of the 1963 season, and negotiations for a new agreement reached an impasse. The city wanted a term of at least four years, and Finley didn't want more than two. He petitioned the league for permission to relocate to Louisville, but his request was voted down by a 9–1 margin. Although the only affirmative vote was Finley's, he didn't give up, flirting with Dallas-Fort Worth, Seattle, and other cities.

The rejection of Finley's proposed move to Louisville came as no surprise, for he had alienated his fellow owners not just with his wanderlust, but with his abrasive personality and radical ideas. They wanted to teach him the same lesson they'd taught another iconoclastic maverick, Bill Veeck. Veeck wanted to move his sinking St. Louis Browns to Baltimore in 1953 but the owners refused and gave him no option but to sell the team, after which the new owners were given permission to move. Perhaps the same strategy could jettison Finley, for he was not doing well in Kansas City.

Finley took the task of adding color to baseball literally, suggesting the use of orange baseballs and outfitting his players in green and gold uniforms. He hired Miss USA to serve as a ball girl[4] and installed a mechanical rabbit called Little Blowhard that popped up behind home plate to provide the umpire with a fresh supply of baseballs. "Charley Finley wasn't the smartest baseball owner I ever knew," wrote Ken Harrelson, "but he sure as hell was the most interesting. Whether or not it made sense, he was always doing something."[5]

Finley had some innovative ideas concerning the way the game was played, much to the consternation of his numerous managers. He employed a full-time pinch-runner, Allen Lewis, known as the "Panamanian Express," whose primary job, which he performed with modest success, was to steal bases.

Lewis was a baseball player who appeared in the outfield on occasion, but in 1974, Finley took the pinch-running concept a step further by signing Herb Washington, a world-class sprinter who hadn't played baseball since high school. He had terrific raw speed, but there were no starting blocks at first base, and the pitcher didn't shoot a starter's pistol when he was going to deliver a pitch. Washington was totally lacking in baseball instincts, and his most ignominious moment was being picked off in a key situation during the 1974 World Series.

When he acquired the Athletics, Finley dismissed the idea that a novice like him should stay on the sidelines, pay the bills, and hire experts to run the team. "It doesn't take any genius to run a baseball team," he said, "as a general manager or a field manager. A monkey could stand out there on the field and wave at the pitchers."[6]

Finley hired insurance man Pat Friday as his GM and attempted to run the operation himself. He orchestrated trades and was very free with advice on how his manager should manage and his players should play. In 1962, when rookie Manny Jimenez was leading the American League in batting average, Finley told him to try for home runs rather than hitting for average, with disastrous results. His average dropped from .398 on May 29 to .301 by the end of the year.

While Finley said a monkey could run a baseball team, the animal he chose to represent the Athletics was a mule. The Kansas City menagerie of animals began when Finley established a zoo in left field, which included capuchin monkeys,[7] China golden pheasants, rabbits, and sheep, all of which were attired in green or gold A's jackets. The star performer, however, was a mule named Charley O, who was sent to a riding academy where, among other things, he learned to bow, a useful talent for any employee of Charles O. Finley. The owner called Charley O. the smartest mule that ever lived.[8]

In New York, Charley O. the owner led Charley O. the mule into the lobby of the Americana Hotel and registered him for a room. Charley O. rode from city to city in an air-conditioned trailer into which Finley piped "mule music" like *Mule Train*. When the White Sox refused to allow the world's smartest mule inside Comiskey Park, Finley displayed Charley O. at a parking facility across the street and posted signs of protest. Then, in the middle of the game, he sneaked a smaller mule into the dugout in a box and let him loose on the field, just as Athletics reliever Jack Aker was preparing to deliver a pitch.

Finley thought it would be wonderful if his ballplayers could ride Charley O. before games. "We were in Los Angeles," recalled catcher Bill Bryan, "and Charley came up to me before the game and said, 'Bill, will you ride the mule around the ballpark for me tonight?'" Bryan grew up on a farm in Georgia, and Finley assumed he must have had some mule jockeying skills.

> I'd walked behind one in the field a couple of times, but I'd never ridden one. But the man owned the ballclub and signed the paychecks, so you can't say, "Hell, no, Charley, I ain't getting on that mule." We didn't make too much money in those days, you remember. So I rode the mule around the ballpark. Charley came into the clubhouse after the game and handed me a hundred dollar bill. I said, "Do you want me to ride him tomorrow night?"[9]

Finley once put Hawk Harrelson on the mule, which got excited and began racing around the field. Harrelson claimed to be a champion at just about everything, but it became quickly apparent he was not a champion mule rider. He nearly fell off and was clinging to Charley O's mane for dear life when the mule finally ran out of gas. Harrelson didn't ask Finley if he could ride the next night.

Charley O. the owner feeds Charley O. the Mule. Charles Finley was a maverick owner who had some great ideas and some terrible ideas. Using a mule for his mascot was probably not one of his better ones.

Each major league acted independently in the 1960s, and thus the National League needed its own eccentric owner, Roy Hofheinz of the Astros. Hofheinz, born in 1912 in Beaumont, Texas, in modest circumstances, was somewhat of a loner as a child, a solitary boy with big dreams. Under his front porch, Hofheinz would build houses and cities, hoping some day to construct the real thing. He wasn't just a dreamer, however, and got a job in a grocery store when he was just nine. In 1924, when he was 12, the family moved to Houston, which was in the midst of a population explosion. As an adult, Hofhienz would leave an indelible mark on his adopted city.

Three years after the family arrived in Houston, Hofheinz's father was killed in an auto accident. Roy was 15 and, like Finley, a high school entrepreneur, promoting dances, running a soda water stand, and producing programs for the school football team. He went to bed late, got up early, and learned to operate with little sleep.

Hofheinz entered Houston Law School in 1930 at the age of 18 and, while still in school, passed the bar at 19. After graduation, he opened a criminal law practice and achieved incredible results, including gaining an acquittal for a man accused of raping his step-daughter. When the man later admitted his guilt, Hofheinz decided it was time for him to exit the criminal law business.

In 1934, the 22-year-old Hofheinz became the youngest legislator ever elected in Texas, and two years later, he became the youngest county judge elected anywhere in the United States. The latter office gave Hofheinz the nickname he would carry for the rest of his life: "The Judge." He became an important figure in Texas politics and worked closely with Lyndon Johnson and John Connally. Like them, Hofheinz became wealthy. After losing an election in 1944, he vowed, "I am not going into politics again until I am a millionaire."[10] He got involved with some business ventures, including broadcasting and a steel slag concern, and began investing in Houston real estate. Hofheinz wasn't afraid of risk and funded many of his ventures with short-term notes, gambling that he could re-finance them when they matured. If the market turned against him, he would have been ruined, but Roy Hofheinz always seemed to have luck on his side. By 1950, he was a millionaire, returned to politics, and was elected mayor of Houston in 1952.

His tenure as mayor was filled with controversy and disappointment. Taxes went up significantly, and Hofheinz battled incessantly with the city councilors, who impeached him. Hofheinz locked himself in his office and survived the impeachment proceedings, but lost the succeeding election. He left office heavily in debt.

Hofheinz had always been a baseball fan, and his station KTHT broadcast Texas League games. One of his financial advisors was R.E. "Bob" Smith, a wealthy oilman 18 years his senior, who was supposedly worth somewhere in the neighborhood of half a billion dollars. In the late 1950s, there were several men, including Smith, George Kirksey, and Craig Cullinan, who were trying to bring major league baseball to Houston. They formed the Harris County Sports Commission, with the intention of building a new stadium. Smith recommended that Hofheinz get involved, and the Judge became vice chair of the Commission and invested more than $300,000 in the venture.

A citizens committee, chaired by attorney Leon Jaworski, who later achieved fame as a prosecutor during the Watergate saga, was formed to encourage public support. The concept of building athletic facilities with public funds was relatively new, and the bond offering for the stadium passed by the relatively narrow margin of 61,658 to 54,127. The approval was sufficient to land the city a National League franchise in 1961, and the following year the Colt. 45s began play in a temporary park that seated 33,000.

Colt Stadium wasn't that impressive, but it had some pizzazz, a foreshadowing of what the new stadium would look like. There was a Fast Draw Club with a saloon and western motif, and sections of the parking lot were named for Wyatt Earp, Matt Dillon, and other Old West figures. Hofheinz was always conscious of attracting female spectators[11] and introduced features that emphasized comfort, although he could do nothing about the infamous Colt Stadium mosquitoes, which attained mythic size and status in future years.

Hofheinz always had a penchant for flashy decor. His home was liberally sprinkled with antiques and circus artifacts, and had a number of themed rooms, including a Circus Room, a French Room, a Gay '90s room, a Harem Room, a Buccaneer Room, and a Brag Room. Hofheinz's goal was to make the permanent Houston stadium an edifice that would be, in true Texas fashion, the most spectacular baseball park ever built.[12] It was formally known as the Harris County Domed Stadium but was invariably referred to as the Astrodome, which was just part of a larger complex that included an Astrohall for livestock shows and rodeos. Future plans called for the creation of a Disney-like theme park.

It was the Astrodome, however, that was the centerpiece of the development—the largest indoor arena in the world and the first covered baseball or football stadium. Sociologist Harry Edwards noted that, like religion, sports had its shrines, and that the Astrodome surpassed even the greatest efforts of the Egyptian Pharaohs.[13] The stadium cost $22 million and the entire project $35.5 million. The dome consisted of 4,596 skylights set in place 218 feet above the diamond. The air conditioning system, which was controlled by a $500,000, rooftop weather station, cost $4.5 million.[14]

The magnificence and grandeur of the Astrodome were impressive, but the innovation that would change the finances of baseball forever was the

There are several domed stadiums today, but when the Astrodome opened in 1965, it was a revolutionary development, the first indoor baseball facility in America.

stadium's luxury boxes. Prior to 1965, the most luxurious accommodations at baseball parks were box seats behind home plate or the dugouts. The Astrodome featured 53 skyboxes, each accommodating 24 to 30 people, that could be leased for $15,000 a year for five years. All were sold out prior to the start of the 1965 season.

Each box bore the mark of an interior designer, and all were laid out with comfort in mind, particularly the comfort of women. Females were out of the elements so that their hair and makeup remained undisturbed for nine innings. The lush furniture was several cuts above the typical folding chairs and bleachers found in other parks, and the food choices went well beyond hot dogs, peanuts, and cracker jack. There was also a private Skydome Club with closed-circuit television that broadcast the game for those who preferred remaining inside. Corporate entertaining became easier and more lavish, and with the high marginal tax rates of the 1960s, deductions were more readily available and much more valuable.

Today, luxury suites are perhaps the key component of any new stadium; selling tickets to the general public is of secondary importance. Ballparks have become restaurants, bars, and entertainment centers, a trend that began with Roy Hofheinz and his Astrodome.[15]

During the first season in the new stadium, the infield and outfield were covered with grass, but grass did not grow well under plexiglass. Groundskeepers painted the surface green, and any outfielder who made a sliding catch was likely to rise to his feet sporting a green jersey. That was not acceptable for the most magnificent stadium in the world, so for the 1966 season, Hofheinz worked with Monsanto Corporation to develop the artificial surface that would be forever known as Astroturf.

No one was sure how a baseball would bounce on a chemically-prepared substance and whether it would dramatically alter the game. When the turf was installed, the ball did not bounce at all like it did off grass. The turf was ripped up and re-installed in the opposite direction, and the bounce was truer. The ball rebounded higher than it did off grass, and balls skipped more quickly past infielders and outfielders. But the bounce was true, with none of the bad hops created by the irregularities of natural surfaces. The game on turf was a bit different, but it was still baseball, and it was better than playing on paint.

Another of Hofheinz's innovations was a $2 million scoreboard that did much more than keep fans informed of the score and the progress of other games. Four stories high, it featured state of the art animation designed to entertain the crowd, using humor and sound effects to cheer the Astros and tease the opponent. A Houston home run initiated a 45-second sequence featuring a raging bull with an American flag on one horn and a Texas flag in the other.

Spectacular scoreboards were a staple for eccentric owners. Finley had also constructed one that went through an elaborate routine each time the Athletics hit a home run. His inspiration was the 130-foot- tall, $325,000 Comiskey Park scoreboard erected by Bill Veeck in 1960. Veeck's board featured flashing neon lights and fireworks, which were ignited for every White Sox homer. It also blasted trumpet calls, foghorns, and the William Tell Overture.

The White Sox's owner received *his* inspiration from a William Saroyan play in which a pinball machine set off an explosive display whenever someone hit the jackpot. Veeck's fireworks expense during the first year was minimal, since the "Go-Go Sox" were next to last in the league in home runs, but on the rare occasions when the scoreboard went off, it was like rubbing salt in the wound of the opposing team.

One player who took particular offense was high-strung Jimmy Piersall, one of the most charismatic players of his generation. The Cleveland center fielder had his own built-in fireworks display, which went off every time an umpire ruled against him on a close play or a pitcher threw too close to him. In 1961, he chased two trespassing Yankee Stadium fans and routed them, dispatching one with a swift kick to the rear. Much of Piersall's erratic behavior was unfortunately due to his mental health problems, but fans didn't know that. They found his eccentricity entertaining and thrilled to his antics. Veeck was a crowd pleaser and so was Piersall, but neither appreciated the way in which the other courted the fans.

"God, it was loud," Piersall wrote of the scoreboard. "All kinds of junk, the debris from the firecrackers, would come floating down on you in centerfield after it went off. It also stunk like hell from all the gunpowder in the fireworks."[16] On May 30, 1960, Piersall's Indians played a doubleheader in Chicago before nearly 46,000 fans, the largest Comiskey crowd of the season. Piersall was ejected from the first game and began throwing bats, balls, gloves, and hats from the Cleveland dugout. He ran across the field to the White Sox dugout and threw a bucket of sand and another bucket filled with orange peels onto the field.

Piersall was booed continuously during the nightcap, and when he caught a fly ball for the final out of the game, someone threw an orange that hit him in the head. He turned and fired the ball against Veeck's precious scoreboard. "I don't care what Piersall throws," Veeck said, "but that had better be the last time he throws anything at my scoreboard."[17]

Veeck's scoreboard became a sore point with the Yankees, who retaliated in a fashion quite unlike the staid franchise that was often compared to U.S. Steel. When Yankee Cletis Boyer hit a home run, manager Casey Stengel and his players lit sparklers on the bench and waved them around. Yogi Berra did the same in the bullpen. "Who's bush now?" Veeck said. "It's typical of George Weiss…. He must have gotten them two for a quarter.[18] I enjoyed it. It was a good idea, and we will reciprocate in kind."[19]

Later that month, when the White Sox visited New York, Yankee Stadium personnel noticed a large, unusual-looking package wrapped in blue paper being delivered to the Chicago locker room. They alerted the New York Fire Department, which opened the package and found a large cache of fireworks inside. As the firemen hauled away the evidence, Veeck described the extensive preparations for his planned incendiary display, and regretted the fact that Yankees fans would not see the fireworks in all their splendor. "Entertaining the fans seems to be contrary to Yankee policy," he said.[20] There was one other problem with Veeck's carefully crafted plan. The White Sox didn't hit a home run that night.

The Yankees won that battle, but by the 21st century, the Yankee Stadium scoreboard took second place to none in terms of noise and "entertainment," blasting commercials and exhorting the fans to make noise, all at ear-splitting volume. Weiss may be spinning in his grave every time the scoreboard erupts, but the staid game of baseball he espoused, like Weiss himself, is long dead. Thanks to men like Veeck, Finley, and Hofheinz, the action on the field is but one facet of an elaborate spectacle. While purists lament the end of a simpler era, the financial results are undeniable. Baseball has expanded its market beyond the hard-core fan, and people with only a casual interest in the sport pay a lot of money to be amused by the frills rather than marveling at a deftly placed sacrifice bunt.

Veeck sold the White Sox in 1961 and Piersall's skills started to fade shortly thereafter, but Finley and Hofheinz took Veeck's place as the resident eccentric owners, and there was another generation of colorful players coming up to replace Piersall. Among them was Bo Belinsky, the man whose exploits supposedly didn't compare to those of Bugs Raymond. *The Sporting News* notwithstanding, few pitchers got as much mileage out of 28 career wins as left-hander Robert "Bo" Belinsky, who spent the 1960s pitching, drinking, dating starlets, and exasperating managers.

Belinsky was an unlikely major leaguer; he never played high school or Legion ball and was signed by the Pirates in 1956 while playing in a sandlot league. "I figured baseball would be just as good as the overalls factory [where he was working at the time]," Belinsky said.[21]

During six years in the minor leagues, Belinsky posted a 43–45 record. By 1958, he was with the Orioles organization, where he struck out a lot of batters, walked a lot, and made it clear that he was not Baltimore manager Paul Richards' type of player. Richards took his baseball very seriously and expected his players to do the same, but Bo Belinsky rarely took anything seriously. In his first year in pro ball he left his Brunswick team twice, the second time for good. In 1961, at Little Rock, he struck out 18 batters in a game and announced afterward he was quitting baseball to study electronics. In 1959, facing a possible statutory rape charge in Pensacola, he was assigned to play for Earl Weaver in Aberdeen, South Dakota, about as far from Pensacola law enforcement as the Orioles could send him. Belinsky supplemented his minor league salary by hustling pool and had a role as an extra in the Jackie Gleason film, *The Hustler.*

Belinsky was drafted by the Los Angeles Angels during the winter following the 1961 season. He'd posted only a 9–10 record with a 3.72 ERA in Double-A ball, but struck out 182 batters in 174 innings. The Angels were in just their second season, and there was opportunity for young pitchers with live arms, even problematic ones. Belinsky shocked the Angels by holding out before his rookie season, but he made the team and opened the season in the starting rotation. On May 5, he got his fourth straight win by pitching the first no-hitter in Angels history, beating the Orioles, 2–0. With a 4–0 record and a no-hitter under his belt, Belinsky reached what would be the pinnacle of his career. He was the toast of Los Angeles and intended to take full advantage of it.

Belinsky took to the LA social scene like a fish to water. Reporters, photographers and, most important, attractive young women sought him out.

He became friends with columnist Walter Winchell, who introduced him to a number of women. He went through a mock wedding in a New York bar. He was sued for $150,000 by a woman who said Belinsky beat her up at the end of a date. He dated a number of celebrities, including Connie Stevens and Queen Saroya of Iran, became engaged to buxom blonde starlet Mamie van Doren, and later married Playboy "Playmate of the Year" Jo Collins.

With so much extracurricular activity on his calendar, time was precious, and Belinsky wasted little of it sleeping. He ignored curfews and sent ulcer-riddled Angels manager Bill Rigney scurrying for his Maalox. Rigney kept fining Belinsky, but it didn't seem to have any effect.

"[H]e never really cared about pitching good and winning," said Angels PR director Irv Kaze. "He never seemed to care about anything. He had a great arm, he could have been a star, but he wasn't motivated. He is the only baseball player I have ever met in my life who didn't care whether he played in the major leagues or the minors."[22]

His night life began to affect Belinsky's performance, and after the no-hitter, his record was spotty. He missed a turn in New York after he "pulled a muscle in his hotel room." The identity of the muscle and the manner in which it had been pulled were not provided. After his 4–0 start, he lost 11 of his last 17 decisions, and a problematic .500 pitcher was not conducive to Rigney's digestive health. Not only was Belinsky pitching poorly, he had become a bad influence on fellow pitcher Dean Chance, an immensely talented youngster who would win the 1964 Cy Young Award.

In late 1962, the Angels "purchased" minor league pitcher Dan Osinski from Kansas City. The transaction was intended to be a trade of Osinski for Belinsky, but when the Angels put the latter on waivers, a prerequisite for any trade subsequent to June 15, the Senators claimed him, blocking the deal. The Angels therefore kept the money and made a gentleman's agreement to deliver Belinsky after the season. Such deals, although they were illegal, were made all the time.

The last thing in the world Belinsky wanted to do was leave Los Angeles for Kansas City, which had great steaks but no starlets. He provided the details of the transaction to the press, which forced Commissioner Ford Frick to step in and rule that Belinsky couldn't be sent to the Athletics. If baseball was looking for publicity, perhaps Frick should have allowed the trade, for a marriage of Bo Belinsky and Charley Finley would have been a journalist's dream.

The Angels were furious at the scuttled trade and more eager than ever to send Belinsky *somewhere*. How about the Mets? "Naw," Bo said, "[Casey] Stengel's 72. He'd have to get a cardiograph if he had me." The Angels had acquired Yankees pitcher Bob Turley on a conditional basis, and if they kept him, they owed the Yankees a player. Might it be Belinsky? "Yeah," he replied. "It'd be good for me to play for the Major [Yankees manager Ralph Houk].

Give me discipline." Belinsky assumed a military stance. "He'd make me stand up straight."[23]

Belinsky wound up going nowhere. He returned to the Angels in 1963 and claimed he was turning over a new leaf. His wild days were behind him, he said, and he was ready to settle down and dedicate himself to pitching. The new leaf was much like the old one, however, and Belinsky overslept and arrived late for the Angels' first spring training session. A few days later, he was tardy again, saying he'd been pulled over by the police, a story later denied by the Palm Springs police chief.

After the season began, Belinsky's pitching was so bad that he was sent to the minor leagues. The Angels' Triple-A team was based in Hawaii, not a bad place for him, but he refused to report for seven weeks. When he arrived, he announced that he was breaking off his engagement with Van Doren, and then he was injured when an elevator door closed on his foot. Belinsky was rarely hurt on the field, but hotel rooms and elevators were apparently more dangerous than opposing batters.

Belinsky was a drawing card in Hawaii, as more than 10,000 fans paid to see his debut and over 16,000 watched his final appearance. He also pitched well—well enough to be recalled by the Angels in September. Following the season, *The Sporting News* ran a headline that said, "All Forgiven—Bo Exhibiting New Attitude."[24] And the next February, "Bo Shunning Bright Lights—It Says Here."[25] The second headline, written with tongue in cheek, appeared over an article from Angels beat writer Braven Dyer of the *Los Angeles Times*, a man who would play a prominent role in the life of Robert Belinsky during the next year.

As expected, the 1964 Belinsky bore little resemblance to a Benedictine monk, but he pitched very well and, for most of the season, managed not to get into any serious difficulty. It would have been out of character for Bo to remain completely silent, however, and based upon his recent good behavior, he asked for a refund of the $750 in fines he had accumulated during his first two years in the big leagues. When the Angels refused, he said he wouldn't get a haircut until they capitulated, a protest that lasted just three weeks.

In early August, Rigney said, "I'd have to say Belinsky has reached maturity."[26] Six days after the article appeared, however, there was an incident at Washington's Shoreham Hotel. On numerous occasions, Belinsky had threatened to quit baseball and find another profession more capable of financing his lavish lifestyle. Dyer questioned Belinsky about an *Associated Press* story in which he said he was going to retire. Belinsky, furious, claimed he had been misquoted and gave Dyer another quote. Dyer had just phoned the story to the *Times* when he received a call from Belinsky. Don't print it, he told Dyer. It was too late, the writer said, and Belinsky let loose a torrent of profanity.

Dyer, a former college football player who'd been a sportswriter since 1923, was from the old school and didn't care for brazen young players like Belinsky. He was also 64 years old, while Belinsky was 27. Good sense would have decreed that Dyer hang up the phone and forget the whole episode. Instead, he decided that Belinsky had insulted him and his profession and that he must demand an apology.

Dyer went upstairs to confront Belinsky, and the next thing he remembered was regaining consciousness with Rigney and the Angels' trainer kneeling over him. He had a black eye, six stitches, some double vision, and no recollection of what had happened. Belinsky, the only witness, claimed that Dyer had attacked him and he punched him in self-defense. He attributed Dyer's injuries to the fact that he must have fallen into the wall.[27]

Belinsky was suspended for the rest of the season, and during the winter he was traded to the Phillies. Philadelphia manager Gene Mauch was even more intense than Paul Richards, and Belinsky's stay in Philadelphia lasted just over a season. He began bouncing back and forth between the majors and minors, and by 1968 he was pitching for the Hawaii Islanders. If he had to be in the minors, Hawaii was probably a good place for him, a lot more exciting than Des Moines or Rochester. He last pitched in the major leagues for Cincinnati in 1970, his final year in professional baseball.

After Belinsky stopped pitching, he fell into a dark abyss. Divorced three times and estranged from his children, he began drinking heavily and developed an addiction to cocaine. His health was also impacted by a lifetime of smoking cigarettes. Eventually, Belinsky managed to right himself, going through drug and alcohol rehabilitation programs and becoming a born-again Christian. He spent the last few years before his death in 2001 working in a public relations capacity for a Las Vegas–area car dealership. The man who'd pitched a major league no-hitter and dated Ann-Margret took great pride in the fact that he was able to keep a regular schedule and show up for work, even though it wasn't much of a job. When he died, he was just 64 years old.

Belinsky's teammate, Angels outfielder Leon Wagner, had an even more tragic end, for he'd been a much bigger star than Belinsky, and in the first years following his retirement from baseball, he appeared to be headed for success in the business world.

Wagner came up in the Giants' organization and hit 51 home runs at Danville in 1956. Unable to displace Willie Mays, Felipe Alou, Orlando Cepeda, and Willie McCovey in the Giants' lineup, he found himself on the Angels' 1961 expansion team. A powerfully built man, Wagner became one of the most feared sluggers in the American League, hitting 193 home runs in six seasons with the Angels and Indians. He made the All-Star team in 1962 and 1963 and hit a home run in one of the 1962 games. "One of these years," he said before the 1966 season, "and it might be this one, I'm gonna hit 55 to 60 home runs."[28] Of course, the year before, he'd said he might hit 70 homers.

Wagner was also one of the most feared fielders in the league, especially by his own pitchers. It seemed as though poor fielding, rather than alcohol, was an integral part of color in the 1960s. Wagner's contemporary, Dick Stuart, was a charismatic first baseman whose horrible fielding earned him the nickname "Doctor Strangeglove". Stuart didn't care about his fielding, often making jokes about it and believing that home runs would keep him in the lineup. Wagner had the same attitude.

Many men come to the major leagues as bad fielders, but with practice and hard work become adequate or sometimes very good. But that required effort, something Wagner didn't think was necessary. In 1969, after he was released by the White Sox, Wagner played for Phoenix in the Pacific Coast League. He let a ball get by him and played it off the wall with such nonchalance that the trainer raced onto the field, thinking he must be injured. No, Wagner assured him, he hadn't run after the ball because he knew that a ball hit that hard would eventually bounce back to him.

Wagner was a good-looking man with high cheekbones that came from his maternal grandmother, a full-blooded Cherokee, and he had a terrific sense of humor. "He and Vic Power," wrote Joe Donnelly, "are baseball's Negro answers to Casey Stengel."[29] The 1950s and 1960s were times of great racial tension, and Wagner dealt with the situation through comedy. In 1965, while leading spring training calisthenics for the Indians, he ordered pushups. "Ten for you white boys," he said, "one for the colored boys and 500

Outfielder Leon Wagner was handsome, witty, and for a few years was one of the top sluggers in the American League. After his baseball career ended, he fell victim to a drug addiction that left him homeless at the time of his death.

for all you guys from Alabama." When he got his first pair of glasses, he put them on in the locker room, looked in the mirror and exclaimed, "Holy cow, I'm colored!"[30]

Once, after colliding with infielder Billy Moran while pursuing a pop fly, Wagner said, ""Imagine me knocking down a man from Georgia and thinking I could get away with it." Between innings, he pretended to cower in the dugout, peeking out to ask, "Has the Ku Klux Klan arrived yet?"[31]

While many players dreaded the end of their playing career, Wagner professed not to care. "I have so much confidence in my moneymaking ability," he said after returning to the minor leagues, "that I blew the $34,000 salary I had in Chicago easier than most guys would give up $10,000. I'd like to go out as an example to those guys who flip out of their minds when they're dropped—the guys who can't face society when their careers are all over."[32]

Wagner last appeared in the major leagues in 1969. For the next two years, he played in the Pacific Coast League and, unlike many former major leaguers relegated to Triple-A ball, he enjoyed it. He liked the fact that he had ten years in the pension plan and appreciated playing without the pressure of major league ball. "I had so much pressure on me," he said, "that I was running and diving for balls that I used to smile at as they went by me in the Pacific Coast League."[33]

When Wagner hung up his spikes (he had hung up his glove long ago) he planned to live off his real estate ventures, his acting career, which included two appearances on *The Man from U.N.C.L.E,* and his record shop and clothing store (whose slogan was "Get your Rags from Daddy Wags"). Unfortunately, his acting career failed to blossom and the store, which was in a bad area, was burglarized several times. "You see any burglars running around in $60 slacks, let me know," Wagner told a reporter.[34]

Wagner had said he wanted to be an example to "guys who can't face society when their careers are all over," but his post-baseball career wasn't an easy one. In 1967, he said, "Mr. [Gabe] Paul has led me to believe that I might be the first Negro to get a good job in baseball when my playing days are though."[35] The job didn't materialize, but Wagner's retirement from the game started out fairly well. In 1976, he was on the Hollywood Park public relations staff. Four years later, when Wagner was 46, he was a salesman and fleet manager for an auto dealer in San Francisco and said he was making $32,000 a year. He'd begun collecting his $8,000 per year pension at age 45.

While on the surface things appeared to going well, Wagner's life had slowly begun to unravel. In 1970, he was arrested for drunken driving in Los Angeles. Two years later, he was beaten and his 24-year-old wife was shot twice by intruders at a friend's apartment. Numerous business ventures failed, he became dependent on drugs and alcohol, divorced three times, and began drifting. Former ballplayers, including Lou Johnson and Mudcat Grant, tried to help. They'd find apartments for him, but he'd get evicted because he spent the rent money on drugs. His two children offered assistance, but his pride would not allow him to accept it.

Pride also drove Wagner to try to keep up appearances. In 2003, the Angels found him and asked him to make an appearance at a school, which he did. "He looked great," said the Angels' Matt Bennett.[36] Wagner may have looked terrific, and he told everyone he was doing great, but by that time he was living in a Lincoln Continental.

Finally, Wagner wound up wandering the streets and living in a shed next to a dumpster, and on January 3, 2004, he died at the age of 69. The man who said he would hit 70 home runs in a season and vowed to be an example for retired players had done neither.

By the late 1960s, baseball's characters reflected the changing times. Belinsky was a playboy of the Frank Sinatra, Dean Martin, Las Vegas variety. He wore his hair slicked back, and he liked Cadillacs and buxom blond actresses. Wagner was a stylish, flamboyant black man who was funny rather than militant. By 1968, some of baseball's most noticeable players had a more rebellious edge and dressed in the mod style that had become prevalent during the second half of the decade.

No one was more stylish, at least in his own opinion, than Boston first baseman/outfielder Ken "Hawk" Harrelson. Harrelson had always possessed the personality for stardom and lacked only the performance. He had good power, and there had been times since entering the American League in 1963 that he seemed on the verge of blossoming. Finally, in 1968, his performance equaled his braggadocio. In the year of vanishing offense, Harrelson hit 35 home runs and led the American League with 109 RBI. At last, he had the numbers to match his image, and he became the darling of Red Sox fans with his hip, mod persona.

Mod fashion was not accepted in the 1968 baseball world. Turtleneck sweaters were too radical for White Sox manager Eddie Stanky.[37] Long hair, beards, and mustaches were forbidden, and the most prevalent manner of tonsorial rebellion was long sideburns. When Mets pitcher Bill Denehy reported to spring training in 1967, he was called to the manager's office to meet with skipper Wes Westrum and general manager Johnny Murphy. "You've been the talk of spring training," Murphy told him, "and it hasn't even started yet. You'll never guess what we were talking about." Denehy hadn't a clue. "It's those fucking sideburns you've got," Murphy shouted. "I want you to cut them off before the first practice tomorrow."[38]

Harrelson had sideburns, wore his hair in bangs and dressed outrageously, with mod Edwardian suits, wide, paisley bell-bottom trousers, white boots, and tinted sunglasses. Occasionally, he topped off his fashion statement with a fake mustache, and he claimed his best outfits cost $300 to $500 each. "I don't care what the Hawk wears," said Boston manager Dick Williams, "as long as he keeps hitting."[39]

Harrelson, a father of three, was in the process of splitting with his wife, whom he'd married when both were 17 and still in high school. He was a hot item on the Boston singles scene[40] and tried to take advantage of his fame by establishing several business enterprises, the most prominent of which was a popular sandwich shop. A song, titled *Don't Walk the Hawk,* was in the works, as was a comic book called *The Hawk.* "The hero would be a guy like Superman," Harrelson revealed, "but he'd wear a Nehru jacket and a medallion with 'H' on it, and he'd have a big nose like mine."[41] Harrelson's lawyer, Bob Woolf, said the Hawk might earn as much as $750,000 per year from his non-baseball activities.[42]

Harrelson acquired his nickname for the size and shape of his nose, and the only thing bigger than Harrelson's nose was his ego. His excerpted auto-biography in *Sports Illustrated* began, "'You handsome son-ofagun, don't you ever die!' I look in the mirror and say that anywhere from one to a dozen times a day—It may sound a little conceited, but when I spot the ensemble, especially the nose that goes with it, I can't help myself."[43]

The Hawk landed in Boston under unusual circumstances, following a bizarre series of events starring Charley Finley. Harrelson had originally been signed by the Kansas City Athletics and, other than a short stint in Washington, played with them for the first five years of his career. In August 1967, during a team flight from Boston to Kansas City, there was an incident, the details of which were vehemently disputed by the parties involved.

The Red Sox spent $125,000 to bring Ken (Hawk) Harrelson to Boston in 1967, and Harrelson spent $10,000 on clothes when he arrived. He brought baseball fashion to a new level and in 1968 had the best year of his career, leading the AL with 109 RBI.

Although the players vigorously denied that any offensive behavior had taken place, and most impartial witnesses agreed that there had been nothing beyond some relatively innocuous horseplay, Finley, against the advice of manager Alvin Dark, fined pitcher Lew Krausse $500 and banned alcoholic beverages from future flights. Why he singled out Krausse was a mystery to the other players, for no one had seen him do anything unusual. Harrelson said Krausse didn't have more than two drinks, and he believed broadcaster Monty Moore told Finley there had been trouble. Finley said he received a letter from TWA about the players' behavior, but an airline spokesman said there had been no letter and that the company had received no complaints from employees or passengers.

Charlie Finley could be a generous man, but only on his own terms. Alvin Dark once said that you could never ask Finley for anything; he had to be the one to offer assistance. Like George Steinbrenner, Finley had a reputation for treating his employees poorly, but like Steinbrenner, he often performed great acts of kindness on his own initiative. He loaned money to players in need and put several into investments that supposedly did very well. Like Steinbrenner, he also liked to recycle people, bringing back Hank Bauer and Dark for repeat management performances.

One thing employees could not do was push Finley into a corner. After Finley issued a statement announcing the disciplinary actions, the players distributed their own statement, calling Finley a meddlesome pain in the neck, or somewhere thereabouts. Finley demanded a retraction, the players refused to back down, and the battle was joined.

Finley summoned Dark to his hotel room and demanded that Dark support him and denounce the players. Dark refused, and Finley fired him. Dark told Finley that he had a fine young team that would win a pennant by 1971 (he was right on the nose) and left the room. A short time later, Finley reconsidered and called Dark to offer him a two-year contract with a raise. When Dark accepted, Finley invited the manager and his coaches up to celebrate.

After about an hour, the party was interrupted by Paul O'Boynick of the *Kansas City Star*. What did Finley think of the players' latest statement, O'Boynick asked? "What statement?" Finley replied. Dark, sitting across the room, realized that he was about to set a major league record for being fired the most times within a three-hour period. "I had to back up my players," he said later. "Everything in their statement was correct." Jack Aker, the Kansas City player representative, asked Commissioner Eckert for a hearing, and the Players Association filed a charge of unfair labor practices with the National Labor Relations Board.[44]

The day after Dark was fired, reporters swarmed the Kansas City clubhouse to get the players' reactions. Harrelson, never shy, was upset and made some very derogatory comments about the Athletics' owner. The next day's paper said he had called Finley "a menace to baseball." Harrelson denied using those words but admitted he had been critical of Finley, who was furious. He had bailed out his spendthrift first baseman with loans on numerous occasions and didn't like the way his generosity was being repaid. Finley called Harrelson and said that if he didn't issue a retraction, he would be released. The Hawk was working on the wording of his statement when Finley called a second time. Forget the retraction, Finley said, he was released anyway.[45]

Harrelson was a free agent, which in 1967 was not, generally speaking, a good thing to be. Since the player could not initiate the process, nearly all of those who were free had become so because their team believed they were no longer worth keeping, nor could they command any value in a trade. Harrelson's situation was different. He was only 25 years old and had been a major league regular for the past three seasons. He had not been released for a lack of ability, and his incident with Finley was unlikely to brand Harrelson as an undesirable. Most of the other major league owners considered Finley a menace to baseball.

At first, Harrelson viewed his release as being "fired" and was afraid Finley had blacklisted him. Gradually, he realized that being a free agent meant that he, a seasoned major leaguer, had the right to sell his services to any of the other 19 major league teams. High school and college players were getting six-figure bonuses to sign; what could a proven regular command?

Harrelson received his first call, from G.M. Ed Short of the White Sox, about a half-hour after he hung up from Finley. Shortly thereafter, he heard from Minnesota, Boston, Detroit, and Baltimore. Luke Appling, who was named Dark's replacement as manager of the Athletics, told Harrelson that Finley had reconsidered and wanted him back in Kansas City. Now the Hawk had his pick of all 20 teams.

Harrelson, who had earned $12,000 the previous year, decided to accept a package deal of $112,000 from the Atlanta Braves. He called Braves GM Paul Richards and told him he was going to sign, but then got a call from Dick O'Connell of the Red Sox. Boston was locked in a bitter fight for the American League pennant, and Tony Conigliaro was out for the season. The Sox desperately needed another outfielder. How much would it take to bring the Hawk to Boston? One hundred and fifty thousand, Harrelson said. "You've got it," O'Connell replied, and, after apologizing to Richards, the Hawk was on his way to Boston.[46]

The Hawk went to Boston and played in the World Series, although he did not hit particularly well. The next season was easily his best in the major leagues, and the best year of Harrelson's life. He was a star in a city he loved, and most of the people of Boston loved him, especially young people. Some people hated him, but everyone noticed him, and that was enough for the Hawk.[47]

Despite Harrelson's great 1968 season, his tenure in Boston was short-lived. He was primarily a first baseman, and not a particularly good one, and since the Red Sox had George Scott at first, Harrelson was moved to the outfield. In 1969, Conigliaro made a heartwarming comeback, and the Red Sox had Harrelson, Conigliaro, Carl Yastrzemski, and Reggie Smith in their outfield. That was one outfielder too many. On the other hand, Boston had too few quality pitchers. On April 19, 1969, they traded Harrelson and pitchers Dick Ellsworth and Juan Pizarro to Cleveland for pitchers Sonny Siebert and Vicente Romo and catcher Jose Azcue.

Harrelson found out about the trade when he received a phone call from the Indians' skipper, who happened to be Alvin Dark, the same Alvin Dark who'd played such an integral role in the Hawk's departure from Kansas City. Harrelson liked Dark, who he said had saved his career by teaching him to stop swinging from the heels. "Welcome, Hawk," Dark said. "Boy, am I glad to have you."[48] What was Dark talking about, Harrelson asked. When Alvin told him of the trade, the Hawk was devastated. How could he be a comic book hero in Cleveland? What about the contract for his autobiography? "But how could they trade me?" he later wrote. "The most popular guy on the team. The most colorful guy in baseball. When hot, the best hitter in the business."[49]

The Hawk couldn't go to Cleveland. He wouldn't. "Boston made me," he wrote. "I didn't know what the hell charisma meant before I went to Boston."[50] He called Woolf and asked if his business enterprises would provide enough income to live on. They would for the average person, Woolf told him, but not for the lifestyle of the Hawk, who estimated that he spent $10,000 on clothes when he arrived in Boston in 1967. Gold and white silk brocade shoes were not cheap, but, as Harrelson said, "You can't save money if you want a really spectacular wardrobe."[51] Despite the fact that he needed his baseball salary, Harrelson, clad in a maize sweater, multi-colored bellbottoms, and white cowboy boots, announced his retirement from the game. If couldn't play in Boston, he said, he wasn't going to play.

After Indians G.M Gabe Paul tried unsuccessfully to convince Harrelson to come to Cleveland, new commissioner Bowie Kuhn asked to meet with him. Harrelson said he wasn't interested, but Woolf convinced him to meet with the commissioner. When Harrelson walked into Kuhn's office, he took hold of Kuhn's lapel and admired the material of his suit. The commissioner failed to return the compliment to Harrelson, who was wearing mahogany-tipped, white cowboy boots, blue bell-bottoms, a white belt, an open-necked, baby blue shirt over a white turtleneck, and a beige ascot.

The commissioner, Paul, O'Connell, and AL president Joe Cronin pleaded with Harrelson to reconsider. They played to his vanity by telling him he would be a star not just in Cleveland, but the entire Midwest. The most powerful men in the game were telling him that baseball needed Ken Harrelson, and he loved it. The Hawk wrote, "[I]t was apparent to everyone that this was a special case—such as had never come up in baseball before and might never come up again. Finally, Woolf convinced me that I had an obligation to baseball that I couldn't ignore."[52] Dramatically, he agreed to go to Cleveland. "I have felt right along," Kuhn said later, "that the loss of Ken Harrelson would be a tragedy for baseball."[53]

A new, more lucrative contract for 1970 had convinced the Hawk to report to Cleveland, and baseball was saved. Upon his arrival, Harrelson was greeted at the airport by a band and a thousand fans chanting, "Hawk, Hawk, Hawk," and was treated like a rock star. Upon learning that a Playboy Club was about to open in Cleveland, he said, "I've been here just a few hours, and already the town is opening up."[54] It might take time, however, as Harrelson's first game in Cleveland was viewed by only slightly more people (fewer than 7,000) than had greeted him at the airport.

Veteran writer Red Smith was incensed by the entire situation. "An utterly absurd spectacle ensued," Smith wrote, "the spectacle of Dick O'Connell, general manager of the Red Sox, Gabe Paul, general manager of the Indians, Joe Cronin, president of the American League, and Bowie Kuhn, commissioner of baseball, pooling their charm to cajole, coax and wheedle a .246 hitter out of leaving the game flat on its face."[55]

But Ken Harrelson was not just any .246 hitter. He was a charismatic figure in a game that desperately needed charisma. He said outrageous things and dressed in an outlandish fashion, and he attracted attention. There were a lot of players with averages higher than .246, but how many fans could recognize Glenn Beckert on the street? There were NFL quarterbacks with better records than Joe Namath, but it was Namath that fans wanted to see. While Harrelson's retirement would hardly be "a tragedy for baseball," perhaps baseball did need Ken Harrelson.

It certainly needed men like Charley Finley and Roy Hofheinz, who realized that 18 men wearing white or gray jerseys playing baseball would not attract new fans to the game. Both men, especially Finley, were frequently ridiculed, but most contemporary teams have colorful uniforms, and they have refined the concept of Finley's mule into humans wearing costumes to make them look like animals. There are a number of domed stadiums, many of which have retractable roofs, eliminating rainouts and lengthy delays. All World Series and All-Star Games are played at night. Luxury boxes can be found even in venerable stadiums like Wrigley Field and Fenway Park.[56]

Baseball also needed a new generation of players who were screwballs, oddballs, and freakish characters, and they got them. When Mark Fidrych burst on the scene in 1976, no one was clamoring for a return of Bugs Raymond and his fifth of rye. After a while, older fans were wondering what had happened to the characters of yesteryear like Bo Belinsky, Leon Wagner, and Ken Harrelson. Someday, they'll miss old-timers like Jonathan Papelbon—-nobody fights in the dugouts anymore, they'll lament. Characters come and characters go, but baseball marches on.

6

I've Just Been Taught a New Trade: I'm a Trained Killer

When he was called up to the Yankees in September 1965, Rich Beck found himself in a place he never could have imagined just a few years earlier. He'd been an average college pitcher who hadn't generated much interest from professional teams, but scout Eddie Taylor, who worked the northwestern United States for the Yankees, thought he saw promise in the young right-hander. Taylor had a good track record, having previously signed Mel Stottlemyre, another Washington native who'd been unimpressive in college. He'd gotten Stottlemyre without offering him a bonus, and by the time Beck was called up, Stottlemyre was on the verge of winning 20 games in his first full major league season.

Taylor's signing of Beck also looked pretty good when the youngster threw a no-hitter in his professional debut. In 1965, his 13–7 record and 2.60 ERA at Columbus got the Yankees' attention, and he was summoned to New York for the final month of the season.

Beck's first visit to the Yankee Stadium locker room was perhaps as great a thrill as actually pitching in the major leagues. "I kept thinking of the team I was joining," he said several years ago. "Mickey Mantle, Whitey Ford, Roger Maris, Elston Howard. I can't even believe now that it happened to me. I watch the Yankees and see [coach] Mel [Stottlemyre] come out to talk to the pitchers, and I have to pinch myself to think that I played with him."[1]

In his first major league start, Beck pitched an excellent game and was the winner on a two-run homer by another September call-up, shortstop Bobby Murcer. In his second start, he pitched a shutout against Detroit. Beck lost his final game, but finished with a 2–1 record and a fine 2.14 ERA, and impressed everyone with his control and poise.

That fall, Beck went to the Florida Instructional League to prepare himself for a run at a position in the starting rotation the following spring. But a funny thing happened on the way to the foursome. In 1958, following his first semester of college, Beck had nearly enlisted in the reserves with some of his buddies. Just as he was about to sign up, however, he learned that his father had terminal cancer and elected to stay home. Had he enlisted, he would have served six months on peacetime active duty, sporadically thereafter, and completed his military obligation.

Now, in 1965, with the Vietnam War escalating, Beck's military obligation remained unfulfilled. He was eligible for the draft, and call-ups had increased to 40,000 per month. Still, Beck wasn't worried, because he was married and the Selective Service wasn't taking married men. "Some ballplayers were putting on a little speed in getting married and starting a family," wrote pitcher Dave Baldwin, "in order to avoid the draft—to have a child or even a pregnant wife earned a ballplayer a 'get out of the military free' card."[2]

As manpower needs increased, however, the exemption for married men was eliminated. Beck was in Florida, working on his breaking stuff, when he got a letter from his draft board in Pasco, Washington, informing him that he had been called for a pre-induction physical. The letter instructed any recipient who was not in the vicinity of his home to take the letter to the nearest Selective Service office. Beck followed instructions and went to the Sarasota office, which scheduled him for a physical in Miami. Prior to the date of the physical, however, Beck's arm began to get a little tender, and the Yankees decided to send him home early. Beck contacted the Selective Service for instructions and was told that his file would be sent back to Pasco, and that he should report there as soon as he arrived.

The delay was to Beck's benefit, for he would be ineligible for the draft when he turned 26 on January 21, 1966. When Beck was signed by the Yankees, Taylor had shaved a year off his age, a year Beck now readily admitted to. Every day was critical, for he could not be inducted until at least 21 days after his physical. Thus, if Beck could delay the exam until after December 31, he would be a free man. The Selective Service office closed for the holidays on December 22 and, by the time Beck arrived back in Pasco, it was early December.

Apparently, someone at the Pasco Selective Service Office was also watching the calendar, and Beck was given a physical on December 21. He passed, but until he received his induction notice, Beck was not in the service, and as January crept along he grew hopeful.

On January 20, one day before his 26th birthday, Beck received his induction notice. "I couldn't believe it," he recalled. "How could this have happened?" He wadded up the draft notice and threw it across the room several times, and then thought of more practical steps. He attempted to enlist in the Air Force, but was told he would have to sign up for at least four years. That would make him a 30-year-old rookie when he got out. The Navy and Officers' Candidate School had the same four-year requirement.

Many baseball players served in the military reserves during the Vietnam War, and a few saw combat. Joe DiMaggio, an old hero and World War II veteran, is shown visiting the troops in 1969.

There was one last glimmer of hope. As soon as he got his induction notice, Beck called Eddie Taylor to see if he could help. Taylor called the Yankees, who found a spot in a reserve unit in Fort Lauderdale. With exemptions being whittled away, joining the reserves was the only way to be certain of avoiding a trip to Vietnam. The demand was therefore great while the supply of openings was extremely low. Still, professional baseball clubs were very good at finding one of those precious places for their young ballplayers.

Pitcher Jerry Hinsley of the Mets recalled getting his draft notice in 1964. He called Mets executive Johnny Murphy, who told him the team would fly him to his home in Las Cruces, New Mexico, and get him enlisted in the National Guard. When Hinsley arrived in Las Cruces, he went to the recruiting office. "I said, 'I want to join the National Guard.' They said, 'Yeah, right, so do about two thousand other people right here in this town. There's no way.'" Hinsley returned to New York and reported his news to Murphy. "He said he'd take care of it," Hinsley recalled. "The next thing I knew I was in the National Guard."[3]

Fellow Mets pitcher Bill Denehy had a similar experience. He also called the club upon receiving his draft notice and was told to call the Governor of Connecticut (his home state), who would take care of it. "I don't know the governor," Denehy thought. His father did know a gentleman named John Tynan, the Commissioner of Motor Vehicles and a leader of the state Democratic Party. "The first day I went to sign up," Denehy recalled, "I was like number 252 on the waiting list. Mr. Tynan made some calls and told me to go back again and see a certain sergeant. I went back the next day, and the following day I was in Fort Dix getting my head shaved."[4]

In 1968, a sergeant and corporal in the Army National Guard were arrested and charged with soliciting a bribe from New York Jets football player Bob Schweickert in order to get him into a reserve unit. Schweickert reported the attempt to the FBI, who monitored him as he turned over $200, and they then arrested the two recruiters.

In 1966, Representative Lucien Nedzi of Michigan discovered that there were 313 professional athletes in military reserve units, and that only two of 960 pro football players had been drafted that year, even though many were of draft age. How could such ratios be possible without rigging the system? In response, Defense Secretary Robert McNamara announced that beginning February 1, 1967, openings in reserve units would be filled on a first-come, first-served basis. He surmised that perhaps athletes had been given preference in the past because of their superior physical fitness, but said that candidates meeting the minimum qualifications would henceforth be accepted in the order of their application.

McNamara's order did not end the controversy, as sports teams continued to use every avenue to exempt their players from active service. In 1969, Boston Celtics guard Jo Jo White enlisted in a Connecticut Marine Corps Reserve unit while he was under an induction notice and ineligible to join. Further, White was not a resident of Connecticut, and the address he gave the reserve unit was that of NBA administrator Carl Scheer.

Connecticut Senator Abe Ribicoff and Missouri Senator Thomas Eagleton were accused of aiding White, although both denied any knowledge of the affair. After some sanctimonious posturing, frantic back-pedaling, and behind-the-scenes maneuvering by Celtics GM Red Auerbach, White was allowed to remain in the reserve unit and was released in six months to join the Celtics. Auerbach had pulled off another in a long line of coups, for he had selected White with the ninth pick in the draft after other teams bypassed him due to the fact that he was expected to spend the next two seasons in the service.

In early 1970, Florida attorney George Foss filed suit against the New York Yankees for $1,984 in legal fees owed him for attempting to help Yankees farmhand Jimmy Babyak avoid the draft. Babyak was no Jo Jo White; he was a 5th-round draft choice who had played just 15 undistinguished games with Class-A Fort Lauderdale in 1967. When Babyak was reclassified as 1-A the following spring, he went to Foss and asked for help.

Foss, Babyak, and Yankees Vice President Johnny Johnson met in a Hollywood, Florida, hotel room, and Foss agreed to take the case. He said he did so only because he had assurances from Johnson that the Yankees would pay him. Johnson denied making any agreement for payment and said that Babyak was responsible for Foss's fees. It wasn't just the money that was at stake, for it would reflect very poorly on the Yankees, whose very name and logo connoted patriotism, if they were hiring lawyers to help young men avoid the draft.[5]

Foss won the case and a judgment against the Yankees. Babyak went to Vietnam and was injured in service. He returned to the Yankees' organization in 1969 and played just two more seasons in the low minors.

Beck hoped for the last-minute reprieve granted so many professional athletes, but just when it appeared that the situation might be redeemed, he learned that the loophole had been closed. Just weeks earlier, a law had been enacted stating that once a man had been drafted, he could not enlist in a reserve unit unless it was for a longer period of time than he would serve if drafted. The final door had been slammed shut.

"I looked in the mirror," Beck recalled, "and said, 'What do you want to do? Do you want to play baseball?' I figured I had 730 days left and I'd take it one day at a time and hope I didn't get shot."

Beck, with his finance degree, spent his entire military career in the Finance Corps at Fort Hood, Texas. "That was incredible for the Army," Beck said, "because normally if you're a cook they make you a truck driver and vice versa." Beck narrowly avoided being shipped to Vietnam on one occasion, but completed his hitch in one piece and arrived in the Caribbean in the winter of 1967 to resume his baseball career.

Following a season of winter ball, Beck reported to Fort Lauderdale in February 1968. He was no longer a 26-year-old with a strong September behind him, but a 28-year-old who hadn't pitched in two years. Things had changed since the fall of 1965, and the window of opportunity which was open that September had closed almost completely. In 1966, while Beck was at Fort Hood, rookie Fritz Peterson won a spot in the starting rotation, and Dooley Womack made the staff as a reliever. One of those spots could have been Beck's.

The inactivity had also taken a toll on Beck's confidence, and it showed in his pitching, He was sent to Syracuse in the final cut. "I never did get it back," Beck said. "That was very frustrating to me."

Beck pitched for two seasons in the minor leagues, retired and became a banker. He always wondered what might have been if someone at the Pasco draft board had been a day or two late processing his papers, but realized that, in the larger scheme of things, he had, in many ways, led a charmed life. With the perspective of nearly 40 years, Beck reflected on his fate.

"I'm no longer the 26-year-old throwing the induction notice around the room and feeling sorry for myself," he said. After his banking career, Beck taught in a Pasco high school, where his students once asked him about his tough break. "I told the kids how upset I was," he recalled.

> I was *really* upset. Then I asked them a question. "What do you think the mother or father, or the brother, or sister of one of the servicemen who was killed in Vietnam would think of my story?" I've got three kids. I'm alive to talk to you today. There were a lot of 18- and 19-year-old kids that I was in basic training with who went to Vietnam and never came home. Maybe they dreamed their dream, but they never got a chance to realize it. By the time I got drafted, I'd already realized my dream.

War and baseball have been intertwined since long before Rich Beck was born. During the Civil War, baseball was in its infancy, and the war greatly curtailed its activity. During the two World Wars of the 20th century, baseball, by then a mature sport, was severely impacted by having many of its players inducted into the armed forces. The 1918 season was ended prematurely due to a shortage of players, and the years 1942–1945 saw a number of 4-Fs, overage veterans, and career minor leaguers replacing stars who were serving their country.

During the 1950s, many players were drafted and fulfilled a two-year hitch in the service. Willie Mays missed most of the 1952 season and all of the following year. Whitey Ford, following a terrific rookie season in 1950, spent the next two years in the military. Mickey Mantle escaped only because of the horrific condition of his legs. After his first season in the minor leagues, he took a physical and was classified 4-F. After an amazing spring training performance in 1951, people began wondering why such a magnificent specimen was not serving in Korea. Mantle agreed to go for another physical, which confirmed the result of the first.

The next year, the Army established a regulation which declared that men with osteomyelitis who had been treated for two years could be inducted into the service. There was no doubt that the rule was directed exclusively at the most famous osteomyelitis case in America. By this time, however, Mantle had other problems. He'd suffered a serious knee injury in the 1951 World Series and, in 1953, failed a third physical.

In the late 1950s, fewer players were drafted, but when crises arose in Berlin and Cuba, they became more vulnerable. In 1960, the Yankees had so many minor leaguers in military service they couldn't field a team in the Florida Instructional League. Even the Mets' statistician had to miss a weekend to serve in the reserves. When the Vietnam conflict began to escalate, draft calls dug even deeper.

Mantle's civilian status during the Korean War had created great resentment in some quarters, and he received a number of hate letters. Athletes of the Vietnam era also faced criticism if they expressed any hesitance to serve.

Star guard Earl Monroe of the Baltimore Bullets told a reporter he would refuse to go in the service if he passed an impending physical. Would he go to prison for resisting the draft? "Prison is nothing. Another day's work, that's all," he replied.

The next day, following the negative reaction to his comments, Monroe denied saying he would not go. When the *Baltimore Sun*, which had published the article, stood by the accuracy of the quotes, Monroe said he was upset in the locker room—he had missed an easy, last-second layup that cost the Bullets the game—and couldn't remember what he said. It all came to naught, for Monroe was never faced with the decision; he failed the physical due to the condition of his knees and was classified 4-F.

The most notorious draft evader of the 1960s was the heavyweight boxing champion known alternatively as Cassius Clay or Muhammad Ali. Ali's request for a deferment was based upon his Muslim beliefs, which would not allow him to participate in war. The Louisville draft board was hesitant to grant a deferment to a famous athlete, perhaps more so since the erstwhile conscientious objector and decrier of violence made his living beating other men senseless. For his refusal, Ali was stripped of his heavyweight title.

Joe Namath, the most famous football player of the 1960s, was 4-F because of his surgically repaired knees, and two Florida congressmen asked for an inquiry. "The Army," replied Selective Service director Lewis Hershey, "can't afford to have four or five trainers around to prepare these people before a fight and take care of them afterwards."[6]

Peacetime military duty for an athlete was not particularly arduous. Former Pirates and Mets star Donn Clendenon spent the winter of 1957–1958 on active duty, mostly playing flag football and basketball. General Mark Clark, of World War II fame, was Clendenon's commander at Fort Jackson, and Clark desperately wanted to win the Third Army basketball championship. Clendenon was the star of the team, and Clark wanted to be sure he had plenty of time to practice. "The life of a jock assigned to special services in the Army isn't bad at all," Clendenon wrote. "We did nothing but hang around the gym, practice, and visit the mess hall any time we wanted to eat. I would receive passes to go home on some weekends when we did not have a game."[7]

With the nation at war, as it was during the 1960s, ballplayers were expected to act like real soldiers, and some demonstrated remarkable proficiency. Denehy, a mortar specialist, recalled a competition in which the reservists were required to shoot a rifle and a .45 pistol, perform bayonet drills, engage in hand-to-hand combat, practice first aid, and demonstrate a few other martial skills. He won the Proficiency Test Award as the best of 250 soldiers and achieved the highest score that anyone in the camp had ever gotten. "I was handed a trophy by a general at Fort Dix," he recalled, "and he said, 'The young man you see in front of you is the finest killer we've ever produced.' Where do you put that on your resume?" Mets pitcher Tug McGraw remarked, after six months on active duty with the Marines, "I'm 21 and I've just been taught a new trade. I'm a trained killer."[8]

In 1970, reservist John Ellis of the Yankees was called upon to quell a disturbance at Yale University. The incident occurred not too long after Guardsmen had killed students at Kent State, and the atmosphere was tense. "If I got killed defending my country somewhere," Ellis said, "it might be worth it, but I'd hate to die 60 miles from home because of a riot. But if I were being attacked by a mob, I would fire. After all, it would be them or me."[9] Fortunately, Ellis didn't have to fire.

One of the few major leaguers to serve in Vietnam was Senators out-fielder Gene Martin, who was drafted in 1965 after his first professional season. He trained as an Army parachutist and was sent to Vietnam in February 1967. Martin served as a parachute rigger and, although he was often within a couple of miles of the shooting, he was never in combat. The only jumps he made were while training in the U.S. Just days before Martin was scheduled to leave Vietnam, the Communists launched the Tet offensive, and Martin feared he might never make it home.[10]

He made it, and there was no one in Pompano Beach during the spring of 1968 happier to run laps or shag fly balls than Gene Martin. "Some nights," he said of the Tet battle, "you got a feeling you'd never pull out of it, so it's hard for me to believe all I'm doing now is playing baseball."[11] After spending the early season with the Class-A Burlington club, he found himself in Washington by July. Martin appeared in just nine games, mostly as a pinch-hitter, but hit .364 and achieved a fame of sorts when he was one of the players sent to Philadelphia in the Curt Flood trade.

During the Vietnam era, one of the most important facets of a ballplayer's resume was his draft status. During spring training in 1966, Tigers minor leaguer George Gmelch was taking correspondence courses in order to maintain his student deferment. The Tigers let him study in their offices during the evening, and one night, while wandering around the building, Gmelch discovered a room where he found a chart on which the draft status of every player in the Tigers' organization was identified by means of a colored star next to his name.[12]

Veterans who were too old to be drafted and were not in the reserves became valuable commodities. "Hal Reniff and Phil Linz may be worth more to us now," said Mets GM Johnny Murphy in January 1968.[13] When discussing the competition for jobs in the Mets' 1968 camp, writer Joe Durso segregated the candidates into military and non-military groups.

Two-week stints in summer camp also opened up opportunities for minor leaguers who otherwise would not have been in the majors, and sent some who would have been major leaguers to the minors. Don Shaw pitched very well for the Mets as a reliever in 1967, before leaving the club in August to fulfill his reserve obligation. Despite a good showing the following spring, Shaw was sent to the minor leagues. "We know he can pitch in the major leagues," said manager Gil Hodges, "but he's going to be lost to us for a number of days in military service this year."[14] Hodges had enough players shuttling in and out of New York and needed one who was going to be around all season. He elected to keep veteran lefty Billy Short, who was beyond draft eligibility.

In 1967, Cubs pitcher Ken Holtzman began the season with a 5–0 record before being called into the service in May.[15] During August and September, he arranged to pitch while on leave and won four more games, finishing with a perfect 9–0 mark. That same year, Tony Conigliaro of the Red Sox spent much of the early season fulfilling his reserve duty before having his military obligation, and the rest of his baseball season, terminated when he was beaned by a Jack Hamilton fastball in August.

Managers juggled pitching rotations in order to start reservists before they departed for duty or when they could obtain a weekend pass. In the spring of 1968, six Mets pitchers were in the reserves, which wreaked complete havoc with the rotation. Manager Hodges not only had to decide upon a four- or five-man rotation—he had to be cognizant of military schedules. Pitchers commuted from Army bases and arrived to pitch with little or no sleep. They were removed from games early in order to catch planes back to base. In July 1970, Angels pitchers Rudy May and Tom Murphy finished working with their reserve unit on Friday, flew to New York on Saturday, and each won his start in a Sunday doubleheader sweep over the Yankees. Then they flew back to California to report for duty Monday morning.

The Orioles' Ron Hansen, who was inducted into the service in 1962, figured he could still play at least 100 games. He was stationed at Fort Meade, Maryland, and could make all 81 home games. He could play in Washington, just a few miles away, which gave him nine more games. He'd save his weekend passes for road trips. Bobby Tolan of the Reds managed to get three passes during his first four days of reserve duty, and commuted 500 miles each way to play against the Mets.

In 1967, Chicago first baseman Tom McCraw was scheduled to leave for his reserve meeting immediately after a game in New York. In order for McCraw to make the flight, a cab, which sat waiting outside, had to leave Yankee Stadium by 10:30. With the Yankees leading, 1–0, McCraw came to bat in the ninth inning. At 10:18, he hit a double. Just before the witching hour, McCraw scored the tying run on a single by Ken Berry, dashed from the field to the locker room and then into the cab. While he was en route to the airport, the Yankees scored in the tenth inning and won the game, 2–1.

Pitcher Danny Frisella of the Mets faced a similar dilemma two months later. He started a game on a night when he had to catch an 11:30 flight from JFK Airport. Manager Wes Westrum placed a curfew of 10:15 on his pitcher. Frisella pitched into the seventh inning and then dashed to a waiting taxicab. He heard on the radio, during the ride to the airport, that the Mets had won and he had his first major league victory.

In July 1968, Senators ace reliever Darold Knowles became the first active major leaguer to be called to service during the Vietnam War. In January, his 113th Tactical Fighter Wing Air Force reserve unit was activated in the wake of the *Pueblo* crisis. Knowles was stationed at Andrews Air Force Base, an easy commute from D.C. Stadium. For the first three months of the season, he managed to appear in 32 games (the most on the Senators' staff) on overnight and weekend passes. Once, after a weekend series in Anaheim, Knowles landed in Washington at 6:30 a.m. and had to report for a full day of duty at 7:30. Ironically, while pitcher Knowles was flying around the country with the Senators, airman Knowles never left the ground. He pitched extremely well (2.18 ERA) despite an exhausting regimen that came to an end in early July when he was sent to Japan.

Losing a player for two weeks in the middle of the season was a major disruption, and occasionally, the consequences were even more serious. In 1969, Carlos May, an outstanding White Sox rookie, blew off the first joint of his right thumb in a mortar accident.

Being away from baseball for extended periods made for a difficult season. "I experienced so much frustration that particular season [1968]," said Nolan Ryan, "in large part because I couldn't focus on my game. I was juggling two worlds, two commitments, all the time."[16]

"It killed you," said Yankees outfielder Steve Whitaker. "It kills you if you're on the DL, let alone not having any practice at all. We were practicing throwing grenades, not baseballs." For a few anxious days, during one of his two-week reserve stints, it appeared that losing his timing was the least of Whitaker's worries. He was put on a plane to Fort Polk, Louisiana, for a secret journey. No one knew where they were going or why.

"It was serious stuff," Whitaker recalled. "I didn't know if the Yankees would be able to protect me and keep me from going over there [Vietnam], because they were calling everybody up then." He arrived at Fort Jackson and was told to wait there until he received his final orders. "I'll bet you," he said, "that 90 percent of the guys went to Korea or Vietnam." Whitaker wasn't one of them. "We got our orders and mine were good and everybody else's were bad. I was lucky and I'm sure the Yankees had something to do with that."[17]

A few years later, Whitaker met one of the soldiers he had served with, who told him about all their buddies who didn't come back from Vietnam. "Shit," Whitaker said, "I was one of the lucky few. I can sit here and cry but, hey, I'm alive. Sure, it could have hurt my career and it was a pain in the ass, but I didn't have to go over there. From that perspective, what's baseball? Guys were losing their lives over there. Shit, I'll never complain about that."[18]

Military service played a major role in baseball of the 1960s. Players had their seasons interrupted, managers had their lineups disrupted, and some players, like Rich Beck, had their careers ended. Yet, Beck's speech to his students placed the situation in perspective. Baseball was inconvenienced, while tens of thousands were killed and many thousands more maimed. None of them got to sit in the Yankees locker room or pitch from a major league mound for even three games. Rich Beck had done both and would be eternally grateful.

7

The Entire Chain
of Events Is of Utter
Embarrassment to Baseball

The 1968 baseball season was scheduled to commence with three games on April 8, including the traditional openers in Washington and Cincinnati, with eight games to follow the next day. None of those games was played as scheduled, however, as for the first time in the history of major league baseball, the opening game of the season was postponed for a reason other than inclement weather. Baseball, which had been played through two world wars, depressions, and natural disasters, fell victim to the internal strife and violence that had been plaguing America for the past year. Nineteen-sixty-seven had been called "The Summer of Love", but it could easily have been known as the "Summer of Hate".

Nineteen-sixty-seven had been one of the most violent years in the domestic history of the United States. During the second half of the 19th century, bitter and deadly labor disputes had wracked the nation, but since that time, there had been nothing to compare to what happened in America during the summer of 1967. There was some form of rioting in 150 cities, ranging from small, localized outbursts that were quickly contained to full-blown riots that continued over several days, destroyed significant portions of cities, and resulted in numerous deaths.

The first disturbance occurred on a sweltering day in Tampa on June 11, when police pursued three black youths following a break-in and fatally shot one of them, a 19-year-old named Martin Chambers. Soon a crowd of several hundred angry blacks gathered and instigated a wave of violence that continued for two days.

On June 12, during the second day of rioting in Tampa, a conflagration erupted in Cincinnati. The cause of the riot dated back about a year, when a black man was convicted of the murder of several white women in a case referred to the "Cincinnati Strangler." One of the condemned man's relatives believed the conviction was unjust and took up the cause. On June 11, another relative was arrested for a minor violation. This, in combination with other incidents, led to some fires, the tossing of Molotov cocktails, and rocks being thrown at police cars. The National Guard was called in and quickly restored order.

On June 17, Atlanta became the scene of the week's third riot. Again, a minor incident, this time an arrest for shoplifting, was the instigating factor. Twenty-six-year-old, Jamaican-born Stokely Carmichael, head of the Student Nonviolent Coordinating Committee, showed up and organized a group of 200 protesters, which faced down about 300 policemen. Fortunately, the violence was short-lived and peace was quickly restored. A petition signed by one thousand residents of the mostly black Dixie Hills section requested that Carmichael leave town so that they could address their grievances on their own.

The riots in Tampa, Cincinnati, and Atlanta scared a lot of people but, in terms of fatalities and property damage, they were but a prelude to the worst episode of the summer, which took place in Detroit, a city with a long history of difficult relations between the black and white races. In early July, H. Rap Brown came to Detroit for a Black Power rally and said, "If Motown doesn't come around, we are going to burn you down!"[1]

In the early morning hours of Sunday, July 24, Detroit police raided an after-hours drinking establishment on 12th Street, interrupting a party for returning Vietnam veterans. After milling around for an hour or so, witnessing the arrests, and accusing the police of using excessive force, the crowd sprang into action. A bottle was thrown through the window of a police car, and someone screamed that there was going to be a riot.

Within an hour, the crowd swelled into the thousands, widespread looting commenced, and the first fires were set. By mid-morning there were 540 officers positioned in the six-block area, and social workers and community activists arrived to try to quell the violence by peaceful means.

The most prevalent activity was looting, and people who otherwise took no part in the rioting sensed an opportunity to acquire goods at a greatly reduced cost. They invaded stores and helped themselves, generally behaving like bargain-hunting shoppers on the day after Thanksgiving rather than rioters.

By late afternoon, the fires were spreading, and by the time they were extinguished, 683 buildings were damaged. Michigan Governor George Romney requested the assistance of the National Guard, which began to arrive around 7:00 p.m. Seven hours later, seven people lay dead and the city was occupied by 2,000 state police and guardsmen. Many of the soldiers were nervous, jittery, and trigger-happy, firing whenever they suspected sniping. They inadvertently shot out a number of street lights, which made nighttime even more dangerous.

On Sunday, while the Yankees and Tigers played a doubleheader at Tiger Stadium, smoke from burning buildings could be seen behind the left field fence. Between games, Tigers general manager Jim Campbell visited the clubhouse, told the players about the violence permeating the city, and advised them to go straight home after the game. He wasn't as concerned about the safety of the crowd of nearly 35,000. "The edict from Campbell," wrote Tigers pitcher Denny McLain, "was that baseball must be in a world of its own. There was a war taking place on the other side of our left-field wall, but Campbell wouldn't even allow a public service announcement for the fans' safety."[2] Broadcaster Ernie Harwell was told not to mention the riots on the air, but the Tigers' next series, scheduled to take place against the Orioles in Detroit, was moved to Baltimore.

While McLain observed the carnage from a distance, his teammate Mickey Lolich was much closer. Lolich was a member of the 191st Michigan National Guard unit and had been assigned to a supply depot and a radio tower, which he guarded with rifle in hand.[3] Another Tiger, outfielder Willie Horton, still in uniform, visited the riot-torn area after the games, climbed atop a car and tried to convince the rioters to go home. "It looked like there was a war out there," he told writer Tim Wendel years later. "I've never seen stuff like that—burning buildings, looting, smoke everywhere." Concerned about his safety, the residents told Horton to go home.[4]

Finally, on Thursday, July 28, Detroit was calm enough to declare the violence ended. Forty-three people, 33 of them black, were dead, and 7,200 more were in jail. Property damage was estimated at $40–45 million.

Detroit's riot was the worst of 1967, but there were others, including disturbances in the New Jersey cities of Newark, Plainfield, Englewood, Jersey City, and New Brunswick. Interestingly, the greatest level of violence occurred not in Southern cities, which had been legally segregated until the early 1960s, but in the North, where there had been no legal segregation or sanctioned discrimination for many decades.

There was *de facto* segregation, however, and riots, not the ideal vehicle for promoting racial harmony, were a rare time when the two races mixed. Blacks encountered white policemen and soldiers who shot at them and arrested them, and whites witnessed blacks threatening to kill them and steal all their possessions. One can understand both the anger of blacks who'd faced discrimination and violence for decades, and the fear and hostility of whites who heard radicals like Carmichael and Brown vowing to destroy them, or saw blacks looting and burning the businesses they'd worked hard to acquire.

By the time 1968 rolled around, the government had learned some valuable lessons about riot control. One was that restraint in the use of firearms spared lives and avoided the type of incident agitators used to fan the flames.

It wasn't long before the police had a chance to apply their lessons. During the evening of April 4, word spread throughout Washington, D.C., that the Reverend Martin Luther King, Jr., had been shot and killed. Carmichael was in the city and went from one business establishment to the next in the area of 14th and U Streets, N.W., demanding that the owners close their shops out of respect for Dr. King.

The young radical, wearing his trademark fatigue jacket, walked up and down 14th Street, animated and vocal, but not violent. Predictably, however, some young blacks began smashing glass windows and damaging both white- and black-owned establishments. "This is not the way," Carmichael shouted at a young boy who'd just broken the window of a theater. Realizing that the night was about to turn violent, Carmichael, who was being watched very closely by the District police, decided that discretion was the better part of valor, jumped into a waiting Mustang, and left town.

There was no stopping the angry mob, whose mood vacillated between violence and celebration. As the *Washington Post* explained, "The evening had started with a hostile, anti-white tone. Now some of the hostility seemed to be forgotten in the carnival excitement produced by the looting."[5]

The police did little to prevent the looting, partly because they were greatly outnumbered and also because they had strict orders to refrain from using firearms unless their lives were in danger. Many store owners kept guns on the premises, and several used them to keep crowds away. While they could not hold off an angry mob by themselves, it was much easier for the looters to go to one of the many undefended stores.

By the early morning hours, it appeared that the situation was stabilizing, but a few hours later, violence erupted once more. Fires broke out and raged out of control, as the crowds threw rocks and bottles at firemen as they attempted to extinguish the blazes. The police had been lulled into a sense of false complacency, many had been sent home to rest and, now, with the riot at full force, the Washington force was disorganized.

At about 3 p.m. on Friday, President Lyndon Johnson ordered federal troops to the area, but deployment was hindered by the lack of communication throughout the city. The phone system was overtaxed, and it was difficult to get a free line. Traffic was hopelessly gridlocked, and any white person stuck in a traffic jam in the area of 14th Street was in grave danger.

The lessons of Detroit had been instructive. Deputy Secretary of Defense Cyrus Vance, who'd been in Detroit, was the point man for many decisions made during the Washington violence. Police and guardsmen were much more restrained in the use of their weapons, and a curfew was imposed on the entire city to keep people off the streets. More tear gas canisters and fewer bullets were fired. National Guard units were better trained and prepared, and contained more black soldiers. Street lights were not shot out by soldiers.

Any report of sniper fire was thoroughly investigated before any shots were fired in response.

There were 12 deaths in the District of Columbia, compared with 43 in Detroit, and many of those were not caused by the police. More than one thousand people were injured, but few of the injuries were serious. Property damage was estimated at $27 million, significantly less than the $40–45 million incurred in Detroit the previous summer.

By April 8, the city was beginning to return to normal, and by the 9th, the day of Dr. King's funeral, it was relatively calm. No one who saw Washington in those days, however, would ever forget the smoldering shells of buildings and the debris filling the streets. The landscape looked like Berlin after the Russian onslaught in 1945.

"It just put a pall over the whole city," recalled attorney Stan Bregman, who later became general counsel for the Senators. "I remember looking out of my office window the next morning and there was nothing but a cloud of smoke over the whole city. People were afraid of everything. I remember driving to opening day with my family and here's the National Guard patrolling the streets. It reminded me of the time I was in the Dominican Republic with the troops in the streets. It was a little scary."[6] "I still recall," wrote Senators pitcher Dave Baldwin decades later, "the cold contrast of burned-out cars against cherry trees in full blossom."[7]

On the evening of April 4, when Stokely Carmichael had gone door-to-door demanding that businesses close, he had not knocked on the door of major league baseball. Precedent for the cancellation of sporting events was murky. Franklin Roosevelt died on April 12, 1945, but baseball seasons started later in those days, and no regular season games were scheduled. In 1963, the National Football League played two days after President Kennedy's assassination, an ill-advised decision that Commissioner Pete Rozelle later regretted. Martin Luther King, Jr., was not a president, but as the spiritual leader of the most dramatic movement of his time, he was one of the most important people in America.

With the ineffectual William Eckert at baseball's helm, the decision as to whether to play was left to the individual clubs. Exhibition games were played on the day following King's death, but in the succeeding days, several were cancelled. One by one, clubs announced plans to cancel their openers, and there were no games on either April 8 or 9. The final game to be wiped from the slate was that between the Dodgers and Phillies in Los Angeles. The Dodgers initially wanted to play, but Philadelphia GM John Quinn stated that his club would risk a forfeit and possible fine rather than play. After meeting with Quinn and National League President Warren Giles, Dodgers owner Walter O'Malley announced that the opener would be delayed.

The Pirates players also took a strong stand, led by first baseman Donn

Clendenon. During Clendenon's days at Morehouse College in Atlanta, King had been assigned as his mentor, and Clendenon visited his home on many occasions. There was no way Clendenon was going to play.

Pittsburgh GM Joe Brown agreed to cancel an exhibition game against the Yankees, but said the decision regarding the Houston regular season games lay with the Astros management. The 11 black Pirates told Brown that no matter what the Astros might decide, they weren't playing. All 25 Pirates met and voted not to play. Roberto Clemente and pitcher Dave Wickersham issued a statement on behalf of the players, affirming their solidarity and stressing that King stood up not just for blacks, but for poor people of all races. The Astros agreed to move the opener from April 9 to 10.

Fan reaction to the postponements was mixed. Many agreed with the players that the games should be postponed out of respect. Others felt that King should not be treated like a head of state, and invoked the example of the NFL's decision to play the weekend of Kennedy's assassination. Still others viewed the situation from a practical point of view. Many ballparks, they pointed out, were in ghetto areas and might be subjected to violence if games were played. It was also likely that there would be tension between black and white players if they were forced to make the individual choice of playing or defying a club order.

The baseball season finally commenced on April 10, but a few major leaguers were missing. Orioles pitcher Pete Richert and shortstop Mark Belanger were called to active duty because of the riot in the Baltimore-Washington area. Richert served as an M.P. in Washington, and a photo in *The Sporting News* showed him posted just outside D.C. Stadium. Belanger was called up by the Maryland Air National Guard and informed that he might be on active status for as long as 24 months. Senators shortstop Ed Brinkman guarded the American University campus and some of the Washington reservoirs. He slept one night on a D.C. Stadium ramp and lost five pounds off his skinny frame during the week he was on duty.

The nation was in crisis, but much of the baseball world was oblivious. The lead story in *The Sporting News* the week after Dr. King's death was "That Pete Rose—He's Got a Line Drive Bat."[8] It was business as usual, except for a story titled "Baseball Leads in Reducing Bias, Negro Players Agree," in which the opening sentence was "The life of the Negro player in the major leagues has never been better and baseball has made more progress than any other sport in eliminating prejudice, major leaguers agree."[9]

Bob Sudyk quoted Willie Mays, Ernie Banks, Lee Maye, Leon Wagner, and others, all of whom said that things were improving. Conditions were certainly better than they had been prior to 1947, when no blacks had been permitted to play major league ball. Spring training sites had been desegregated during the early 1960s, and most overt vestiges of racism had been removed. The players recalled racial incidents from their early careers in the minors and contrasted them with current conditions, under which restaurants and hotels were open to them and fans didn't shout racial epithets from the stands.

Things were not quite as rosy as *The Sporting News* inferred. Most of the black players of the 1960s were minor leaguers during the 1950s, and many who grew up in the North or West had their first encounter with overt, virulent racism in Southern minor league towns. Californian Curt Flood began his professional career at High Point-Thomasville of the Carolina League. "One of my first and most enduring memories," he wrote, "was of a large, loud cracker who installed himself and his four little boys in a front row box and started yelling 'black bastard' at me."[10] When Flood was called up the Reds for the final weeks of the season, he said it was like escaping from prison. For the first time all season, he could stay in the same hotels as his teammates and eat in the same restaurants.

Many Southern minor leagues remained lily-white into the 1960s. "There wasn't a written rule as such," wrote Dave Baldwin, who played in the Southern Association in 1961, "but every one of the eight teams in the league was entirely white, and that wasn't a coincidence. The Southern Association was in denial."[11]

"People think the [Negro] players are satisfied," said Cardinals first baseman Bill White. "They don't understand."[12] The biggest negative, black players agreed, was that they did not make as much money in endorsement income as white players. After his Triple Crown 1966 season, Frank Robinson earned less than $10,000 for appearances and endorsements, a fraction of what Carl Yastrzemski would earn for the same feat a year later.[13] After *his* great performance in the 1967 World Series, Bob Gibson earned about $2,500 in endorsements.

A second grievance was a strategy known as stacking, in which black players were concentrated in the same positions, thereby limiting the total number of blacks on major league rosters. A Baltimore scouting report on young Giants players in the late 1950s read, "The Giants have three colored first basemen—Cepeda at Memphis, McCovey at Dallas, and White who is in the service. All these fellows are very young. On the premise that they are getting over stocked on colored players and are deep in this position, probably it would be worthwhile making a deal for one of them."[14]

A study of major league rosters for the years 1956–1967 by sociologist Harry Edwards showed that while 32 percent of outfielders had been black, blacks represented just 5 percent of catchers and 9 percent of shortstops, generally considered the most responsible and intellectually demanding defensive positions.[15] Further, while a minority of players were black, they represented a majority of the best players. In 1967, only one of the players with the top ten batting averages in the National League (Rusty Staub of the Astros) was white.

In 1966, Emmett Ashford became the first black major league umpire. Ashford was a former semi-pro player and postal worker who'd been a minor league umpire since 1951. In 1954, he was promoted to the Pacific Coast League, and in 1963 was named umpire-in-chief. In September 1965, Ashford was offered an American League contract, and the following April, in the presidential opener at Washington, he became the first black man to umpire a major league game.

It is always said that the best compliment an umpire can receive is that no one remembers who they were after the game is finished. No one watching a game umpired by Emmett Ashford, however, could ever forget that he was on the field. Ashford was a showman who dusted off home plate with a pirouette and a flourish, sprinted down the foul line to keep his legs loose, and had a dramatic strike call that often infuriated players he rang up on strikes.

Throughout Ashford's five years as an AL umpire, there was a spirited debate as to his ability. Was he just a flamboyant showman, or was he a good umpire? His fellow umpires believed Ashford was adequate, but that he was handicapped by the fact that he was more than 50 years old when he first came to the big leagues, and his eyesight was not perfect. No one, however, questioned Ashford's hustle or the fact that he brought excitement to any game he officiated.[16]

In 1968, there were no high-profile racial incidents in other major sports like football and basketball, and there were no blacks in hockey. The event that served as the vehicle for African-American dissent was the Summer Olympic Games. The Winter Games were held in Grenoble, France, in February, but there were virtually no minorities who participated in winter sports. In the summer Olympics, however, the U.S. track and field and basketball squads were dominated by African-Americans.

Four years earlier, comedian Dick Gregory had urged a boycott of the 1964 Tokyo games, but no action was taken. In the fall of 1967, led by Dr. Harry Edwards, a 26-year-old sociology professor and former college discus thrower, black athletes formed the Olympic Project for Human Rights (OPHR) and planned to boycott the following year's summer games. A number of prominent college basketball players, most notably Lew Alcindor, Lucius Allen, and Mike Warren of UCLA, declined invitations to participate in the Olympic trials. Alcindor, now Kareem Abdul-Jabbar, reflected on his actions when U.S. athletes contemplated absenting themselves from the 2008 games in protest of China's human rights violations. "Any other year I would have been proud and elated at the prospect of playing for my country against the world's elite athletes," he said. "But 1968 wasn't like any other year."[17]

One of the goals of OPHR was the removal of reactionary Avery Brundage as head of the United States Olympic Committee. The 80-year-old Brundage had a troubling history of supporting Nazi Germany's hosting of the 1936 games and in 1968 was grappling with the issue of South Africa and its apartheid regime. When the Olympic Committee agreed to allow South Africa to participate, the Soviet Union and a number of black African nations threatened to boycott. In late April, Brundage announced that South Africa would not be allowed in the Olympics. That, of course, did not affect Edwards' cause, which was predicated upon racism in the United States.

California Governor Ronald Reagan spoke out strongly against a prospective boycott and hinted that the athletes were simply puppets of Edwards, a remark that infuriated Alcindor and others. In response, Edwards called Reagan "a petrified pig, unfit to govern."[18] Jesse Owens, who had made a definitive statement against racism by winning four gold medals during Hitler's Olympics, also disagreed with the idea of a boycott. "I believe," he said, "Negroes would do themselves infinitely more harm in a boycott."[19]

After the Olympic trials, no final decisions were made on team selection because of the uncertainty as to which athletes might be willing to go. In the event, the desire to compete in the Olympics prevailed and the boycott movement was abandoned. The U.S. team, black and white alike, went to Mexico City, where the games began on October 12.

The 1968 Summer Olympic Games were known as much for the politics that permeated them as for the athletic competition. There was the threat of the Russian and African boycott, and then that of the U.S. blacks. The games were also the first occasion on which separate Olympic teams represented East and West Germany. Exacerbating the tension was the fact that just ten days before the Games began, police in Mexico City fired into a group of students protesting against the government, killing 267 and wounding more than 1,100.

There were two political protests during the games. Czech gymnast Vera Caslavska won four gold medals, and each time she stood on the winners' platform as the Soviet anthem was played, she turned her head away in a symbolic protest of the Soviet invasion of Czechoslovakia that summer.

The second protest was the defining moment of the Games. After the men's 200 meter event, while the U.S. national anthem was played, gold medal winner Tommie Smith and bronze medalist John Carlos stood on the victory platform with black-gloved fists held high in the air in the Black Power salute. Australian Peter Norman, who captured the silver, wore an OPHR badge in sympathy.

The International Olympic Committee immediately dismissed Smith and Carlos from the U.S. team, and eventually they were banned from the Olympics for life. The two men had made an impact on the American psyche, however, for the scene had been broadcast on national television, and its poignancy gave some people who'd given little thought to racial relations reason to think about them seriously for the first time.

One of those people was columnist Joe Falls, a writer for the *Detroit Free Press* whose column graced the inside cover of each week's *Sporting News*.[20] Falls liked to write about soft subjects like the best major league city in which to find a hot fudge sundae or his 50 favorite things about spring training, but after the Olympics he wrote a column about Smith and Carlos. Most sports page editorials condemned the actions of the two men, but Falls tried to understand their motivation. He said he wished Smith and Carlos had not done what they did, and set forth the reasons why he believed so. Then he wrote a phrase that, coming from conservative, baseball-mad Joe Falls, was somewhat remarkable. After noting how many people thought the act made the United States look bad, he wrote, "Maybe, on the other hand, it actually made us look pretty good ... that an individual citizen could voice his opinion without fear of punishment. Isn't that what our country is built on, too? As I say, I don't agree with what Smith and Carlos did, but I can also try to understand why they did it ... because if you don't think the Negroes in our country have a problem that the white population doesn't have, then you're still living in medieval times."

From there, Falls went on to talk about what the world must think about our riots, the internal conflict over Vietnam, and the assassinations, before lapsing into a discussion of Ray Oyler's selection in the expansion draft and moving on to one of his favorite subjects, Denny McLain.[21] For a brief, shining moment, however, Smith and Carlos's actions had forced Falls and his readers into an area where they rarely ventured.

They didn't play baseball in Mexico City, but the politicization of sport could not help but reach the game Americans called their National Pastime. If baseball were to sidestep the burning issues that faced America in 1968, would it continue to be known as the National Pastime? Or would it become an anachronism, a minor sport steeped in nostalgia and tradition but out of step with contemporary mores? Would it become the cricket of the 20th century?

"[W]hat happens," wrote Tim Wendel in *Summer of '68*, "when events in the outside world become so chaotic, so divisive, that it's no longer possible to fully escape them? When larger issues begin to permeate sports in such a way that it impacts our ability as fans to follow the action and the story line in the usual way?"[22]

It was not just spectators who were conflicted. As the summer of 1968 played out its unique scenario, many baseball players who were the same age or the same race as the revolutionaries wondered how they fit into the American scene. Despite evangelist Billy Graham's statement, "Athletes, you notice, don't take drugs,"[23] some of them did. Players who gravitated toward team sports tended to be more conformist than those who didn't, but the counter-culture was so pervasive that even ballplayers were affected. Most players had lived a sheltered existence, shielded by their talent, but reality was rapidly encroaching upon the world of baseball. If the young players melded with mainstream American youth, would they have a place in the atavistic world of baseball?

"I don't recall that players showed much interest in social issues until the late 1960s," said Dave Baldwin, who began his professional career in 1959. "In 1970 I was with the Milwaukee Brewers and there was a strong 'hippie' movement among the players. I remember nearly everyone (including me) read Hermann Hesse's *Siddharta* and *Steppenwolf,* and we would discuss those books as if we really understood them."[24]

The Brewers were the relocated Seattle Pilots of *Ball Four,* and included Jim Bouton's buddy Steve Hovley, known as "Orbit" for his spacey personality, and several other of the free-spirited Pilots who brought the pages of Bouton's book alive. But baseball hippies needed to keep their beliefs to themselves if they wanted a long career in the major leagues. "Whole gaggles of players dropped out," Baldwin wrote, "but did so only from October through early February. As soon as spring training opened, they dropped in again."[25]

In 1968, it was hard to avoid coming in contact with political reality. Bob Gibson and Curt Flood of the Cardinals met Muhammad Ali, who intro-duced them to the philosophy of the Black Muslims, but both Flood and Gib-son were turned off by the violence of the movement.[26] "When I was playing in Oakland," said outfielder Jim Gosger, "they had the Black Panthers out there. We were scared to death. You didn't know from one day to the next whether there was going to be a race riot at the ballpark."[27]

In August 1968, during the riots at the Democratic Convention in Chicago, Ken Holtzman's National Guard unit was activated and he was uncomfortably close to the action. Meanwhile, the Astros flew into town for a series with the Cubs. Astros pitcher Larry Dierker recalled smelling smoke and tear gas as he and his teammates entered their hotel through the back entrance (it was too dangerous to go through the front door). Dierker and his roommate, Jim Ray, went up to their room and watched out the window as police fought with demonstrators, sirens blared, and loud voices from bull-horns pierced the night air.

"I was in the same age group as the people who were upset about the war," Dierker said. "I knew I was part of the generation that was boiling up down below. At the time, I was more selfishly concerned with my own life and career. I didn't feel a great kinship with the ones protesting. But once you see something like that, you don't forget it so easily. Looking back on it, that night changed me."[28]

Some baseball players took an active interest in national affairs. Cubs pitcher Rich Nye had a brother who was a professor at the left-leaning University of Wisconsin, and while Rich was a student at the University of California, he supported Mario Savio and his Free Speech Movement.

Jim Bouton of the Yankees was one of the most opinionated ball players. He had always been outspoken, but when he first came up to the major leagues, his eccentricity took the form of silly humor, such as impersonations of drunken Crazy Guggenheim from the "Jackie Gleason Show". When he became a 20-game winner, Bouton began to venture into the fields of religion and politics, two subjects rarely discussed among ballplayers. He supported the exclusion of apartheid South Africa from the Olympics, appeared at rallies for liberal Presidential candidate Eugene McCarthy, and went to Haight-Ashbury to see how the hippies lived and learn a little about the drug culture. In 1972, Bouton attended the Democratic Convention as a George McGovern delegate.

Bouton won 39 games, plus two in the World Series, in 1963 and 1964, but his arm went bad in 1965 and he became a marginal performer. He and his liberal opinions were thus expendable. Tom Seaver opposed the war in Vietnam and made no secret of it, but by the late 1960s, Seaver was a Cy Young Award winner, while Bouton was a sore-armed reliever who'd won just nine games in four years. In 1968, Yankees management tired of his iconoclastic views and sold him to Seattle.

Some of the violence that permeated American society found its way to baseball stadiums. On June 7, 1968, Tigers fans, incensed by a call of umpire Jim Honochick, bombarded the field with beer cans and garbage. A couple of weeks later, the Tigers played miserably in a loss to the Red Sox, and the disgusted home fans again threw debris at the players. One threw a cherry bomb that exploded behind Boston first baseman Ken Harrelson and shattered his much-prized aplomb. He left the field, but was persuaded to return and played the last inning deep and very wide of first base, as far from the fans as he could be.

Fans of the 1960s and 1970s were much more involved in the game, in a literal sense. In some stadiums, they were allowed to bring their own beer, and beer sold at the park, often dispensed in bottles or cans rather than plastic cups, could become lethal weapons. Videotapes of old games show fans running on the field to celebrate, and in 1969, when the Mets captured perhaps the most improbable and unexpected World Series win in baseball history, fans tore up Shea Stadium on three occasions—the pennant clinching, the NLCS win, and the World Series finale.

Film of Hank Aaron rounding the bases following his 715th home run shows him covering the ground between second and third with an escort of two young men, neither of whom was wearing a Braves uniform. When Yankees first baseman Chris Chambliss won the 1976 pennant with a ninth-inning home run, he had to fight his way through what seemed like half the fans who'd been in the stands. It was all part of the game, for in the 1960s and 1970s, an increasing tolerance of anarchic behavior and the attitude that drunken escapades were entertaining often created a dangerous atmosphere.

In June, four months prior to the Smith-Carlos incident, a second tragic assassination brought baseball into the spotlight once more. During the early hours of June 5, 1968, at the Ambassador Hotel in Los Angeles, following his stunning victory in the California primary, Senator Robert Kennedy was shot in the head by Palestinian militant Sirhan Sirhan. Over the next four days, baseball proceeded to shoot itself in the foot.

In the days that followed the killing of Martin Luther King, Jr., baseball, despite the haphazard leadership of William Eckert, responded with appropriate respect, canceling games and avoiding controversy. Eckert hadn't made a decision; he'd asked the owners what should be done and, miraculously, they did enough to avoid public outrage. During the aftermath of the Kennedy shooting, however, the "Lords of Baseball" seemed to bumble whenever possible, and the backtracking and apologies that followed underlined baseball's lack of leadership. It was the worst moment of Eckert's sorry reign.

The principal question was who, if anyone, was in charge? Joe Reichler, public relations director for the commissioner's office, stated that Eckert had ordered that weekend games be played as scheduled, but that on Saturday, no game would be commenced until the rites for Senator Kennedy had been concluded. The funeral service would be held in New York City, and the body would then be taken by train to the burial site in Arlington National Cemetery.

The instructions sounded relatively simple, but their implementation was confused and uncoordinated. The Yankees and Senators, in contravention of Eckert's directive, announced that they would postpone their Saturday games. New York, of course, was the state represented by the late Senator, and Washington was the scene of the Kennedy family's greatest triumphs.

New York's other team, the Mets, were in San Francisco, where the Giants, in compliance with Eckert's orders, intended to play. Saturday was Bat Day, and a crowd of 30,000 to 40,000 was anticipated. The Giants' attendance was down, and, dead senator or no, they were not about to give up a Bat Day crowd.

The Mets' players voted unanimously not to play, even if it meant forfeiting the game. The decision was supported by the Mets' management. The Giants offered a compromise, under which the start of the game would be moved back from 1 p.m. Pacific time to 4 p.m.

The Giants appealed to National League President Giles, asking for a forfeit or for the Mets to pay the Giants $80,000, the amount they claimed they would lose, but Giles declined to forfeit the game or impose any financial penalty on the Mets. Then, according to Reichler, the Giants asked the commissioner's office for permission to postpone the game, which was granted. The team said they were deluged with phone calls following the announcement of the cancellation, almost evenly split between those who approved and those who were furious at the club for "breaking the hearts of the kids who had planned on Bat Day."[29] There was no mention of owner Horace Stoneham's broken heart over the loss of the Bat Day revenue.

The commissioner's instructions stated that no game should begin until the funeral services had ended. Eckert made many mistakes during his reign in the commissioner's chair, but on this occasion circumstances conspired against him. Kennedy's services were scheduled to begin at 10:00 a.m., and the train was to depart for Washington immediately after their conclusion. It was assumed that the burial would be concluded prior to the start of night games.

The special train left New York at 12:30, but what would normally have been a four-hour trip became eight hours when mourners lined the track and forced the cars to proceed at a snail's pace. By eight o'clock Eastern time, the scheduled start of most games on the East Coast, the procession was still quite a way from Arlington Cemetery. Cincinnati GM Bob Howsam, with a stadium full of people, called the commissioner's office and asked for advice. He and Eckert decided that the game should start and, about 45 minutes later than scheduled, it did.

Before the players took the field, however, a drama had been taking place in the clubhouse. The Reds took a vote as to whether they would play, and the first ballot was 12 to 12, with one abstention. Manager Dave Bristol gave a brief talk encouraging his men to play the game and invited nine of them to follow him on the field. A second ballot produced a 13–12 margin in favor of playing.

Reds pitcher Milt Pappas had been a very vocal participant in the discussions. Pappas was in the midst of a controversial and mostly successful major league career, during which he won 209 games in 17 years. He came up as a cocky 18-year-old in 1957, and four years later faced Roger Maris in the Yankees' 154th game of 1961. Maris had 58 home runs, and under the standards imposed by Commissioner Frick, had to hit two more that night to tie Babe Ruth. Before the game, with the pennant race essentially over, the brash Pappas told Maris he would throw him only fastballs. He did, and Maris hit #59 and nearly cleared the fence a second time. Five years later, Pappas established his legacy as the man traded for Frank Robinson, who was the 1966 American League MVP and led the Orioles to four World Series during the next six years.

Pappas was the Reds' player representative, but he was not popular with his teammates.[30] After his first season in Cincinnati, fellow pitchers Jim O'Toole and Joe Nuxhall accused him of malingering, missing starts because of a sinus problem they thought trivial.[31] Pappas had been adamantly against playing, and as his teammates took the field, he shouted, "You guys are wrong. I'm telling you you're all wrong. If you guys play, you'll have to find another player rep."[32]

The fiasco of Saturday was followed by further controversy on Sunday, the official day of mourning proclaimed by President Johnson. Trouble was brewing in the president's home state, where Rusty Staub and Bob Aspromonte of the Astros and Maury Wills of the Pirates refused to play in the Pirates-Astros game.

During the game, Wills sat in the trainer's room reading Kennedy's book, *To Seek a Newer World*.[33] "This is an individual thing," said Wills, "not a team matter. You must let your conscience be your guide." Roberto Clemente also intended to sit the game out, but after a meeting with Pirates manager Larry Shepard, Clemente agreed to play.

The Houston players twice voted unanimously not to play, but under the threat of fines and disciplinary action from Astros GM Spec Richardson, all but Staub and Aspromonte agreed to take the field. "We still have strong convictions about this," said Astros player rep Dave Giusti. "We changed our position after the strongest economic pressure had been brought to bear against us by the general manager."[34] Staub and Aspromonte were docked a day's pay. In Boston and Baltimore, Sunday games were postponed by management.

The aftermath of the weekend was filled with accusations and conflicting stories. When the commissioner's office announced that the Yankees had been ordered not to play on Saturday, Yankees president Michael Burke replied, "By way of clarification, the Yankees made a unilateral decision early Thursday morning [June 6] to cancel the Saturday game with California."[35] Burke said he communicated his decision to American League President Joe Cronin, who passed it along to Eckert.

Eckert, according to Burke, said that virtually all teams would play on Saturday, and the Yankees risked a forfeit if they didn't. When the Angels agreed to the postponement, the issue of a forfeit was eliminated, but Burke was still livid with Eckert. "The Yankee club's decision not to play on the day of the funeral was dictated by its own subjective moral judgment.... Any reports that the Yankee ball club was directed by the commissioner's office or league office not to play on Saturday are incorrect."[36] The Yankees had the foresight to schedule *their* Bat Day for Sunday and played in front of 56,614, the largest crowd of the season.

A few writers and fans supported Eckert. One letter writer to *The Sporting News* asked rhetorically how many businesses had closed out of respect for the Senator's death. Harold Kaese of the *Boston Globe* added, "More is always expected of sports than other businesses, and more is always expected of baseball than other sports."[37]

Most feedback was critical of the vagueness of Eckert's directives, particularly the decision to start games after the funeral, which put club owners in a difficult position, with the stands filled and players voting on whether to play. "It was," wrote Dick Young, "as though someone was standing by the side of the bier with a stopwatch and a starter's gun."[38] "Baseball again returned to normalcy—," said Pittsburgh writer Les Biederman, "confusion."[39] Bob August wrote in the *Cleveland Press*, "Baseball's observance of Sen. Kennedy's death was disorganized, illogical and thoroughly shabby."[40]

Letters poured in to *The Sporting News*. Among them was a missive from Wesley Tom of Flushing, New York, who wrote, "The commissioner's inaction allowed all 20 clubs to run off in 20 directions. The entire chain of events is of utter embarrassment to baseball."[41]

"Management is money hungry," added another reader, "for even thinking of playing on such a day."[42] Mrs. Phillip King of Bowie, Maryland, said she had been a fan since she was a little girl, but was now ashamed of baseball. She said the Mets [then one of the worst teams in baseball] had more character than the others combined.[43] A Reds scout wrote that he had resigned his post rather than be associated with an organization that "put monetary factors over a day of national mourning."[44]

Kennedy's press secretary, Frank Mankiewicz, sent letters of thanks to Pappas, Wills, Staub, and Aspromonte, and one to manager Gil Hodges of the Mets. Pappas, who'd been pitching poorly, was immediately traded to the Atlanta Braves, where he would have the opportunity to practice his labor organizing skills against Atlanta GM Paul Richards, perhaps the most reactionary of anyone in baseball management.[45] Eckert was left to try to piece together the shreds of his rapidly vanishing credibility.

8

Let's Not Permit the Inmates to Run the Asylum

Ever since baseball players began getting paid in the 1860s, there has been a conflict between capital and labor. The tide of battle has ebbed and flowed, but from the 1920s through the mid–1960s, capital achieved an almost unbroken string of victories. Any discussion of current player compensation inevitably includes a comparison with salaries of decades ago, and the conclusion that baseball players of the 1960s received very modest wages and played not for the money but for "the love of the game."

A reading of contemporary sources provides a dramatically different picture. Although the stakes were much lower, players were just as concerned with salary as they are today, and the attitude of management and the media was that they were every bit as overpaid and pampered as today's players. One got the impression that the players were in control, and their salary demands were driving the owners to the brink of insolvency.

In March 1960, Dan Daniel wrote in *The Sporting News* that the upper limit of salaries had been reached. "Salary demands of the players continue to rise," he said, and suggested to Yankees general manager George Weiss, "George, the player salary problem appears to have become acute." Not surprisingly, Weiss agreed, although he said that while the growth of salaries needed to be curtailed, a "state of outright alarm" had not yet been reached. "However," he said, "we definitely are near our limit, and salaries will have to level off."[1]

In 1966, columnist Arthur Daley wrote, "[T]he hired hands have virtually no grievances."[2] If today's players operated under the conditions of the 1960s, they would have plenty of grievances, but while the players of the 1960s weren't totally content, they weren't ready to rebel. The owners had convinced star players that they had a great situation and shouldn't rock the boat. They reinforced the notion that marginal players were expendable and in no position to negotiate for more. If they didn't like their situation, there were hundreds of minor leaguers eager to take their places, and would they be better off carrying a lunch pail?

Most ballplayers, although earning a small fraction of today's salaries, were paid more than the average working man, and all they had to do, management constantly reminded them, was play a game. What working stiff wouldn't trade places with them? Holdouts were portrayed as selfish ingrates who were hurting the team by not reporting to camp and getting in shape. "I don't know what the hell they're arguing on salaries for," fumed Yankees manager Casey Stengel in the spring of 1960. "They ought to be signed and in here. They've got a job to do."[3]

In 1962, Daley railed against the greed of the players for wanting to continue holding two All-Star Games each year in order to bolster their pension fund. "The ballplayers are insisting on it," Daley wrote, "because they have become as greedy as the owners. Because receipts swell their pension fund, they have become so money-mad that they would even be willing to perform in twenty All Star games if the owners would let them. They make demands on their bosses and then back down in exchange for that second builder-upper of the pension swag."[4]

The key to manipulating public opinion was clubs' control of the media, which depended on them for access and information. When a player was engaged in a salary dispute, news reports spoke of general managers shaking their heads over preposterous "demands" even though the players, in the reserve clause era, had no leverage to demand anything. Teams made offers, players made demands, and the media obediently informed the public, in words conveniently provided by management.

When longtime Yankees star Phil Rizzuto was suddenly released in 1956, *The Sporting News* downplayed the fact that the Yankees had jettisoned perhaps their most loyal player and dutifully reported that, during his career, Rizzuto had earned $342,631 in salary and World Series shares.[5] Since salary information was ostensibly confidential, there is no doubt that the information came from the Yankees' front office.

With all the cards firmly in their hands, management took advantage of every opportunity to keep salaries down. In 1960, the Braves wanted to cut the salary of star pitcher Lew Burdette after his record "dropped" from 20–10 to 21–15. Following a 16–8 record in 1967, Pirates pitcher Bob Veale was asked to take a pay cut because his ERA went up.

There were ingenious methods of dealing with difficult ballplayers. Jim Bouton, a 21-game winner in 1963, held out the following spring, stating that he thought winning 20 games was worth a $10–15,000 raise. Yankees GM Ralph Houk believed it was worth somewhat less, and devised a clever strategy for getting Bouton to capitulate. It was against the rules to fine a player for holding out, so Houk said he would reduce his offer to Bouton by $100 for each day that he remained out of camp. With few alternatives, Bouton signed. His 21 wins earned him a raise from $10,500 to $18,500.

One of the favorite tricks of Dodgers GM Buzzie Bavasi was to leave fake contracts with low salary amounts around his office where players could see them, in order to convince them that their teammates were getting less money than they themselves were being offered.[6]

In the spring of 1966, Bavasi found himself on the wrong end of a unique strategy that struck fear into the hearts of the baseball establishment, for it involved a collaborative effort and a third-party negotiator. Pitchers Sandy Koufax and Don Drysdale, who had carried the light-hitting Dodgers to the 1965 World Championship, decided to negotiate as a team, and both held out well into spring training, vowing that neither would sign until the other agreed to a contract.

The two pitchers began negotiating individually, asking for raises similar to what they'd previously gotten after having good seasons. The problem this time, Drysdale believed, was that the increases would put each of them over the $100,000 level, and no major league pitcher had ever earned $100,000.

According to Drysdale, it was his wife Ginger who suggested that, rather than let Bavasi play them off against each other, Koufax and her husband should negotiate together. Their initial discussions as a duo were not fruitful, and therefore the two pitchers took a second step. Koufax had been represented by Hollywood attorney and talent agent J. William Hayes, who began talking to Drysdale and agreed to represent both men.

Hayes told the two pitchers they should ask for a combined $1 million over three years, or $167,000 per year for each. There were four things Bavasi didn't like about that proposition. First, a million dollars was much, much too high. Second, he didn't want three-year contracts; third, he didn't want to combine the negotiations of the two players and; fourth, he didn't want to deal with an agent. Other than that, the proposal was fine.

As much as Bavasi wanted to take a hard line, the Dodgers were clearly in a quandary. They had captured the National League title the previous year despite being eighth in the league in runs scored and last in home runs. They hit just 24 home runs in Dodger Stadium, and Willie Mays hit more homers in a single month than any Dodger hit all year. The Dodgers' pennant clincher was indicative of their season. They beat the Braves, 3–1, and scored their runs on a passed ball and two bases-loaded walks. They had such a feeble offense that veteran infielder Gene Freese once said, "I hear the Dodgers just came into town. They're taking batting practice in the hotel lobby."[7]

Koufax and Drysdale had started 83 of 162 games and accounted for 49 of the 97 Dodgers victories. Moreover, Drysdale had been the Dodgers' only .300 hitter. Trying to play without the two pitchers would be suicidal, but the prospect of dramatically altering the economics of baseball was even more daunting. "The Dodgers were not only battling for the sanctity of O'Malley's treasury," wrote Arthur Daley, "but for the preservation of the entire baseball structure."[8] "We can't give in to them," Walter O'Malley said. "There are too many agents hanging around Hollywood looking for clients."[9]

Prior to William Hayes, there had been a few agents in baseball, the most noted of whom were Christy Walsh, who represented Babe Ruth, and Frank Scott, who'd been traveling secretary for the Yankees from 1946 through 1951. After he left the Yankees, Scott served as an agent to many top major league players. The principal job of Walsh and Scott, however, was to line up paid appearances for their clients, not negotiate their salary. When negotiating salaries with veterans or bonuses with youngsters, teams insisted on dealing directly with the players or, in the case of those under 21, their parents.

Some parents, such as Carl Yastrzemski's father, were bull-headed negotiators. In most cases, however, a business-savvy executive dealt with people who had never negotiated anything more complex than the purchase of a used car. Management liked it that way and, after all, they were giving these youngsters the chance to be a major league ballplayer and, in many cases, offering more money than they had ever dreamed of.

"My father was a coal miner," said former pitcher Joe Grzenda. "After we signed, he came over to me and said, 'Juzep [Polish for Joseph], I did my best.' I didn't know the difference. I got $4,000, and found out later I could have gotten a lot more."[10]

Prior to the implementation of the free agent draft in 1965, a youngster signing his first contract had some leverage, for he could negotiate with any team. There were a number of sizable bonuses paid in the 1950s and early 1960s, which sent big league executives scrambling for ways to keep themselves from competing with each other. The solution of the 1950s was a rule stating that any player receiving a bonus greater than $4,000 had to be kept on the big league roster for two seasons. First imposed in 1946, discarded in 1950, and re-instituted in 1952, the rule was uniformly unpopular and did little to stop the payout of large bonuses. It also encouraged falsifying the amount of a player's bonus.

Tying up a roster spot with an unseasoned, virtually useless player discouraged many teams, but a number of players were still given large bonuses. Many wound up never realizing their potential because they rusted on a major league bench for two years rather than learning the game in the minor leagues.

Bob "Hawk" Taylor signed with the Braves in 1957 for $100,000 and was immediately placed on the Milwaukee roster. From a high school campus to the major leagues was a monumental leap, and the euphoria of receiving $100,000 was soon dulled by the reality of trying to compete in the major leagues without any professional experience.

"That was sort of a mixed blessing," said Taylor. "Here I am just out of high school going into the major leagues with the Milwaukee Braves, who were in the middle of a pennant fight. On one hand it was a great experience. Here you are rubbing elbows with all these guys whose pictures were on your wall at home. They were my heroes and now they're my teammates."[11]

The other side of the story was that many of the Braves' veterans were not happy having to carry Taylor on the roster while they tried to win a pennant. "He took a lot of heat," said teammate John DeMerit. "The guys used to get on him and give him a hard time about a lot of things."[12] In order to make room on the roster for Taylor, the Braves had to sell popular veteran (and future manager) Chuck Tanner to the Cubs. "He could have made a much greater contribution to the team than I could," Taylor said, "and they had to let him go."[13]

In addition to Taylor, the Braves were carrying DeMerit, a second bonus player who rarely left the bench. Still, playing with just 23 effective men, they won the National League pennant and beat the Yankees in the World Series. Although Taylor was with the team for more than half the season, he was voted a World Series share of only $1,000, about one-eighth of a full share. Apparently, the veterans felt he didn't need the money.

Despite the two-year rule, big bonuses continued to be paid because market forces were allowed to prevail. The risk associated with signing an 18-year-old to a huge bonus contract was overwhelming, for the youngsters had been judged against uneven competition, their mettle hadn't been tested in pressure situations, and they hadn't matured physically or emotionally.

Not surprisingly, there were more failures than successes among the bonus signees. Perhaps the worst investments were the Dodgers paying pitcher Paul Speckenbach $100,000 in 1962 and the Indians giving 18-year-old Billy Joe Davidson $120,000 in 1951. Speckenbach came down with a sore shoulder almost immediately after cashing his check and never pitched an inning in the major leagues. Davidson likewise never made it out of the minor leagues and wound up working in a cotton mill. Paul Pettit, the first $100,000 bonus boy, pitched in just 12 games for the Pirates in the early 1950s. The Yankees gave Ed Cereghino $85,000, while those who got $80,000 included such forgotten names as Gus Keriazakos, Frank Quinn, and Tookie Gilbert.

The Cardinals struck paydirt once with the three McDaniel brothers. Lindy spent 21 years as a top relief pitcher, Von had a meteoric rise followed by an immediate and inexplicable decline, and Kerry Don never made it to the major leagues. Each cost the Cardinals $50,000.

The institution of the amateur free agent draft in 1965 cooled the bonus ardor to some degree, but teams still paid good money to their high draft choices. In 1966, the Mets used the first overall choice to select Steve Chilcott, a 17-year-old, left-hand-hitting catcher from California, and signed him for a $75,000 bonus. Chilcott and Reggie Jackson, an outfielder from Arizona State, were the top two prospects that year, and most experts rated them about even.

Chilcott didn't hit too well in the Appalachian League, so the Mets sent him to Auburn of the New York-Penn League. He didn't hit there, either, batting just .155 in 25 games. Johnny Murphy attributed Chilcott's problems to the fact that he wasn't accustomed to hitting under lights. That could be a problem, unless he was traded to the Cubs.

In 1968, Chilcott found himself in the service after playing just 19 games at Visalia of the California League. While crawling across the ground during a drill at Fort Ord, he felt something pop in his shoulder. He worried that if he said anything, it would delay his release from service, so his injury went untreated until he was discharged a month later. The bad shoulder made it impossible for Chilcott to catch, so the Mets moved him to first base. He never made it past Triple A ball, and the Mets were left wondering whether they should have drafted Reggie Jackson.

Rather than play the high-risk game of giving huge sums to untried youngsters, it might have made more sense to bid on known commodities, veterans who had proven themselves in major league competition. But with the reserve clause in place, that couldn't happen, resulting in a system where raw reserves like Taylor and DeMerit, with their bonuses, were compensated much better than Braves stars Hank Aaron, Warren Spahn, and Eddie Mathews. The idea of open bidding for veterans was anathema to the owners, who were wedded to the reserve clause like drowning men clinging to a lifeboat.

When Bill Hayes took the case of Drysdale and Koufax, he couldn't threaten to have them sign with the Giants or the Reds, and needed to come up with a viable alternative. He got both pitchers a contract to appear in the film *Warning Shot,* a Paramount Pictures production starring David Janssen, and made arrangements for a Japanese tour that would supposedly earn each player a six-figure sum. Koufax signed a contract with Viking Press to write his autobiography for $150,000. Drysdale discussed an ongoing role in an ABC series titled "Iron Horse." More ominously, Koufax began thinking about testing the reserve clause in court if he and Drysdale couldn't reach agreement with the Dodgers.[14]

Meanwhile, both pitchers were working out privately, trying to stay in shape, for despite the smoke screen of acting and writing offers, they really wanted to pitch for the Dodgers. Once they'd failed to report for spring training and officially became holdouts, the Dodgers began to employ the media to make their case, while Hayes went silent. He issued no press releases, wouldn't take phone calls, and carefully monitored public opinion. "Hayes was just amazing," Drysdale wrote much later. "He had the greatest instinct for judging just how the wind would blow. He could practically name the day that certain publications would take the Dodgers' side in the dispute or ours."[15]

When the holdout continued into late March, the Dodgers said they would carry on without their star pitchers. One of the major tenets of management's strategy against labor was to insist that no player, no matter how skilled he might be, was indispensible. Branch Rickey famously told slugger Ralph Kiner that the Pirates had finished last with him and could finish last without him. Kiner, of course, might have retorted that they also could have finished last without Rickey and *his* large salary.

The Dodgers had finished first rather than last, and there was no way they were going to repeat without Koufax and Drysdale, but they maintained a brave front. Pitching coach Lefty Phillips said that if the two pitchers signed, they would have to work their way into the rotation.

It was all whistling in the dark, for without Koufax and Drysdale, the Dodgers would be fighting the Mets and Astros to stay out of last place. Moreover, attendance was likely to plummet, for each pitcher, especially Koufax, drew large crowds whenever he pitched, generating far more incremental revenue than the two were asking in salaries. The Dodgers averaged 31,526 fans per game in 1965, but when Koufax started, the average was 37,540. Moreover, overall major league attendance was less than 15,000 per game, but when Koufax started on the road, he drew an average of 28,816 fans, while Drysdale drew 23,847.

On March 24, with the start of the season just 18 days away, Hayes said the odds against either Drysdale or Koufax pitching for the Dodgers in 1966 were 100 to 1. Koufax said two days later, "The ball club is defending the principle that it really doesn't have to negotiate with a ballplayer because we have no place to go."[16] Drysdale said, "We are making plans based on not playing this year."[17]

Meanwhile, Hayes was doing a little legal research. He found a California statute enacted to deal with contracts under which Hollywood studios owned the rights to actors and actresses in perpetuity. The law limited personal service contracts to seven years. A similar New York statute set the limit at ten years. Hayes had one of his partners prepare briefs in case his clients wanted to challenge the reserve clause in court.

On March 29, O'Malley said the team had given up on its efforts to sign the players for 1966, but Drysdale, who was certain the Dodgers knew about Hayes' research, thought there was still hope. Former major league player turned actor Chuck Connors arranged a meeting between Bavasi and Drysdale on March 30 (Koufax declined to participate), and the two men brought the drama to a close.

Bavasi said he was willing to offer Drysdale $115,000 and Koufax $125,000.[18] Drysdale went to a nearby phone booth and called Koufax, who accepted. The crisis was over, and Hayes could put his briefs aside. At the press conference announcing the signing, the Dodgers tried to push Hayes into the shadows, but Koufax insisted that (as his "attorney") Hayes had played a major role.

Whether the Dodgers admitted to the influence of Hayes or not, baseball had not seen the last of the player agent. In 1969, pitcher Al Downing of the Yankees employed Eugene Kass as his representative, and Kass told the Yankees that they could only negotiate through him. The Yankees were as insulted as the Dodgers had been by the presence of Bill Hayes. Let one agent in, the rest would follow, and the fragile walls would crumble. The Yankees insisted on speaking only to Downing.

Downing's situation was drastically different from that of Koufax and Drysdale. The once-promising left-hander, troubled by arm injuries, had pitched in just 15 games in 1968. Unlike Koufax and Drysdale's six-figure requests, Downing was attempting to avoid taking a cut from the $32,000 he'd earned the previous year. While the Dodgers could only bluff, the Yankees could play hardball, for they could well afford to start the season without sore-armed Al Downing. There was another implication to the Downing case, however; he claimed that under the reserve clause, he was actually under contract with the Yankees, and that his contract renewed annually whether he signed or not.

As usual, the Yankees made their case through the media, claiming they could not reach Downing. "Why does the club say they can't reach me?" Downing asked George Vecsey of the *New York Times*. "You reached me, didn't you?"[19] Finally, in mid–March, in a very unusual move, the Yankees and their holdout pitcher agreed that he would report to camp and play without a contract. If the two parties couldn't reach an agreement, the Yankees would pay Downing 20 percent less than his previous year's salary, the maximum reduction allowed under the new bargaining agreement. It was the first time anyone could remember a player participating in training camp without a signed contract.

On March 31, Downing was sent to the minor leagues. Even though 1969 was an expansion year and pitchers were at a premium, all 11 American League clubs waived on the rights to a 27-year-old left-hander who had been on the All-Star squad less than two years earlier. Why wouldn't a pitching-starved club like the Seattle Pilots risk the $20,000 waiver price, plus Downing's salary? They'd dropped $175,000 in the expansion draft for pitchers like Paul Click, Robert Richmond, and John Miklos. Perhaps the Pilots, the Royals, and all the other clubs passed on Downing because it was time to circle the wagons and send a message to anyone else contemplating a similar strategy.

On April 20, Downing signed a contract stipulating that if his arm was sound and he was able to pitch for the Yankees, he would receive the same

$32,000 he was paid in 1968. If he played at Syracuse, he would accept a 12 percent cut. Downing's arm bounced back, and he was soon called up by the Yanks and became one of their most effective pitchers, finishing with a 7–5 record and a 3.38 ERA. At one point late in the season, he was *the* best Yankee pitcher, allowing only three earned runs in 41 innings. Two years later, Downing was a 20-game winner for the Dodgers.

Prior to the actions of Koufax, Drysdale, and Downing, there had been some isolated incidents of rebellion. In 1962, holdout pitcher Joey Jay of the Reds offered to buy his contract and gain control over his own destiny. He started by offering more than $100,000 and eventually increased his offer to $250,000. Where Jay would get $250,000 he didn't say, since he had earned less than $20,000 in 1961. He supposedly had made money drilling for oil, but if he didn't have enough, would someone put it up for him in order to control the contract of a 20-game winner? In any event, the offer was refused without thanks, and Jay signed for an estimated $27,500.

In May 1967, Orioles first baseman Mike Epstein refused to report to Baltimore's Rochester farm club. Epstein was 24 years old and had led the California League in batting in 1965, while hitting 30 homers and driving in 100 runs. He'd been the minor league "Player of the Year" in 1966 and didn't see what more he could prove at Rochester. The Orioles had Boog Powell, coming off a big 1966 season, at first base, and rather than try to learn to play the outfield in the minor leagues, Epstein wanted to be traded to another major league team.

Epstein was not a typical ballplayer. He majored in social psychology at the University of California and was fond of quoting Frost, Shakespeare, Socrates, and Emerson. Epstein had been a fullback in college, but decided to play baseball after reading *The Pursuit of the Millennium* and becoming enamored of the individual challenges of baseball, as opposed to the more anonymous team atmosphere of football. He'd been christened "Superjew" in the California League and liked the nickname. It was one word, he said, like Superman. Superjew was not about to have the moguls of major league baseball tell him what to do. Would Emerson have reported to Rochester?

The Orioles decided to trade Epstein. The Yankees, always looking for left-handed power hitters, particularly Jewish ones who would bring fans to Yankee Stadium, were interested, but wouldn't surrender star pitcher Mel Stottlemyre in exchange. At the end of May, the Orioles traded their rebellious first baseman to the Senators for starting pitcher Pete Richert, and a crisis was averted. Still, Epstein had forced a trade, and though he didn't have his choice of teams, he had gotten away from the team that held his rights under the reserve clause.

Epstein's case was a rare one, for he had an education, could have made a career outside of baseball, and was willing to take a chance and challenge the system. Most players were not, for the system was rigged against them. "We didn't have any leverage," said Bob Friend, the Pirates pitcher and National League player representative.[20]

The players did have a union, but it was not a strong or militant one. The players' "demands" were usually not very demanding and never struck at the heart of the relationship between owner and player. Two issues emerged from a July 1961 meeting of player representatives: the continuance of the system of two All-Star Games per year and an end to segregation in spring training accommodations. "On neither of those points," Dan Daniel wrote, "did the delegates take a firm stand. On both, they placated the club owners to a point at which they appeared to be trying to wheedle concessions out of them. The players used to make demands. Now they suggest."[21]

For the most part, players accepted the fact that owners and managers controlled their destiny. "I wanted to play baseball so bad," said outfielder Billy Cowan, "that I didn't want to do anything that might jeopardize my getting a chance. I knew I had the ability, but in those days most players had the fear of pissing off the wrong people and they could bury you. There was no place to go. There was no free agency. You had no options. You did what you were told."[22]

The owners claimed, and many sincerely believed, that free agency would lead to a catastrophe, for they had enough difficulty controlling salaries in a monopolistic situation. The legal basis for the reserve clause was shaky, based upon a 1922 case in which the Baltimore Club of the defunct Federal League had sued the National League. Supreme Court Justice Oliver Wendell Holmes, in his opinion, wrote that baseball was a local exhibition rather than interstate commerce and therefore not subject to anti-trust regulation.

The concept of professional baseball, with franchises throughout the United States, as local business was tenuous, made even more so by the advent of radio and television. In 1947, outfielder Danny Gardella of the Giants, who had been banned from baseball for jumping to the Mexican League, sued on the basis that the sport had changed so much that it should be considered interstate commerce. The case never reached the courts, as the Giants settled by giving Gardella $60,000.

The foundation of the anti-trust exemption was so fragile that any change in the structure of the game was liable to tip the balance. The institution of the amateur draft in 1965 was just such a change, but the owners were willing to assume the risk if they could find a way to keep themselves from paying big bonuses to people like Paul Speckenbach. Walter O'Malley called the draft the beginning of socialism, but apparently his fellow owners preferred socialism with bigger profits to free enterprise with large expenditures.

The draft, similar to that used by professional football and basketball, had been discussed by baseball owners for several years. In 1963, *The Sporting*

News endorsed the concept as a solution to large bonus expenditures. In January 1964, the owners approved a plan, and three months later, Commissioner Frick announced that the initial draft would take place in June 1965. O'Malley urged that each league hold its own draft and bid against each other, but his proposal was voted down. Players would continue to be the property of one team for their entire careers, and now they had lost the ability to choose that team.

While bonuses had been high, controls on the free market for labor had enabled teams to keep their payrolls down. In 1967, the players' union stated that the average salary of a major league player was $19,000. Over the years, salaries had increased in absolute numbers but had declined from 50 percent of team revenue during the 1930s to 30 percent by the 1960s.

While major league salaries were higher than those of the average American (median household income in 1967 was $7,200), players who hadn't reached the majors weren't earning a living wage. Minor leaguers earned an average of $1,000 per month in Triple-A, $7–800 per month in Double-A and $5–600 per month in A ball. The monthly pay, of course, was received only during the season, which meant that the average Triple A player made about $5,000 a year.

Expense reimbursements were rarely enough to cover actual expenses. In spring training, major league players were given $25 per week for incidentals, and while some minor leaguers got $14 a week, most got nothing at all. The players had to pay for their own shoes and gloves, unless they had a contract with a distributor.

During the regular season, major and minor leaguers received meal money when the team was on the road. If teams left before noon, major leaguers got $12 for the day; if after noon, they got $6. If they arrived home before six, they got only $6, under the assumption they would get home in time for dinner. Typically, teams deducted breakfast money when leaving after 10 a.m. and all money when meals were served on plane flights.

One could eat reasonably well on major league meal money, but not in the minors. In 1965, the meal money paid in the Mets' organization was as follows: New York, $10 per day; Buffalo $5; Williamsport $4; Auburn and Greenville $3. Admittedly, it was more expensive to eat in Los Angeles, Chicago, and other National League cities, but was it possible to eat for three dollars a day in the South Atlantic League? The answer is that it wasn't, and as a result the diet of the typical minor league player was poor and/or subsidized by his family back home.

By 1966, the most attractive benefit the players had obtained was a pension plan, under which payments ranged from $88 per month for a five-year veteran who began collecting at age 50 to $550 per month for a 20-year veteran at 65. Those who played less than five years in the majors received nothing. In addition to the owners' contribution, each player was required to put $344 per year into the plan.

Most major leaguers had to work during the off-season to supplement their income and prepare for a career after baseball. "You had to have a job," said former pitcher Clem Labine. "You would be very stupid if you didn't have one. You couldn't support your family."[23] Orioles pitcher Dick Hall was an accountant. Ed Kranepool was a stock broker. Al Jackson worked for Howard Clothing Stores. Greg Goossen was a private investigator.

Mickey Mantle worked in the Oklahoma mines while playing in the minor leagues. "I worked in an engineering office," said Ed Bressoud, "I taught driver education and I ran a jackhammer."[24] Ron Hunt drove a truck, while Jim Hickman, between the 1964 and 1965 seasons, worked part-time in a cotton factory. "We have a large tobacco farm here in Maysville," said former pitcher Herb Moford, "which is seasonal. The season starts in November and ends in February. It worked out just right for me. I worked on the tobacco farm all winter."[25] Can one imagine Alex Rodriguez harvesting tobacco after the baseball season ended?

Off-season jobs were sometimes dangerous. In 1963, promising Twins farmhand John Strzyzewski lost his pitching hand in an industrial accident. The Phillies wanted pitcher Jerry Johnson to quit his construction job, which required him to be up to 300 feet above the ground. "I worked construction," said Mets outfielder Don Bosch, "which was hard on my body. I was crawling around concrete floors on my knees and lifting heavy planks. I was climbing scaffolding. It wasn't conducive to taking care of your body for an athletic career."[26]

Although everyone knew that the money earned during a player's career could not sustain him for the rest of his life, outside business interests were frowned upon, for they supposedly detracted from a player's concentration on the game. Further, general managers didn't like dealing with players who had other sources of income, for there was nothing better than a player who had to sign or else starve. After the Yankees' poor 1959 season, a fan sent in a poem which someone, believed to be George Weiss, posted on the locker room bulletin board. It read:

> Although you were defeated, Yanks,
> You shouldn't feel too blue
> Just think of all the bars and banks
> And bowling alleys, too
> As businessmen you guys are tops
> It really seems a shame
> That you should have to leave your shops
> Just for a Lousy Game.[27]

Dan Daniel, writing in *The Sporting News*, lamented the fact that not all youngsters were eager to show up for early spring training instructional camps, for which they were not paid. "They say they cannot afford to take two or three weeks out, minus salary," Daniel wrote. "This is to be deplored. But that is how things stand."[28]

One option for off-season employment was playing in the Caribbean, where one could earn up to a $2,000 a month by the mid–1960s. The Caribbean season generally started in October and ended with playoffs in February, after which the players reported to spring training. Pitchers threw as many as 150 innings during the winter which, combined with their regular season work, might mean 400 innings over a calendar year.

Playing winter ball, moreover, was a much more adventurous activity than being a stockbroker. Paydays could be irregular and sometimes life was downright dangerous, for Caribbean fans took their baseball seriously. In 1953, a 21-year-old fan, distraught after Caracas lost to Santurce in the Caribbean tournament, hung himself in his room. Managers and players had fist fights on the field, and fans threw fruit, rocks, bottles, and other objects at the players.

In 1958, the Venezuelan season was suspended for nine days following the rioting that took place after the overthrow of President Marcos Perez Jiminez by a military junta. Fortunately, the leader of the junta, Rear Admiral Wolfgang Larrazabal, was a baseball fan who allowed the season to resume once the violence tapered off.

"The umpires [in Cuba] were known for keeping guns in their pockets," said pitcher Danny McDevitt.

> I was there in the winter of 1957–58. They had this guy named Armando Rodriguez. He was a big guy. He wasn't giving me anything, and I was yakking at him. I walked up there and the next thing I knew he hit me over the head with his mask. I got up and had him around the neck. [Catcher] Harry Chiti came out and jumped on Rodriguez and everybody was trying to get out there. I ended up getting several stitches sewn up right in the clubhouse. After that, everybody knew me, especially after I went around town with that big white bandage on my head.
>
> People would come up to me and say, "Don't go to the movies tonight." Then you'd read the next day that they bombed the movie theater. A lot of the guys who worked at the ballpark were in the underground.[29]

Mets pitcher Larry Bearnarth pitched in Venezuela after the 1965 season. Letters Bearnarth wrote to Maury Allen of the *New York Post* about conditions in the country offended a number of the natives, who loudly and obscenely made Bearnarth aware of their displeasure every time he pitched. One night, he was pitching a shutout in the ninth inning when he suddenly turned and fired the ball into the first base stands. "I just couldn't take it any more," he said, "not even in Spanish."[30] The umpire ordered Bearnarth out of the game for his own protection and told him the fans would kill him if he didn't leave.

Following the game, the police backed a van up to the locker room, loaded Bearnarth aboard, and took him to the local jail, again for his own protection. The next day, he hastily apologized and left the country. Mets manager Wes Westrum observed that Bearnarth had gone to Venezuela to work on his control and aggressiveness. "Judging by what happened," Westrum said, "I would say he succeeded in both."[31]

The victories of Drysdale, Koufax, and Epstein were isolated events, for by the mid–1960s, owners held the upper hand in their relationship with the players. An article in the *Georgetown Law Journal* by Erwin G. Krasnow and Herman M. Levy expressed the opinion that the labor situation left the players open to exploitation by the owners. Formation of a strong union, they claimed, was the logical remedy.

"The official view, then," said the *Wall Street Journal* in 1969, even after the players had made several gains, "appears to be that those who run the business of baseball should do pretty much as they please, with no effective regulation by themselves or anyone else. And their employees ought to be thankful that the bosses let them work.... That, of course, is largely the way many businessmen operated half a century or so ago. But somehow we can't help thinking that baseball requires remedies more rational than merely turning back the clock."[32]

Few thought of the *Wall Street Journal* as a mouthpiece of militant labor, but when it came to baseball's labor situation, it was as far to the left as *The Daily Worker* when compared to *The Sporting News*. TSN was in favor of change, as long as it was "reasonable," that is, reasonable as defined by *TSN*, which generally meant no change at all. Whether the subject was playing rules, baseball tradition, or economics, the Spink family was against any radical alteration of the sport that had made them wealthy.

Yet even the Spinks were beginning to realize that change was inevitable. In the spring of 1969, an editorial read, "Perhaps baseball's old methods are too high-handed for the modern era. Maybe the reserve clause as presently constituted restricts players' rights too severely. Maybe players are entitled to job security. Maybe ... and maybe not." Then Spink regained his head. "Meanwhile," he continued, "let's not permit the inmates to run the asylum."[33]

The owners had taken a hard line when it came to unions and outside representation. In 1953, players Ralph Kiner and Allie Reynolds brought attorney Norman Lewis to a meeting with Commissioner Frick, but Frick refused to meet with Lewis. Kiner and Reynolds met briefly with the commissioner (without Lewis) and then issued a statement stating that there would be no more meetings unless an attorney was allowed to accompany them.

Shortly afterward, Frick announced that the reason he had wanted to meet with the players was that the owners were planning to vote on ending the pension plan. Since Kiner and Reynolds didn't want to discuss the matter, he said, the owners would vote on eliminating the plan without their input. They decided not to end the pension plan, but Lewis quickly disappeared from the scene.

There were some militants among the players, but for the most part, they accepted their lot. "I don't believe," said retired future Hall of Fame pitcher Bob Feller in 1959, "—to paraphrase the old Charley Wilson story about General Motors—that's what's good for [the owners] always is good for the players, but generally speaking, that's probably right."[34]

When the player representatives met at the 1963 All-Star Game, Bob Friend came out strongly against the idea of a strong union. He gave a lengthy interview to *The Sporting News* in which he refuted the claims made in the *Law Journal* article. "During the thirteen years I have been in the National League," Friend said, "I know of no player who has been exploited." A union would lead to antagonism between the players and owners, he claimed, and would hurt baseball's image. "Stan Musial picketing a ballpark would look great, wouldn't it?"[35]

In February 1966, Jimmy Hoffa tried to form a sports division of the Teamsters Union that would include baseball, football, and basketball players. He was silent on the connection between athletes and teamsters, perhaps considering the players' riding of Charley Finley's mule a sufficient link. Milt Woodward, assistant commissioner of the American Football League, retorted, "[T]hey ought to organize the owners; the players are getting all the money."[36]

Within 20 years, the situation would change dramatically. Players would no longer need to work in the off-season to make ends meet. They might play in the fall or winter to hone their skills, but not for the money. They might take jobs, but only to prepare for life after baseball. Eventually, most major leaguers would spend the winter months in a rigorous workout program, for the best investment they could make was in a career that in just five or ten years could earn them enough money to support their families for the rest of their lives. One of the primary reasons they were able to do so was the appearance on the baseball scene of a gentleman named Marvin Miller.

9

We May Have Been Overly Optimistic in the Spring

In 1968, the National League had its second consecutive lackluster pennant race. St. Louis was expected to repeat, and they didn't disappoint, taking the flag relatively easily and removing any drama from the race by mid–September. The team had talent and spirit, and the latter quality was perhaps the most interesting.

The Cardinals were a racially and culturally heterogeneous combination that somehow avoided the tension that charged so many locker rooms of the 1960s. Why did the Cardinals get along so well? There is an age-old argument in sports as to the value of intangibles and whether spirit and good chemistry breed winning or vice versa. Baseball is primarily a game of skill rather than emotion, and of individual confrontations between batters and pitchers rather than scripted plays in which everyone must cooperate. Football and basketball are more dependent on teamwork and emotion, and players who hit harder and play with more intensity generally get better results. The fine motor skills needed to throw a curve ball or hit a knuckleball may be more difficult for the overly intense baseball player, and coaches and managers often urge them to relax. Trying too hard is frequently as detrimental as not trying hard enough.

Spirit is more often found on good teams because, particularly in older days, it was considered *de rigueur* to act despondently after losses, sitting before one's locker with head hung low, muttering one-word answers for reporters. Last-place teams didn't hold raucous kangaroo court sessions. Championship teams had a lot more wins to celebrate and a lot more reasons to be happy. Further, the higher salaries and the World Series shares earned by players on a winning team generally make for a more cheerful atmosphere.

Whatever it was, the Cardinals had it. Roger Maris, who'd suffered through some painful years in New York, was ready to retire before he was traded to St. Louis after the 1966 season. Once he joined the Cardinals, he had a spiritual rebirth. "Everybody pulls for everybody else," he said. "It's a great club. Close to a perfect club."[1]

Orlando Cepeda, who was traded from the Giants to the Cardinals in 1966, said it was one of the few clubs he'd been with on which there were no fights. "Every ball team has fights," he said. "You don't read about it in the paper, but fights break out in the locker room, or on the bus, or in the hotel. But not the Cardinals. Never since I've been here."[2]

For Cepeda, the atmosphere in St. Louis was a welcome relief from the tension in the Giants' clubhouse, where former manager Alvin Dark had alienated his black and Latino players.[3] Bill Veeck said that the Giants had three teams—one white, one black, and one Hispanic—and that Willie Mays was the only player who got along with all three groups. Cepeda said that the racial divisions that were prevalent with the Giants were virtually non-existent in the Cardinal clubhouse.

First baseman Orlando Cepeda was traded from the Giants to the Cardinals and became a leader in the clubhouse as St. Louis won NL pennants in 1967 and 1968. He was a unanimous choice as NL MVP in 1967.

"[T]he Cardinals of 1967 and 1968," wrote center fielder Curt Flood, "must have been the most remarkable team in the history of baseball. The men of that team were as close to being free of racist poison as a diverse group of twentieth-century Americans could possibly be. Few of them had been that way when they came to the Cardinals. But they changed."[4] "And so there we were," he continued, "including the volatile Cepeda, the impossible Maris and the impenetrable Gibson, three celebrated non-candidates for togetherness. There we were, Latinos, blacks, liberal whites and redeemed peckerwoods, the best team in the game and the most exultant."[5]

Part of the reason for the placid Cardinals clubhouse

was the easy-going manner of manager Red Schoendienst, who was smart enough to leave his talented players alone. He wasn't as sensitive to challenges to his authority as many managers and listened to suggestions from his players on strategy.

Cepeda had been a big slugger in San Francisco, but his last years there had not been happy ones. He had a great rookie season in 1958, but the following year the Giants brought up Willie McCovey, who was voted the best rookie of 1959. McCovey's best position, like Cepeda's, was first base. Through 1964, the Giants tried to figure out how to get both bats in the lineup, which meant playing either Cepeda or McCovey in the outfield, where neither was particularly adept. McCovey was willing but not particularly able, and Cepeda was not especially willing, expressing on several occasions his dislike of outfield play.

When the Giants first went to San Francisco, Cepeda was more popular with many fans than Willie Mays, for Cepeda was the Bay Area's own while Mays was New York's hero. Yet, on a national level, Mays was the superstar, and Cepeda would always be in his shadow. He would never be the leader of the Giants.

In 1965, Cepeda missed almost the entire season after knee surgery, leaving McCovey to play first base every day, and he hit 39 home runs. When Cepeda's knee still appeared gimpy at the beginning of the 1966 season, he was traded to the Cardinals for left-handed pitcher Ray Sadecki, a 20-game winner in 1964 who had slumped badly the next year.

Cepeda's father, Perucho, had been a star player in Puerto Rico, known for his prodigious slugging and his mercurial temper. He had on occasion gone into the stands to take on hecklers. Orlando appeared to have inherited his father's temperament, and columnist Jim Murray once wrote, "Orlando Cepeda has sometimes seemed to have less a career than a long-term tantrum."[6]

Cepeda had trouble with most of his managers before and after he played in St. Louis. His first major league manager was Bill Rigney, and after the Giants finished third in 1959, Cepeda said, "That man lost the pennant for us. He can't manage, he doesn't know baseball or baseball players and he always was picking on me."[7]

Cepeda's problems with Dark were well-documented and justified, as was his dissatisfaction with Dark's successor, Herman Franks. Franks thought Cepeda was not working hard enough to recover from knee surgery and, like Dark, said that Cepeda choked in the clutch, one of the most damning things that can be said about a ballplayer. Dark had a complicated system of plusses and minuses, primarily related to performance in clutch situations, and told reporters that in 1961, Cepeda had the worst rating of any Giants player.

After he left the Cardinals for the Braves in 1969, Cepeda again had trouble with the manager. By 1972, his knees were hurting again, and Luman Harris gave him more rest than Cepeda thought he needed. In June, he left the team in protest and wound up finishing the year in Oakland, but was released after the season. "I never liked Oakland,"[8] he said.

The following year, he was a beneficiary of the new designated hitter rule and had a good season with Boston. When he was released in the spring of 1974, he blamed new Red Sox manager Darrell Johnson.

In St. Louis, however, Cepeda emerged from Mays' shadow and became the spiritual leader of the Cardinals club and a role model for the young Latin players. In 1967, he visited the Cardinals' minor league camp and convinced a number of homesick young players not to quit baseball. It was in the Cardinals' locker room, however, that Cepeda was most influential. He was one of the first players to bring a tape player into the clubhouse, where he played his music loud, talked a lot, and was a master of the friendly insult. After a Cardinals victory, he would deliver a raucous speech celebrating the win, dish out a few jabs, and lead cheers for El Birdos.

In 1968, the Cardinals moved into first place on April 21 and stayed there until May 23, when they fell behind those divided, unhappy Giants. St. Louis was plagued by that common 1968 problem, a lack of hitting. When they fell out of first place, they'd lost seven of eight games in which they scored a total of just 11 runs. A few days later, the team was still slumping and found themselves in fourth place.

The swoon was short-lived, and on June 2 the Cardinals swept the Mets in a doubleheader to move back into first, a position they never left. They won 21 of their next 25 games, and as the club widened its lead, Stan Musial said that the Cards were building a dynasty that would exceed the achievements of the great Cardinals teams of the 1920s, 1930s, and 1940s. He noted that Maris, 34, and second baseman Julian Javier, 31, were the oldest regulars.

The Cardinals also had depth. Maris was planning to retire at the end of the season, but speedy young Bobby Tolan was ready to take his place. John Edwards, who'd been an All-Star catcher in Cincinnati, backed up Tim McCarver. Veteran Dick Schofield, who'd filled in admirably at short for the World Champion Pirates in 1960, was the backup infielder. And there were more reinforcements on the way. Tulsa, the Cardinals' top farm club, won the Pacific Coast League playoffs, and with youngsters like pitchers Mike Torrez and Jerry Reuss and catcher Ted Simmons in the high minors, Musial thought his Cardinals had a long string of pennants ahead of them.

In the year of the pitcher, the Cardinals had perhaps the best in baseball in Bob Gibson. For the first half of the season, right-hander Nelson Briles and lefty Steve Carlton, just 22, provided terrific support behind Gibson. Briles extended a two-year winning streak to 14 games, and Carlton won eight of his first ten decisions. Neither was particularly sharp down the stretch, but Briles won 19 games and Carlton finished 13–11.

Briles was one of baseball's Renaissance men. He was a punter on his high school football team; he'd done some boxing at Santa Clara University; he spoke Spanish and French; he had minor roles in Shakespeare's *Twelfth Night;* he played the guitar and sang, and he wanted to have a career in acting after his baseball career ended.

Had right-hander Dick Hughes been able to duplicate his 1967 form, the Cardinals might have had the best starting rotation in the major leagues. A very near-sighted farmer from Arkansas who carried a rifle with him on the road, Hughes spent nine years in the minor leagues before bursting on the major league scene and earning *The Sporting News'* "Rookie Pitcher of the Year Award" in 1967. In the bullpen when the season began, Hughes wound up winning 16 games. Midway through the season, the Cards tore up his contract and gave him a $2,500 raise.

Before the Cardinals even left Florida in 1968, Hughes was getting cortisone injections for a sore shoulder. He appeared in a few games in relief, but went on the disabled list in June. Hughes threw only 63⅔ innings all year, mostly in relief, and won just two games. When he pitched, he pitched well, allowing only 45 hits, but his shoulder was so badly damaged that he would never pitch in the majors again.

The St. Louis bullpen, led by left-hander Joe Hoerner, wasn't needed much when Gibson pitched, for he completed 28 of 34 starts. When Gibson wasn't pitching, the bullpen adequately backed up the other starters. The 31-year-old Hoerner, who had an 8–2 record, 17 saves and a 1.47 ERA, was an unusual character. One day when no bus driver appeared to take the Cardinals to their hotel after a game, Hoerner got behind the wheel and managed to get the bus into gear and out on the highway, where he amused most of the team, but angered and frightened others, who felt it was a foolish and dangerous thing to do. On another occasion, he climbed aboard a luggage transportation vehicle on the tarmac at the Philadelphia airport and took a few of his teammates for a ride.[9]

Hoerner was also a great fungo hitter, and one night he set a record by hitting the Astrodome roof five times. That broke the mark of four he'd set the previous evening. The Astros were not pleased, for the club had issued orders that no one was to attempt to hit the roof. The Astrodome was one of the wonders of the world, and the far reaches of the wonders of the world were not to be reached by middle-aged pitchers with fungo bats.

It was fortunate that the Cardinals' pitching was strong—leading the league with a 2.49 ERA and 30 shutouts—for the hitting was not nearly as potent as it had been a year earlier. The team average declined from .263 to .249, runs scored dropped from 695 to 583, and home runs were down from 115 to 73.

The greatest decline was that of Cepeda, the 1967 National League Most Valuable Player. After receiving a raise to $85,000, the Cardinals' first baseman came to spring training well rested, having played only occasionally in Puerto Rico during the winter. Yet when the season began, Cepeda didn't hit like he did in 1967. In early May, he was benched after a 1-for-23 slump. In July, he was pulled for a pinch-hitter for the first time in his career. When the season was over, his average had dropped from .325 to .248, his home run production from 25 to 16, and his RBI total from 111 to 73.

Off the field, Cepeda also had a difficult season. In April, he lost an appeal of a $1,000,000 libel suit against *Look* magazine, which had published an article about him in 1963 that contained uncomplimentary references to his lack of motivation and portrayed him as a selfish player. In June, the Internal Revenue Service said he owed over $9,000 in back taxes from 1965. In October, the Supreme Court declined to hear an appeal of his libel suit.[10]

Center fielder Curt Flood was the club's only .300 hitter, barely nosing over the coveted mark with a .301 average. Lou Brock also had an excellent year at the plate, batting .279 with 66 extra-base hits, including 46 doubles and 14 triples, and stole 62 bases.

Brock and Flood got on base and Mike Shannon, who led the club with 79 RBI, drove them in, but the rest of the Cardinals struggled. One of the bright spots was shortstop Dal Maxvill, who surprised everyone by hitting .253 (he batted .175 the following year). Maris hit two home runs on April 14, but the man who once hit 61 in a season hit just five in his final year.[11] McCarver had an off-year and wound up sharing time with Edwards, who got into 85 games. Even with a lackluster offense, the Cardinals won the pennant handily, finishing nine games in front of the Giants and 13 above the third-place Cubs.

After the Giants fell out of first place in May, they never mounted a meaningful threat. Juan Marichal was the only starter who was consistent throughout the season. Mike McCormick, the 1967 Cy Young Award winner, faltered so badly that he wound up in the bullpen. Ray Sadecki slumped to a 12–18 record, despite a 2.91 ERA.

Willie McCovey had a fabulous season, leading the league with 36 home runs and 105 RBI, while batting .293. Thirty-seven-year-old Willie Mays was no longer a superstar, but he had a good year, batting .289 with 23 home runs and 79 RBI. He even stole 12 bases, the most he'd pilfered since 1964. The Giants finished second for the fourth straight year, and cranky manager Herman Franks, who had pondered retirement all season, departed at the end of the year in favor of the more affable Clyde King.

Third place was occupied by the Cubs, who never seriously contended for the pennant. Leo Durocher had been hired in 1966 to rejuvenate a moribund Chicago team that had been led for the past several years by owner Phil

Wrigley's "college of coaches", who took turns acting as head coach. The experiment was novel but unsuccessful, as the Cubs hovered near the bottom of the National League standings. Durocher took over, vowing to do better, but in fact did worse, landing the Cubs in the basement in 1966, suffering the ignominity of finishing behind the hapless Mets, who climbed out of the cellar for the first time.

Durocher brought the Cubs from last to third in 1967, a remarkable achievement that included some time spent in first place around the All-Star break. The Cubs had sluggers like Ernie Banks, Billy Williams, and Ron Santo in the middle of the lineup, and Banks, second baseman Glenn Beckert, shortstop Don Kessinger, and third baseman Santo formed a solid infield. In Randy Hundley, the Cubs had a young iron man catcher who appeared in 149 games in 1966, 152 in 1967, and a remarkable 160 in 1968.

Chicago also had good young starting pitching. Early in the 1966 season, the Cubs acquired 6'5", Canadian right-hander Ferguson Jenkins from the Phillies for two veteran pitchers. Jenkins, given a chance to start regularly, was 20–13 in 1967 and was the only 20-game winner to repeat in 1968, finishing with a burst to end the season at 20–15, despite being the victim of five 1–0 losses.

Behind the 24-year-old Jenkins was 22-year-old lefty Ken Holtzman. After his 9–0, military-interrupted 1967 season, Holtzman predicted 20 wins in 1968 for both himself and Jenkins, and said that the other two Cubs starters, Joe Niekro and Rich Nye, might win 20 as well.

Unfortunately, Holtzman was not finished with the National Guard, which in 1968 probably inflicted more damage on him than did National League hitters. He missed his first scheduled start of the year when he was called to serve on Chicago riot duty, and later in the summer he did weekend stints, went away for two consecutive weeks, and thus never achieved a consistent rhythm. After a poor start against the Mets in June, Durocher blasted him for a lack of effort. In late July and early August, he pitched three straight shutouts, but tailed off and finished the season with a disappointing 11–14 record.

One of the Cubs' main shortcomings early in the season was an ineffective bullpen, a problem solved by the acquisition of Dodgers relief ace Phil Regan, who won the "Fireman of the Year" Award in 1966 and would do so again in 1968. With their starting pitching behind Jenkins inconsistent, however, the Cubs never mounted a meaningful challenge to the Cardinals and again finished third, as the top three clubs in the league, the Cardinals, Giants, and Cubs, finished in exactly the same order they had in 1967.

The one National League club that could hit in 1968 was the Cincinnati Reds. Pete Rose won the first of his four batting titles by getting a hit in the season's final game to edge Pittsburgh's Matty Alou, .335 to .332. The Reds also had a rookie catcher who, before the season even started, was being hailed as one of the best prospects in many years. Johnny Bench had just turned 20 the previous December and, after tearing up the International League in 1967 with 23 home runs in 98 games, was promoted to the major leagues, but he batted only .163 in 26 games with the Reds. It wasn't the minor league home runs that got everyone's attention; it was the youngster's powerful arm and the masterful way he handled himself behind the plate.

Bench was handed the Reds' catching job long before the 1968 season began, and John Edwards, the number one receiver for several years, was traded to the Cardinals. Bench got off to a slow start offensively, and his average was only .171 on May 5. By the time the season was over, however, he had played in 154 games—an astonishing number for a catcher—and hit .275 with 15 home runs and 82 runs batted in. Those numbers were nowhere near the statistics Bench would achieve during the next few years, but in the dark offensive days of 1968, they were mighty impressive, especially for the best defensive catcher in baseball. In November, Bench was voted the National League "Rookie of the Year".

Rose had been an All-Star in previous years, and Bench's performance was no surprise to those who'd seen him play in the minor leagues, but there was a third Reds player whose batting prowess was a most pleasant surprise. Alex Johnson was a six-foot, 205-pound outfielder who led the Florida State League with a .313 average in 1962 and hit .329 and paced the Pioneer League with 35 home runs and 128 RBI the following year. He came up to the Phillies in the middle of the 1964 season and hit .303 in 43 games. After batting .297 in 97 games the following year, Johnson was traded to the Cardinals, where something went terribly wrong. He had two awful years and acquired a reputation as a troubled sort who wouldn't listen to his manager and coaches. "I didn't pay any attention to what they told me," Johnson told a reporter.[12] "He doesn't seem to want to improve," said Cardinals coach Dick Sisler. "He doesn't have concentration."[13]

During the 1967 World Series, Cardinals manager Schoendienst was looking for Johnson to pinch-hit but couldn't find him. Finally, someone located him in the clubhouse, eating a sandwich. "Alex," Flood once said to him, "you ought to find something to do that you like better than baseball."[14]

When Johnson played with the Phillies, manager Gene Mauch sought to inspire him by telling him he could be a $40,0000-a-year ballplayer, but Johnson told Mauch he didn't need that much money. He wouldn't listen when his teammates tried to change his positioning in the outfield. He had an altercation with Cardinals outfielder Bobby Tolan. He trotted to first base on infield grounders. The final straw, however, was that Johnson didn't hit. "Ball clubs will put up with some problem athletes, if they happen to produce well," wrote St. Louis correspondent Neal Russo, "but Johnson had flopped."[15]

Russo pointed out that Johnson had exactly as many homers (one) as light-hitting, 155-pound shortstop Dal Maxvill.

The Cardinals traded Johnson to Cincinnati in January 1968 for outfielder Dick Simpson. Flood said that he didn't care if Johnson hit .400; he was glad he was gone because he didn't hustle.[16] The Reds were hopeful that manager Dave Bristol, known for his patience, could mine Johnson's great offensive potential. Bristol managed to get Johnson to hit, but he couldn't get him to talk. The bubbly Rose was the life of the Reds, and he tried to draw Johnson out by teasing him. All he ever got in return was an impassive stare. "Mr. Personality, that's Alex," joked Reds second baseman Tommy Helms.[17]

Earl Lawson, who served as the Reds' *Sporting News* beat writer for many years, liked to portray the Reds as a happy team.[18] In a May 1969 profile of Johnson, Lawson quoted a "grinning" Jim Merritt, who said, "sometimes I don't think Alex hears very well." "I just want to keep hearing Alex's bat," chuckled Dave Bristol. "Just give Alex a bat to swing and someone to pitch to him and he's happy," cracked Rose. A "grinning" Bristol pointed out the size of Johnson's bat, a subject he found so amusing that he laughed.[19] It seemed as though everyone on the Reds was cracking jokes, laughing, and grinning.

Everyone, that is, except Alex Johnson. Even Lawson never described him as grinning, chuckling, chortling, or guffawing. He rarely quoted him, relying on what others said for material on Johnson. Some viewed Johnson with amusement, interpreting his detachment as a sign that he was worry-free, aloof, or a man of few words. None recognized the mentally troubled individual he was found to be in the early 1970s after winning a batting title in California.

Bristol decided to leave Johnson alone and let him hit the way he wanted, and that proved to be the solution. Johnson reached the .300 mark early in 1968 and stayed there all season. The increase in his average caused his image to morph from that of an anti-social loner to the "strong silent type." When coach Vern Benson asked him how many hits he had in a certain game, Johnson replied, "I don't count 'em." When a writer reminded him that he was hitting over .300, he replied, "too bad."[20]

Johnson's final average was .312 in 603 at-bats, although he did not display the power he'd shown in the minor leagues. The fact that he hit just two home runs was considered a tribute to his selfless virtue in trying for singles and a high average. In November, Johnson was voted *The Sporting News'* National League "Comeback Player of the Year". "All I needed was a chance to play," he said.[21]

With Rose, Bench, Johnson, Tony Perez, and Lee May, the Reds had plenty of firepower. Their total of 690 runs scored was 78 ahead of the second-best

Cubs, and their .272 team average was 20 points higher than that of the next highest clubs, the Braves and Pirates.

Unfortunately, the Reds' pitching was not equal to their hitting. In the spring, Bristol thought he had a strong rotation in Milt Pappas, Jim Maloney, Mel Queen, and Gary Nolan. Maloney was an All-Star who won 23 games in 1963 and 20 in 1965. Queen was a converted outfielder who blossomed and won 14 games in 1967. Nolan won 14 games that year as a 19-year-old and was strong-armed and cocky. Pappas was an 11-year veteran and former American League All-Star who was just as cocky but no longer quite as strong-armed.

All of the Reds starters except Nolan had a history of injury, and in spring training Nolan began experiencing pain in his shoulder. He received a shot of cortisone and a ticket to Tampa to rehab in the Florida State League. Maloney's shoulder, which had given him trouble in the past, kicked up just before the start of the season. Queen went down in the second game of the year. He didn't have a lot of pain, but he couldn't throw hard. He got a shot of cortisone and Bristol got a major headache, as his entire rotation imploded before the season was barely underway.

Queen pitched only 18 innings all year and didn't win a single game. Maloney and Nolan pitched effectively when they were able to take the mound, but their arms bothered them all year. Ace reliever Ted Abernathy suffered from a sore shoulder, and lefty reliever Billy McCool was also sidelined.

With the Reds' starters on the shelf, Bristol pressed right-hander George Culver into service, and he threw 226 innings while finishing 11–16, including a no-hitter. Big right-hander Tony Cloninger, acquired from the Braves in mid-season, had won 24 games for the Milwaukee Braves in 1965. After pitching on a frigid Opening Day in Atlanta the following year, his arm had never been the same. Cloninger fit right in with the gimpy Cincinnati staff.

The Reds finished last in the league with a 3.56 ERA and surrendered 573 walks, a horrendous 3.5 per game, by far the worst ratio in the league. The poor pitching doomed the Reds to a fourth-place finish at 83–79, 14 games behind the Cardinals.

The Braves were in their third year in Atlanta, with a new manager, Luman Harris, and a new shortstop, Sonny Jackson, who received a big winter buildup. The young shortstop, just 23, had burst onto the scene with the Astros in 1966, batting .292 and tying the major league record for most steals by a rookie with 49. The next year, his performance fell off dramatically, and the Astros traded him to the Braves.

Perhaps the Braves should have been suspicious that Houston had given up so quickly on a player who just a year earlier was touted as a coming star. Jackson's greatest shortcoming was his defense, for he had an erratic arm and led the league's shortstops in errors in each of his two seasons. Although Jackson's fielding wasn't any better in Atlanta, he didn't lead the league in errors, primarily because he missed so much time with injuries. His offensive production was also poor. He batted .226 and was sent to the Arizona Instructional League to learn how to bunt.

Before the season began, the Braves lost slugging outfielder Rico Carty for the year when he was diagnosed with tuberculosis. Clete Boyer, who'd been so eager during the winter to tell his teammates how they might improve, didn't do much to help the Braves in 1968. He hit poorly and on July 12, the Dodgers' Don Drysdale hit *him*, flush on the hand. The injury kept Boyer out the rest of the year, leaving him with a .227 average and just four homers and 17 RBI. That was just four more homers and 17 more RBI than Carty.

The Braves were devastated by injuries. In addition to Carty missing the entire season and Boyer being out for about half the year, catcher Joe Torre was hampered by a series of mishaps. He had ankle surgery before the season, missed a few days with a fractured finger when he was hit by a foul tip, and then suffered a hairline fracture of his cheekbone and the roof of his mouth when he was beaned by the Cubs' Chuck Hartenstein. As soon as he recovered from being hit, he hurt his arm. In late May, he injured his hand and missed a few more days. Torre never got going and didn't come close to equaling his excellent 1966 stats, or even his decent 1967 figures.

The Braves might have survived all of the injuries if Henry Aaron had hit like he was capable of hitting. But for the first half of the season, Aaron hit like Clete Boyer. At the end of June he was batting .237 with 15 homers. That wasn't horrible in the Year of the Pitcher, but it wasn't what the Braves needed from their top slugger with Carty and Torre out. On July 14, Aaron hit the 500th home run of his career off Mike McCormick of the Giants, and he finished strong, but by that time the Braves were out of the race. Aaron ended the season with a .287 average, 29 home runs and 86 runs batted in, and the Braves came home fifth at 81–81.

The Pirates had been contenders in 1966 and disappointing in 1967. During the winter, the acquisition of Jim Bunning was the major reason for the optimism of freshman manager Larry Shepard. During his first two starts, Bunning looked like his old self, but then he suffered a physical collapse. He had an ankle injury, a groin pull, a hip injury, and a pulled muscle in his leg. Knowing how much the Pirates were counting on him, Bunning tried to return too soon and kept aggravating his ills and creating new ones.

To add to the Pirates' indignity, the pitcher sent to the Phillies in return for Bunning, Woodie Fryman, got off to a terrific start. Fryman had gone just 3–8 with the 1967 Pirates, but after 11 1968 starts, he had a 7–4 record and a 1.75 ERA. Meanwhile, Bunning was 3–5 with a 3.71 ERA. The rest of the year was even worse, and the man who was supposed to be the savior of the Pirates' franchise would up with a record of 4–14.

Big lefty Bob Veale was the Pirates' best pitcher, but he had trouble winning. In Veale's first five starts, he gave up just eight runs, but didn't win a game as his mates scored a total of just four. He was 0–3 with a 1.77 ERA. Veale's luck didn't get much better as the season progressed. He got into a dispute with Shepard when he missed a turn because he refused to take an early flight to Houston if he could not bring his dog. One couldn't blame him, for the dog probably supported him better than his teammates, who were shut out eight times when he pitched. Veale's final record was 13–14 despite an excellent ERA of 2.05.

The Pirates' best pitcher turned out to be 26-year-old right-hander Steve Blass. Blass had been with the Pirates since 1964, winning 22 games and losing 23, and hadn't been overly impressive. A 1966 scouting report misspelled his name as Blas and stated that he was not an overpowering pitcher and suffered from a lack of control and poor stamina. When the 1968 season began, Blass was in the bullpen, which in the 1960s was the place for pitchers who weren't good enough to start. When the Pirates needed a fifth starter, Blass got the call, and he kept moving up in the pecking order. He won nine straight starts down the stretch, including six complete games, and finished 18–6.

In June, the Pirates called up another young pitcher, 23-year-old Dock Ellis, whose greatest notoriety to that point had come when he held out in the spring of 1968. After his 7–7 record at Macon and Columbus in 1967, Ellis thought he was entitled to a hefty raise. When he didn't get one, he became, according to general manager Joe Brown, the most stubborn holdout in Brown's 13-year tenure. It was audacious behavior for a rookie, but the world would soon learn that audacity was a significant part of the personality of Dock Phillip Ellis, Jr.

The Pirates could hit for average and had the second-highest mark in the league but, playing in cavernous Forbes Field, managed just 80 home runs. Willie Stargell,[22] with 24, accounted for nearly a third of the total. Roberto Clemente added 18 and first baseman Donn Clendenon had 17, but no one else had more than *four*.[23]

The Forbes Field infield was hard as a rock, and players like Matty Alou, Manny Mota, and Clemente concentrated on pounding the ball into the dirt and beating out infield hits or driving the ball through the infield. The Buc with the highest average was Alou, who was in the race for the batting title until Pete Rose nosed him out on the final day of the season.

The 1960s were a decade during which players with high batting averages were considered the most valuable. Modern analysis would diminish the value of Alou, a slap hitter with no power who rarely walked, had a weak arm, and contributed little beyond the .330 or so he batted in several years.

Clemente, the Pirates' best all-around player, was troubled by a shoulder injury all season, missing 30 games, and it took a strong finish to get his average up to .291. Shortstop Gene Alley, an All-Star in 1967, also injured his shoulder. Playing in pain all season, he managed to get into 133 games, but had trouble throwing and was not the player he was in 1966 and 1967.

When the Pirates got off to a slow start, their rookie manager suffered badly. "[S]hepard feels," wrote Les Beiderman, "every game is a crisis; a sort of World Series contest early in the season."[24] Not only was Shepard's club losing, they seemed to have to discovered a knack for doing so in a dramatic and heartbreaking fashion that would test the nerves of any manager. After a ninth-inning loss in the opener, Shepard sat silently in the clubhouse, sat staring straight ahead on the bus, and appeared to be catatonic at the airport.

Baseball has a long season, and if Shepard was going to take every loss that hard, he would not survive for 162 games. When Danny Murtaugh managed the Pirates, he took wins and losses stoically. During the 1960 World Series, after his club took three horrendous thrashings from the Yankees, he reminded everyone that each counted as only one loss. Shepard's immediate predecessor, Harry Walker, responded to adversity the way he reacted to everything—loudly. He blasted his players, the umpires, and the fans, but he never sat in silent agony.

After a losing game, Shepard often didn't eat, didn't speak, and had trouble sleeping. No doubt he wanted to show his bosses how much he cared, but the drama did little for his club's confidence. By the time the season was over, Shepard had been silent, hungry, and sleepless 82 times, and his club finished in sixth place, a tremendous disappointment for a veteran club that entered the season with such high hopes.

The story of the 1968 Phillies was the story of Richie Allen. During the previous summer, Allen had been pushing his vintage 1950 car up a hill when his hand went through the headlight, and he severed two tendons connecting the little and ring fingers. He underwent five hours of surgery to reconnect the tendons, but nerves take time, sometimes months or years, to regenerate, and for most of the winter Allen wore a shoulder-to-fingertip cast and had no control of two fingers on his right hand. He was scared.

When the cast was removed, Allen saw stitches and pins and a very abnormal-looking hand, one with which it would be very difficult to throw a baseball or swing a bat. He insisted he would play in 1968, but where? He probably wouldn't be able to throw well enough to regain his third base job. He could play first, but what would the Phils do with veteran Bill White, who couldn't play anywhere but first? Perhaps left field was the answer.

As 1967 turned to 1968, Allen slowly began to regain mobility as the nerves in his hand regenerated. No one, including Allen, knew if he would ever have full use of the hand or if he would have the ability to hit like he had in the past. While Allen was driving to Clearwater for spring training, he stopped at a batting cage and decided to test himself. His hand was still a bit numb, but he hit the ball hard and felt he had cleared the first mental hurdle.

Allen was able to hit in Florida, and when the season opened in Los Angeles, he played left field and hit a double. In order to cope with the early-season cold in Philadelphia, Allen wore two gloves and talked about wearing a heated glove.

Allen had never been a particularly good fielder, and after he separated his right shoulder in 1966, he had difficulty throwing from third base. When infielder Cookie Rojas was injured early in the 1968 season, however, Allen was moved back to third and made three throwing errors in his first three games. But he was hitting for a team that didn't have many good hitters, and the Phillies needed to find a place for him somewhere on the field.

Many thought Allen's biggest problem was not his hand but his head. After pitcher Dick Ellsworth was traded to the Red Sox, he said, "His behavior on and off the field has been disgusting. People would be amazed at what the guys think of him. He drags us down."[25] Beat writer Allen Lewis noted that Allen "talks only to writers who don't criticize him and refuses to speak to those who point out times when he fails to hustle."[26]

Richie Allen was one of the most feared sluggers and enigmatic personalities of the 1960s. In 1968, he was at the center of numerous controversies that led to the firing of Philadelphia manager Gene Mauch.

Many fans didn't care much for Allen either. Dan Miller of Long Beach, California, wrote to *The Sporting News*, urging the Phillies to rid themselves of their problem child. "The trouble is just starting," he warned.[27] Philadelphia fans rode Allen all season, and he was the only player who was consistently booed in the genteel Astrodome.

Allen's personality had hardened during his early days in baseball, when he was the only black player on the

Little Rock, Arkansas, club. Fans put racist flyers under the windshield wipers of cars in the parking lots, and Allen's teammates tried to gather them up before he could see them. They accompanied Allen to his car to provide protection from the violent Arkansas fans. Allen fought back on the field, hitting 33 home runs and driving in 97 runs, but the bitterness came with him when he arrived in Philadelphia, which, although a Northern city, had a history of racism, including the protests against Jackie Robinson playing in the city in 1947.

Allen thought his problems in Philadelphia stemmed from a batting practice fight with teammate Frank Thomas in 1965. Thomas, a notorious needler, kept referring to African-American outfielder Johnny Briggs as "boy," which led to an argument between Allen and Thomas. Thomas hit Allen in the shoulder with his bat, and Allen punched Thomas in the jaw. Thomas was immediately placed on waivers and sold to the Astros, but Allen felt that the press and fans had blamed him for the incident, and from that moment on they treated him unfairly.

Allen didn't help his image with his penchant for finding ways to get into trouble. Allen drove his own car from Philadelphia to New York for an April 30 game against the Mets rather than taking the team bus. He got caught in traffic and arrived just 20 minutes before game-time. Manager Gene Mauch said Allen had not asked for permission to drive, and sat him on the bench when he arrived.

In late May, Allen injured his groin horseback riding and missed several games. A couple of days later, he showed up late and Mauch fined him a second time. When Mauch called for an afternoon workout before a night game, Bill White quipped that it was the only way he could get Allen to the park in time for the game.

Shortly afterward, Allen said he wanted to be traded and sat out a few games, either because (a) his groin still bothered him; (b) he didn't want to play, or; (c) Mauch didn't want him to play. Finally, owner Bob Carpenter intervened and met with Allen. He told Mauch to put the troubled star back in the lineup.

Mauch followed orders, but he was not happy about it. He was an intense disciplinarian and did not make adjustments to accommodate problem personalities; either they adjusted to his way of doing things or, like Alex Johnson, they found themselves with another team.

On June 15, Mauch was fired. The Phillies were not playing well, but the timing and circumstances of the dismissal were troubling. First, Mauch was given the news while he was at the bedside of his sick wife, rather than being told in person. Second, the firing came just five days after Carpenter's meeting with Allen, which led many to speculate that Allen had given the owner a "he goes or I go" ultimatum.

Worst of all was general manager Bob Quinn's comment regarding Mauch's dismissal. "The Allen problem was a factor," Quinn admitted, "but not the entire reason. We know Gene had some personal problems that would have affected his managing that I won't discuss." Were the problems related to his wife's health? No, Quinn said, but he wouldn't elaborate.[28]

Former major league outfielder Bob Skinner, 36, who'd been managing the Phillies' top farm club in San Diego, was given the job of managing Allen and the rest of the Phillies. He said Allen was a great player, looked forward to managing him, and didn't anticipate any problems.

For the first month of Skinner's reign, Allen delivered. In 30 games, he batted .356 with 12 home runs and 27 RBI. Both Allen and Skinner said the hot streak had nothing to do with Mauch's departure and was attributable to the warmer weather and the passage of time, both of which did wonders for Allen's right hand. Allen said he knew his hand would never be the same as it was before the injury, but he had adjusted his swing and could still hit. Skinner praised Allen as a winner and a team player.

A month later, the honeymoon came to an abrupt end when Allen was involved in an altercation in a bar. The bartender pressed charges against Allen, whom he refused to serve because he was intoxicated, and he claimed that Allen had threatened him. Allen insisted the entire incident was the result of an unrelated personal vendetta and complained about the treatment he and his family received from the Philadelphia fans. He said once more that he wanted to be traded. Carpenter said he needed to grow up. The charges were dropped, but now Skinner was as upset as Carpenter and the fans, who became even more restive when Allen's offensive production fell off. In September, he again encountered traffic problems and missed a flight to St. Louis.

In his final game of the season, Allen hit three homers and drove in seven runs against the Mets, giving him 33 homers and 90 RBI for a season during which he missed ten games for a variety of reasons. The 33 home runs placed him second in the league behind Willie McCovey.

"I'm disappointed in Allen's production," Carpenter said. "I think he should give you a .300 average and 120 runs batted in."[29] He talked about trading Allen, who clearly wanted to go somewhere else. The Mets wanted him, but not for what the Phillies expected in return. After a year in which offensive production was at a premium, one would think there would have been a line of teams looking for a hitter as productive as Allen, but unless the Phils wanted to accept less than market value, there were no takers. They had been so successful in publicizing Allen's negative attributes that they had severely diminished his trading value.

By the end of the 1969 season, Skinner, following several confrontations with Allen, was no longer the manager, and by December, Allen was no longer a Phillie. He was traded to St. Louis in a transaction that would rock baseball history—not because Allen was traded, but because one of the Cardinals sent to Philadelphia was Curt Flood, who refused to go.

With Allen, the Phillies' offense was adequate, but in a year in which pitching seemed plentiful, the Phillies didn't have much. Woodie Fryman, who began the season with such promise, faded badly in the second half, went a month without a win, and finished with a record of 12–14.

Fryman had an interesting background. When he was 17, he attended a Pirates tryout camp and was offered a contract. There was no bonus, however, so he went back to his family's tobacco farm. The government provided generous subsidies for growing tobacco, much more than the $300 per month Fryman could have earned pitching in the minor leagues. He worked the farm during the week and played semi-pro ball on weekends, once pitching a 13-inning perfect game in which he struck out 25.

Tobacco subsidies were reduced, the farm became less profitable, and Fryman decided that, even without a bonus, he might have a better future throwing fastballs than harvesting tobacco. After just one year in the minors, he joined the Pirates in 1966 and won 12 games. The National League "Green Book" listed his birth date as 1943, making him a 23-year-old rookie. Two years later, the records were revised to show that Fryman was born in 1940. When the Pirates had signed him, they shaved three years off his age.

Lefty Chris Short won 19 games and veteran Larry Jackson won 13, but those two, plus Fryman, were the only reliable hurlers on the Philadelphia staff. Neither Mauch nor Skinner could find a fourth starter, and none of the relievers was consistent. A 1968 club without pitching was not going to be successful, and the Phils ended the season tied for seventh place with a 76–86 record. They were 27–27 under Mauch and 48–59 under Skinner.[30]

The team that tied the Phillies was the Dodgers, only two years removed from consecutive World Series appearances. After losing four straight to the Orioles in the 1966 Series, the Dodgers' roster underwent dramatic changes. Cy Young Award winner Sandy Koufax retired, All-Star shortstop Maury Wills was traded to the Pirates, and two-time batting champion Tommy Davis was traded to the Mets.

In 1967, the Dodgers slipped to eighth place, 22 games below their pace of the previous year and their worst record since 1944. As always, a lack of spirit and desire was believed to be the reason. Don Drysdale said the team wasn't hungry, as if a hungrier pitcher could have replaced Koufax's 27 wins or a starving shortstop could have stolen bases like Wills. Although many were tried at shortstop in 1967, all were found wanting, which is why the Dodgers had acquired Zoilo Versalles from the Twins.

Like the Yankees team that collapsed in 1965, the Dodgers were certain they'd bounce back in 1968, with renewed spirit and a few new players. Versalles had worn out his welcome in Minnesota with indifferent play and didn't appear to be bringing the spirit Drysdale was looking for. He wasn't the savior; struggling with a new league and a bad back, Versalles hit just .196 and showed little range in the field. By the end of the year, the Dodgers' shortstop was journeyman utility player Paul Popovich.

Willie Davis, the Dodgers' immensely talented center fielder, had been a mystery since he arrived in Los Angeles eight years earlier. Davis was perhaps the fastest player in the National League and showed flashes of brilliance with the bat, but he never achieved the stardom predicted for him when he arrived in Los Angeles in 1960 after hitting .346 at Triple-A Spokane, with 217 hits and 81 extra-base hits, including 26 triples. With the Dodgers, he hit .318 in 22 games.

Davis always seemed on the verge of stardom, but he could never quite get there. He sometimes had troubling gauging fly balls in the outfield. He experimented endlessly at the plate, acquiring the nickname "The Man of a Thousand Stances."[31] His inconsistency from season to season was almost consistent, as his average went up and down in alternate years:

1960	.318
1961	.254
1962	.285
1963	.245
1964	.294
1965	.238
1966	.284
1967	.257

Walter Alston and the Dodgers' coaches never understood how a man with Davis's speed and hitting ability could have such low batting averages. Further, after hitting 21 home runs in 1962 at the age of 22, Davis hadn't hit more than 12 since, and had just six in 1967.

Davis's prior pattern indicated he was due for a good season in 1968, but he started slowly. In fact, the entire Dodgers offense got off to a dreadful start, being shut out in three of their first four games. Bob Bailey, who was supposed to provide power from the third base position, didn't drive in a run until May 2, not that there were many Dodgers on base to drive in. When told his RBI was timely, Bailey replied, "Any run batted in on this club is timely."[32]

Al Ferrara, the powerful, right-handed-hitting outfielder, broke his ankle in the second game of the season and missed the rest of the year. Rocky Colavito, acquired over the winter from the White Sox, didn't hit and was released. The only player who hit well all season was veteran catcher Tom Haller, who played in 144 games and batted .285, but hit only four home runs. The husky, former University of Illinois quarterback had been in double figures in the home run department the last six seasons in San Francisco and had hit as many as 27 in a single year. What happened in Los Angeles?

During the 1960s, players who sacrificed power to hit for a higher average were praised for their selflessness, but Haller said he would have been a better hitter had he hit more home runs, even if his average suffered. In the large confines of Dodger Stadium and with the dominant pitching of 1968, no one was going to hit a lot of home runs, and the Dodgers connected for just 25 in 81 home games.[33] Len Gabrielson, platooned in left field after Ferrara's injury, paced the club with ten, and Haller led in runs batted in with just 53.

The Dodgers had great pitching from the top to the bottom of the staff, with a rotation of Drysdale, Claude Osteen, Bill Singer, and Don Sutton, plus an excellent bullpen, but the pitching couldn't overcome the feeble offense. Only Drysdale, who finished at 14–12, was able to post a winning record. Eight of his wins were shutouts, including the record six in a row. In 12 of his 31 starts, Drysdale did not allow an earned run.

In 1965, the Dodgers won the pennant without much offense, but Drysdale was able to help his own cause by batting .300 with seven home runs in just 130 at-bats. Since Jim Lefevbre and Lou Johnson tied for the team lead with 12 that year—each in more than 450 at-bats—Drysdale was the best power threat on the club. Apparently the Year of the Pitcher affected Drysdale at the plate, for in 1968 he batted just .177 with no home runs. The other three Dodgers starters, despite not having an ERA higher than 3.08, lost a combined 14 more games than they won.

At the beginning of September, the Dodgers were in last place, behind even the Mets and Astros. They had been shut out 23 times, the most in the league. Eliminated from the pennant race, the Dodgers brought up some of their kids, the most notable being third baseman Bill Sudakis. Sudakis homered in his big league debut and hit a triple and single in his second game. Then he hit a grand slam. Two home runs in a week by a single player was enough to get Dodgers fans excited, and they also liked the youngster's personality. He was tough—a feisty scrapper who played with the spirit Drysdale had been looking for.

Sudakis, hampered by knee injuries, did not become the next Dodgers star, but he was the vanguard of a phalanx of youngsters who would lead the club to a series of pennants in the 1970s. After the dismal 1968 season, former Dodgers star Duke Snider said his old team would not be a power for years to come, but the Dodgers always prided themselves on being able to develop youngsters on the farm, and in 1968 they had a bumper crop. At Ogden of the Pioneer League, the lowest rung on the ladder, manager Tommy Lasorda won the pennant with third baseman Steve Garvey, first baseman Bill Buckner, and outfielders Bobby Valentine and Tom Paciorek. Shortstop Billy Grabarkewitz was tearing up the Texas League before he broke his ankle. Catcher Joe Ferguson was in Tri Cities and outfielder Bill Russell in Bakersfield. Better days were ahead.

The Mets were one of the few National League teams that was satisfied with their 1968 performance. Under new manager Gil Hodges, the Mets had the best season in the seven-year history of their franchise. Finishing ninth with a 73–89 record would not have excited the fans of most teams, but it was the most games the Mets had ever won, only the second time they had avoided 100 losses, and the second time they'd escaped the basement.

In a era where pitching mattered, the Mets had good young pitchers. They'd gone through a number of teenage phenoms since 1962, and almost all had succumbed to arm trouble or ineffectiveness. In 1967, however, rookie Tom Seaver, whose name had been drawn out of the commissioner's hat when it was determined that the contract he'd signed out of USC with the Braves was invalid, won 16 games and was named NL "Rookie of the Year".

The following year, the Mets unveiled a rookie left-hander, Jerry Koosman, who won 19 games. Seaver won 16, giving the Mets the nucleus of a good pitching staff. That was fortunate, for at .228, they had the lowest team batting average in the National League. The previous winter, they'd traded Tommy Davis, their best hitter, to acquire Tommie Agee, who they thought would fill a hole in center field. Agee was a major disappointment in 1968, batting just .218 and driving in only 17 runs in 132 games. But with Agee and fellow outfielder Cleon Jones, the Mets had speed, something they'd never had before.

The Mets flirted with the magic .500 mark until late July, coming within a game on several occasions, but were never able to get over the hurdle. In September, their goal was to set a team record for wins (eclipsing the 66 posted in 1966) and stay out of last place. The second Mets ninth-place team was different from the first, for in 1966 the Mets had imported veterans like Ken Boyer, Bob Shaw, Bob Friend, and Ed Bressoud, who were able to lift the Mets out of the basement, but were at the end of the their careers. The 1968 Mets had promising youngsters like Jones and Agee, shortstop Bud Harrelson, Seaver, and Koosman, and young pitchers Nolan Ryan and Jim McAndrew. First baseman Ed Kranepool seemed as though he'd been around forever (and he had—seven years), but he was only 23. The core of the 1968 team had a chance to get better.

The Mets achieved both of their goals, but manager Hodges was not around to celebrate. The Mets' manager began smoking cigarettes while serving in Okinawa during World War II, and as the pressures of managing intensified, he smoked more. In August 1968 he experienced chest pains, but eventually they went away. A month later they returned, and this time they didn't go away. For five days Hodges suffered in silence, although the pain was so intense he could barely function.

Somehow he kept going, and kept smoking—two or three packs per day.

On September 24, despite the boring pain in his chest, Hodges pitched batting practice on a humid evening in Atlanta. During the second inning, he told pitching coach Rube Walker he didn't feel well and was going to lie down in the clubhouse. Mets trainer Gus Mauch had suffered a heart attack in 1960, and as soon as he saw Hodges, he realized what was happening. He summoned the Braves' team doctor, and the two men, over Hodges' protests, got him to the hospital, where doctors informed the Mets' manager he'd suffered a mild heart attack. They told him that a winter of rest should enable him to resume his duties in the spring, but the best season in Mets history ended with the open question of whether the man who'd led them to their glorious ninth-place finish would be able to take the reins in 1969.

Nineteen-sixty-eight was the Houston franchise's seventh year in the National League and their fourth season as the Astros. They'd begun their existence in 1962 as the Colt .45s and finished eighth, ahead of the Cubs and Mets. Since the Colts finished 24 games ahead of the Mets, their sister expansion franchise, it appeared that the Houston organization was on the road to success.

The next five years, however, did not bear out that hypothesis. They finished ninth four times, climbed as high as eighth in 1966, and never finished higher than any team other than the woeful Mets and Cubs. Houston's win totals in their first six seasons were 64, 66, 66, 65, 72, and 69. While consistency is admirable in many instances, it is not when a baseball team repeatedly loses nearly 100 games a year. Part of the reason for the lack of success was that Houston was attempting to build for the future, bringing youngsters like Joe Morgan, Rusty Staub, Sonny Jackson, Jim Wynn, and Larry Dierker to the major leagues before they were ready. Morgan, Staub, Wynn, and Dierker eventually made good, but they were accompanied by many youngsters who failed and did little to help the club. For one game at the end of the 1963 season, the Colts started the following lineup:

	Age
Sonny Jackson ss	19
Joe Morgan 2b	20
Jimmy Wynn cf	21
Rusty Staub 1b	19
Aaron Pointer rf	21
Brock Davis lf	19
Glenn Vaughn 3b	19
Jerry Grote c	20
Jay Dahl p[34]	17

By 1968, Astros fans and owner Roy Hofheinz were tired of talking about the future. Hofheinz said he expected the club to be in the first division and, with a few breaks, he thought they might win the pennant. Manager Grady

Hatton had an edict to win now, for the youngsters who'd been brought up as teenagers were in their mid–20s. It was time to start showing tangible progress.

Hatton decided he needed to strengthen his defense and moved the slugging Wynn from center field to left, shifted Staub from right field to first base, and installed slick-fielding but light-hitting Ron Davis in center. The maneuvers may have made tactical sense, but they were a strategic failure in that they antagonized Staub and Wynn, the club's best hitters. Wynn, the Astros' biggest power threat with 37 home runs and 107 RBI in 1967, was particularly incensed by being moved out of the glamour outfield position, which he considered a lack of confidence in his ability. He certainly wasn't an embarrassment in center, and perhaps Hatton might have been better off keeping his superstar happy, particularly after Davis failed to hit.

The season got off to a very bad start when Morgan injured his knee in the fifth game of the season and missed most of the rest of the year. Rookie catcher Hal King didn't hit, and base runners took great liberties on his arm. Davis, after batting .212 in 57 games with just one home run, was traded to the Cardinals, and Wynn resumed his old position in center. With three members of the starting eight injured or unproductive, the Astros found themselves near the bottom of the standings by mid–June. "We may have been overly optimistic in the spring," assistant GM John Mullen conceded.[35]

On June 17, Hatton was fired and replaced by former Pirates manager Harry "the Hat" Walker. The Astros had lost 14 of 16 and were in tenth place, six games out of ninth. When he fired Hatton, GM Spec Richardson said that Hatton was not being blamed for the club's failure, but that it was merely time to make a change. The reason it was time to make a change, however, was that the club was failing. "In a pea-pod," Hatton said when he was dismissed, "the problem is hitting. We have not hit since the day we left spring training."[36] Neither had anyone else, but the Astros' pitching was eighth in the league in ERA, and the fielding wasn't that good.

Hatton was right about the club not hitting, and it was particularly deficient in power, managing just 66 home runs all season. The Astrodome was not conducive to power hitting, and the club went nearly a month without hitting a round tripper at home. Wynn hit 26 of the 66 homers, and no teammate had more than six.

The Astros didn't have any power and didn't have much speed, stealing only 44 bases, ninth in the league. Again, Wynn led with 11 and no one else had more than 6. Houston's fielding average was tied for last, as they made 156 errors. The bullpen was shaky after burly reliever Fred Gladding was lost for the season with an elbow injury after pitching just 4⅓ innings. Other than Wynn and Staub, who hit .291 and drove in 72 runs, the only bright spot was the starting pitching. The entire staff set a club record with its 3.26 ERA.

That was good for only seventh in the league, however, and with so little support, none of the starters was able to post a winning record. Don Wilson was the leader in victories, but his record was just 13–16.

One category in which Astros pitchers led the league was strikeouts, with 1,021. On July 14, Wilson struck out 18 Reds, tying the modern major league mark, and matched another record by fanning eight in succession. Typical of the Astros' season, Wilson was later rendered *hors de combat* when he injured his ribs while sneezing.

With no offense, no defense, no speed, and no bullpen, the Astros, despite tying their all-time franchise high of 72 wins, finished last for the first time in their history. The club played better under Walker (49–52) than they had under Hatton (23–38), but it wasn't enough to escape the cellar.

At the end of every season, all clubs but the pennant winner are somewhat disappointed, but the 1968 National League race seemingly saw a greater number of teams ending the season unhappily. Among the happy teams were the Cardinals, who won the pennant, and the Mets, who won seven more games than they'd ever won before.

The disappointed teams were far more numerous. Even the pennant-winning Cardinals ended the season glumly after squandering a 3–1 game lead in the World Series. Six times before, they'd played a seventh game and each time they had won, but in 1968 they lost.

The Giants finished second, but they'd already done that three years in a row. The Cubs had surprised everyone in 1967, but did no better in 1968. The Dodgers were confident they'd come back from the depths but didn't. The Pirates and Reds expected to contend for the pennant, but both fell out of the race early in the season. The Braves and Phillies were wracked by internal dissension, and even the Astros' modest quest for mediocrity was unfulfilled.

The disappointing performance of nearly every team, in addition to the lack of offensive production, made 1968 a very unexciting year, other than for those who liked shutouts and strikeouts. A close pennant race might have mitigated the concerns about the lack of scoring, but luck was not with either major league in that regard. The season did nothing to dissuade those who thought that baseball was dying.

10

Don't Worry About the
Tigers, They Always Manage
to Find a Way Not to Win

Nineteen-sixty-eight was the final year for ten-team pennant races; beginning in 1969, the division champion would have to win a playoff series before it could advance to the World Series. Baseball purists lamented the demise of the good old-fashioned, six-month pennant race, but the last old-time races did not help their cause, for they were not exciting ones. Each league champion pulled away from the pack early and clinched the flag with several games remaining.

For the first time since 1945, the American League pennant went to the Detroit Tigers. During the past several years, Tigers general manager Jim Campbell had been nurturing prospects in the farm system, slowly working them into the Detroit lineup. By 1968, a number of them were young veterans, and they were playing so well that manager Mayo Smith had difficulty finding a spot in the lineup for future Hall of Famers Eddie Mathews and Al Kaline. Mathews was 36 and battling a bad back, and Kaline, 33, had been hampered by injuries the past few years and hadn't played as many as 150 games since 1961. With young outfielders Mickey Stanley, Jim Northrup, and slugging Willie Horton available, Smith wondered if he should try Kaline at first base. If he did, what would happen to Mathews and veteran Norm Cash?

Cash had a fabulous year in 1961, winning the batting title with a .361 average, hitting 41 homers, and driving in 132 runs. The following year his average plummeted an astonishing 118 points, and he hadn't come close to batting .300 since. Cash continued to hit for power, but he was inconsistent and often incurred the wrath of Tiger Stadium fans, who expected the Cash of 1961. Still, he got most of the playing time at first base, while Dick McAuliffe and Don Wert, both products of the farm system, played second and third. During spring training in 1968, weak-hitting Dick Tracewski was beaten out for the shortstop job by even weaker-hitting Ray Oyler. Solid All-Star Bill Freehan was the catcher.

The starting pitching was strong but the bullpen was inexperienced, populated by youngsters like John Hiller, Pat Dobson, Daryl Patterson, and Jon Warden. Warden got off to a fast start, winning three games in his first eight days in the major leagues while pitching a total of just three innings, but then he tailed off. In 1968, starters were expected to throw complete games, and bullpen usage was much different from today. There was no closer, no lefty specialist, and no set-up man. The relievers merely pitched as needed, and when Smith told the Tigers' relievers to pitch, they did well enough.

The Tigers got off to a flying start, ripping off nine straight wins after an Opening Day loss. Some Detroit fans saw the streak in person, and others watched on television or listened on the radio, but none read about the Tigers in the local papers, which were in the midst of a lengthy strike. Former Detroit pitcher Billy Hoeft said that if the strike continued all season, the Tigers might win the pennant, for he believed the reporters had been so tough on the players that it affected their performance. Cash said the press had encouraged the fans to boo him. "You could start a fire in the press box," said Denny McLain, "lock the door and watch the flames spread—then we'd get a new ball park and new writers."[1]

The Tigers moved into first place for good on May 10. Chicago manager Eddie Stanky said in June that Detroit would probably win the pennant by ten games, but if the race was close, the Tigers would choke, as they had in the past. "They'd better win it big or they won't win at all," he said. "Don't worry about the Tigers," added Boston manager Dick Williams. "They always manage to find a way not to win."[2]

By the All-Star Game, Detroit had a 9½ game lead, the largest margin at the break since the 1958 Yankees. They'd been consistent all season, with records of 12–5 in April, 16–11 in May, 20–11 in June, and 17–12 in July. By mid–August, the Detroit press, which was back in business, was confident enough to establish a Magic Moment contest, in which readers were invited to pick the day and time the Tigers would clinch the pennant.

A couple of weeks later, it looked as though the press might have returned just in time to curse the Tigers, who lost four straight to the Yankees, cutting their lead over the hard-charging Orioles to five games. Within a week, Baltimore sliced off another game, and everyone was poised for a Detroit collapse. This time, however, the Tigers rallied, and the Magic Moment occurred on September 17, when they beat the Yankees, 2–1, on a single in the bottom of the ninth by Don Wert.

Wert's big hit was one of the few he got in 1968. He had been seriously beaned in June, and when he returned to the lineup, he didn't hit, ending up with a final average of just .200. The Tigers got virtually no offense from the left side of their infield. "We may have had the worst hitting trio at shortstop in baseball history," wrote Denny McLain.[3] The regular shortstop, Oyler, batted an anemic .135, with just 29 hits in 215 at-bats. Dick Tracewski wasn't much better at .156, nor was rookie shortstop Tom Matchick at .203. None could compare to pitcher Earl Wilson, who batted .227 with seven home runs. While the Tigers' shortstops couldn't hit, they could field, and the team's 105 errors were the fewest in the major leagues.

Fortunately, the rest of the lineup made up the slack. In cozy Tiger Stadium, Detroit easily led the majors in home runs with 185, well ahead of runner-up Baltimore's 133. Four Tigers, including Horton (36), Freehan and Cash (25), and Northrup (21), hit more than 20, and the latter led the team in RBI with 90.[4] Cash got off to a dreadful start and was batting just .195 in late July, but he went on a tear and hit .333 for the rest of the season. Gates Brown, used primarily as a pinch-hitter, batted .370 in 92 at-bats. Kaline, who missed time after his arm was broken by a pitch from Lew Krausse of the Athletics, played in only 102 games.

In addition to being the first Detroit pennant winner in 23 years, the team's 103 wins were the most by a Tigers club to that point, and their 12-game margin over Baltimore was the largest since the 1947 Yankees finished 12 games in front.

For the Orioles, it was a second consecutive disappointing season, for in 1966 their fans had been talking about a dynasty. Baltimore won the pennant easily that year and swept the Dodgers in four games in the World Series, as their pitching staff, led by youngsters Jim Palmer, 20, Wally Bunker, 21, and Dave McNally, 23, shut out the Dodgers over the last 33 innings.

Within a year, everything had changed. Frank Robinson, winner of the 1966 Triple Crown, had 21 homers, 59 RBI and a .337 average less than halfway through the 1967 season and seemed headed for another phenomenal year. Then, on June 27, he slid into second base trying to break up a double play and was hit in the head by the knee of Chicago's Al Weis. Robinson suffered a concussion, was out a month, and had blurred vision for the rest of the season. Palmer came down with a sore shoulder and won just three games. A sore-armed Bunker won another three. McNally managed to win seven despite *his* bad arm. The combined 13 wins were 25 fewer than the three youngsters won in 1966. As a team, the Orioles won 21 fewer games in 1967, going from first place and a 97–63 record to 76–85 and a tie for sixth place.

Injuries were not confined to the players, as everything seemed to go wrong in Baltimore in 1967. A member of the ground crew was hurt while dragging the infield and had to be carried off on a stretcher. The scoreboard operator fell and suffered a head injury.

Orioles manager Hank Bauer considered injuries, especially pitchers' sore arms, to be a personal insult. Bauer had fought the Japanese in World

Earl Weaver's career as a major league manager began when he replaced Hank Bauer as skipper of the Orioles in July 1968. He's seen here in a typical pose, voicing his displeasure to an American League umpire. In Weaver's pocket one can see an outline that shows, as author Paul Hensler pointed out, that his cigarettes were always close to Weaver's heart.

War II and believed that a little toughness could cure any arm miseries. He made it clear in the spring of 1968 that he would not tolerate any more injuries. "I'm bringing back 11 pitchers," he said, "and they're all going to be healthy. Maybe this'll give these guys something to think about."[5] A headline in *The Sporting News* in early March read: "Oriole Hurlers Please Note: Bauer is Sick of Sore Arms."[6] "[I]f a pitcher shows up who hasn't got his arm in a sling," Bauer told a reporter in Florida, "you can waken me. I'd like to see one."[7]

Bauer had a reputation as a tough man and strong leader. "Do you want a cheerleader or a manager?"[8] he once asked Charley Finley when he managed the Athletics. Some thought the image was unjustified. "The paradox of Hank Bauer," wrote Bill Tanton, "is that his public image is so vastly different from his true self. The public image would have made a great manager, or at least a great leader."[9] He claimed that when times got tough, Bauer retreated into a shell and ignored his players.

Rather than trying to scare lame arms back to life, perhaps Bauer should have been dealing with the numerous off-the-field problems that had plagued his club in 1967. The troubles began in spring training when the players said they would no longer give interviews for free. When the season opened, rookie first baseman Mike Epstein refused to report to the minor leagues and forced a trade to the Senators. Left-hander Steve Barber, who pitched and lost a no-hitter in April, experienced major control trouble, jumped the club, and got himself traded to the Yankees. Outfielder Curt Blefary battled with the press. Frank Robinson said some of his teammates were jealous of him. As the problems multiplied and the Orioles sank in the standings, Bauer, who had quit smoking, started up again.

In mid–March 1968, it appeared that Bauer's stern approach had worked, for not a sore arm was to be found in Miami. Just before the season started, however, Palmer's shoulder kicked up again, causing him to miss the entire season. Bunker began the year at Rochester, and although he pitched well and was recalled in mid–June, he won just two games for the Orioles. McNally, rookie Jim Hardin, and Tom Phoebus combined for 55 wins, but the Orioles were never able to find a reliable fourth starter.

In late June, with rumors of his impending dismissal swirling around him, Bauer had an operation to remove a nodule from his vocal cord. On July 10, the Orioles decided to perform surgery to remove Bauer from the dugout, replacing him with first base coach Earl Weaver. The team was struggling, attendance was down more than 160,000, and the Orioles had a team batting average of .218.

Weaver, 37, was a scrappy little 5'7" former infielder who'd neither played nor managed in the majors. "There comes a point," he once said, "when you realize that you're not going to make it to the major leagues [as a player]."[10] For Weaver, the realization came early, and he became a player-manager at Knoxville in 1956 at the age of 25. The following year, he was sent to Fitzgerald, Georgia, in the Class D Georgia-Florida League to begin his long climb up the Baltimore minor league ladder.

Harry Dalton, then the assistant farm director for the Orioles, was sent to Fitzgerald to check on the Orioles' farmhands, but left with an indelible memory of their manager. "That year in Fitzgerald," Dalton recalled, "he got heated up and charged into the other dugout. He went in alone to fight a whole team and got the hell beaten out of him."[11]

At first, Weaver had no expectations of managing in the major leagues; he wanted to work in the minors as long as he could and then become a scout. But the Orioles liked the fiery little skipper and kept moving him up, to Elmira of the Double-A Eastern League for four years and then to Baltimore's top farm club in Rochester in 1966 and 1967. After posting losing records in his first two years as a manager, Weaver's teams were over .500 for the next ten seasons, and he won three pennants. His Red Wings won the International League pennant in 1966 and finished a game behind the following year. It was in Rochester that Weaver began to believe that he could manage in the big leagues.

In 1968, Weaver was named first base coach of the Orioles. The Orioles needed a replacement because, following the disappointing 1967 season, all three of Bauer's coaches were fired and Bauer was supposedly asked to resign.[12] He refused to do so unless the Orioles paid him in full for the final year of his contract. Dalton wanted to fire Bauer, but was overruled by Frank Cashen and Jerry Hoffberger.

Dalton thought the Orioles had been complacent in 1967 and wanted the enthusiastic Weaver on the coaching staff to light a fire under the youngsters who'd played so well in 1966. Bauer was not pleased to have a 37-year-old, highly successful minor league manager in the first base coaching box. Weaver had managed 15 of the young Orioles players in the minor leagues and in winter ball, and they believed in him. Bauer believed Weaver was after his job.

"I didn't want him around. I was knifed in the back once before," Bauer said a day after he was fired, referring to his replacement in Kansas City by Eddie Lopat in 1962.[13] "As soon as he was made coach," said Brooks Robinson, "I think we all knew that Earl would be made manager eventually. He was Harry Dalton's boy."[14] After his dismissal, Bauer said that if he had been given the choice, he would have appointed third base coach Billy Hunter as manager. Hunter shared Bauer's opinion, but Dalton chose Weaver, giving him a contract only through the end of the season.

Weaver thus began his tenure with Hunter looking over his shoulder from the third base coaching box and Bauer's wrath dogging him. When Weaver went to use the manager's shower for the first time, someone said he be should careful, for perhaps the muscular Bauer had shut the water off as hard as he could, or that he had switched the hot and cold knobs.

Sports editor John Steadman of the *Baltimore Sun* defended Weaver. He claimed that Weaver had done nothing to undermine Bauer, was thrilled just to be in the big leagues for the first time, and would have been happy to remain first base coach. Steadman also noted that Bauer had been the third base coach for former Orioles manager Billy Hitchcock and took Hitchcock's place when he was fired.[15]

Many had their doubts about Weaver, a career minor leaguer until just a few months earlier. He had a reputation as a hothead, and he'd never managed veteran players. Dalton felt otherwise. "He was tremendously competitive," Dalton said, "got players to respond and his strategy was exceptional. A lot of times he was a couple innings ahead of the opposing manager as he set up changes."[16] In the Baltimore system, Weaver had been influenced by Paul Richards, a legendary strategist who made more moves in an inning than some managers made in a game.

As so often happens when a new man takes the helm, the Orioles caught fire. They won Weaver's first six games and 30 of his first 45 to kindle hopes that there might be an American League pennant race after all. On August 27, they swept a doubleheader from Oakland while Detroit was losing to the White Sox, to creep within four games of first place.

Four games was as close as the Orioles would get. The next two nights, they lost to the lowly Senators, who they'd beaten 12 times in a row, and then dropped two of three to the Tigers, which essentially sealed their fate. Baltimore finished 91–71, 12 games behind, but had gone 48–34 (.585) under Weaver. For a 162-game season, a .585 winning percentage equates to 95 wins, often good enough for a pennant, which is what Weaver won in each of the next three years.

One of the most pleasant surprises of the 1968 season was the Cleveland Indians. After being one of the better teams in the AL during the 1950s, the Indians were having a rough decade. They were a bad team playing in an obsolete park in a decaying city. One Angels player said the reason the Indians didn't have a better home record was because, since there was nothing to do in Cleveland, visiting players were much more rested than they were in other cities.[17]

Under disciplinarian Joe Adcock, the Indians finished eighth in 1967 with a 75–87 record. They had not been eighth since 1914 and had not won as few as 75 games since 1946. Adcock was fired and replaced by Alvin Dark, the tenth Cleveland manager in 13 years. Dark was a star shortstop during the 1950s and managed the Giants to the 1962 pennant before being fired two years later after making derogatory remarks about his black and Latin players.

Dark was hired by Charley Finley to manage his Kansas City Athletics in 1966, but managing for Finley was generally a short-term proposition. The Athletics began their existence in Philadelphia and, for their first 50 years, were managed by one man, Connie Mack. Finley bought the team in 1961, and Dark was his sixth manager. Finley not only fired Dark, he fired him twice the same day in 1967 (see Chapter 5), which left Dark available when the Indians jettisoned Adcock in October.

Major league managers are a mobile population, departing one venue in disgrace, only to reappear as a prospective savior somewhere else. Dark left San Francisco under a cloud and departed from Kansas City after a dramatic, late-night clash with Finley. Now, in the spring of 1968, he appeared in the Indians' camp as a wise, sober, and capable man, spoken of reverently by ballplayers he had yet to cut, trade, bench, or criticize.

"Alvin Dark was the best manager I ever played for in the major leagues," said Jim Gosger. "If you weren't playing, he kept you involved in the game. He'd come up to you on the bench and say, 'What do you think we should do in this situation?' He'd tell you exactly what your job was and what he expected of you."[18]

For the first half of the season, Dark appeared to be a miracle worker. On the morning of July 2, his Indians were in second place, 7½ games behind the Tigers, mainly on the strength of the right-left pitching combination of Luis Tiant and Sam McDowell.

The offense was not equal to the pitching, as one of the men counted upon to provide power didn't provide much. Before the season began, Leon Wagner vowed to hit 40 home runs if he played regularly. He based his prediction upon the fact that he was only 32 (actually 33), had quit smoking, didn't drink much, was in great shape and, well, because he was Leon Wagner. Wagner fell just 39 homers short of his goal, hitting one in 211 at-bats with the Indians and White Sox.

The Indians spent much of the season in second place, surprising nearly everyone and greatly increasing attendance at Municipal Stadium. By the end of the year, the Tribe had drawn 857,944 fans, an increase of 195,014 from the previous season. At the All-Star break, the Indians had a record of 47–39, and Dark predicted they would win the pennant. Cleveland had a history of collapsing in July, but at the end of the month, they were 58–44, and in third place, eight games behind the Tigers. People were even starting to worry about the fact that the National Tire Dealers and Retreaders Association had reserved 3,100 of the city's 4,200 hotel rooms for their convention the weekend of October 5. That was World Series week, and there would be a problem if the Indians were playing.

The tire boys had the city to themselves the first week of October. In early August, Cleveland was 8½ games back with seven games coming up against the Tigers in a span of nine days. The first game was a typical 1968 affair. Tiant gave up one run in nine innings, and Detroit's John Hiller, who tied a major league record by striking out the first six Indians, one in eight. There was no more scoring until weak-hitting Tigers shortstop Dick Tracewski singled home the winning run in the 17th inning.

The Indians lost the final three games of the series and then lost two of three to the Tigers the next week in Cleveland, which put them 13½ games out. They wound up third, 16½ games behind, but with a record of 86–75, 11 ½ games better than the previous year; third place was their best finish since they were second in 1959. The pitching was great all season, and the Tribe barely missed winning the team ERA championship with a mark of 2.66 to Baltimore's 2.65.

The Red Sox and Cardinals had won their respective pennants in 1967, and just about everybody expected the Cards to repeat. They were not so sure about the Sox. Miracle teams rarely duplicate the magic, for miracles don't often recur in successive years. Boston followed the disappointing path of most Cinderella teams, especially those that lost the Cy Young Award winner before the season began.

Jim Lonborg's recovery from knee surgery was slower than expected. At the beginning of April, he was exercising and lifting weights, but had yet to throw a baseball and was still limping. On April 22, he pitched a little batting practice and said he thought he'd be ready to appear in a game in about two weeks. Lonborg had developed another problem, however, for while his knee was in a cast, his leg had atrophied.

In mid–May, the Red Sox hoped he'd be ready to pitch by Memorial Day. That was before he had to take a cortisone shot for his aching shoulder. Finally, at the end of May, he was placed on the active roster. After a handful of relief efforts, Lonborg made his first start on June 16 against the Indians. On June 23 he left a game after pitching to only two batters and hitting them both. His shoulder was bothering him again and would for the rest of the year. Lonborg won only six games while losing ten.

In Lonborg's absence, right-hander Jose Santiago emerged as the ace of the Boston staff. He put together a streak of 27 scoreless innings and stretched his two-season winning streak (not including two losses in the 1967 World Series) to 12 games. "He's our new stopper," said manager Dick Williams.[19] "I've never been in better shape in my life and I've never felt better," Santiago said.[20] Soon, however, Santiago's right elbow wasn't feeling very good. He tried to pitch a number of times in July, but had to leave when the knife-like pain returned. With a 9–4 record and a 2.25 ERA, his season was over.

By the end of the year, the two best Boston pitchers were lefty Dick Ellsworth and righty Ray Culp. Both had been acquired from National League teams the previous winter after having had success early in their careers and then suffering from arm trouble and losing records.[21] Neither Ellsworth nor Culp started well in 1968, but both finished like Seabiscuit coming down the stretch, winning a combined 22 of their last 25 decisions. Ellsworth became the first Red Sox left-hander in 15 years to win as many as ten games. His final record was 16–7, a ten-win improvement from the 6–7 mark he posted for the Phillies in 1967.

Culp was even better. In his first two starts, he gave up 13 runs in 7⅓ innings, which earned him an exile to the bullpen. There, he re-discovered his fastball and quickly regained a place in the rotation. Late in the season, Culp pitched four straight shutouts and seven straight complete-game victories, and finished with a 16–6 mark.

Ellsworth and Culp compensated in large part for the loss of Lonborg and Santiago, but the miracles that marked the 1967 season were absent in 1968. It would have been difficult for Carl Yastrzemski, the biggest miracle-maker, to duplicate his Triple Crown MVP season, and he didn't.

There was so much opportunity to earn money in the off-season that Yastrzemski couldn't resist. An officer of Portland Printing, where Yastrzemski was employed during the off-season, claimed the outfielder's 1968 income potential was $350,000, an assertion Yastrzemski quickly denied. Agent Frank Scott said Yaz was getting $1,500 per speaking engagement,[22] and in January he signed an exclusive contract with Licensing Corp. of America to handle all of his endorsement activity.

In December, Yastrzemski went to the Colonial Country Club in Lynnwood to begin his off-season workouts, and found the environment a little different from the year before. This year the small gym was packed with reporters and photographers, for the good player of 1966 had become the superstar of 1967, whose every move was newsworthy. Despite his intention to limit his personal appearances, Yastrzemski made a lot of them, and when he didn't play as well as he did in 1967, the fans blamed him for overextending himself during the winter.

Yaz started the season with two homers on Opening Day, giving promise that 1968 might be another 1967. He soon went into a slump that dropped him below .250, and he didn't hit a home run from April 17 until May 24. In June and July, Yaz had another homerless streak, this one lasting 21 games. He said his mechanics were all messed up, and shortly afterward, he injured his wrist.

One of the reasons Yastrzemski was having trouble was that he was not getting a lot of good pitches to hit, for none of the other Red Sox players except Ken Harrelson was having a good year. Tony Conigliaro was out with impaired vision. Rico Petrocelli spent much of the season out of action or subpar with an injured elbow. George Scott was healthy but his bat was ailing.

Scott had arrived on the scene in 1966 after winning the Eastern League Triple Crown and MVP Award and made the All-Star team as a 22-year-old. He batted only .245, but hit 27 home runs and drove in 90 runs. The following year, he hit 19 homers and drove in 82 runs, and boosted his average to .303; he appeared to be on his way to stardom. At a banquet in Scott's home town of Greenville, Mississippi, after the World Series, Boston coach Eddie Popowski said he expected Scott to develop into a consistent .300 hitter who would hit 35–40 homers a year.

In addition to his offensive prowess, Scott was just about the best defensive first baseman in the league. He had terrific range, great hands, and excelled at digging low throws out of the dirt. Williams said he was a better fielder than his former Dodgers teammate Gil Hodges, considered the finest fielding first baseman of the 1950s.

About the only thing people complained about was Scott's weight, which was listed at 215 but was often much higher. During the winter following the 1967 season, Scott married 20-year-old Malvina Pena, and therefore had a full-time cook at his disposal. Sure enough, he showed up in Winter Haven several pounds over his prescribed weight. Still, he was hot in the early exhibitions, and Larry Claflin wrote, "Scott looks as if this is going to be the year he fully arrives at stardom."[23]

When the season began, however, Scott was headed for the bench rather than stardom. By May 5, he was 6-for-62 and was being criticized for not hustling. As the season went on, Scott didn't threaten the .200 mark and ended the year with a pathetic .171 average, a 132-point decline from 1967. He hit just three home runs and drove home only 25 runs in 350 at-bats. It was by far the worst season of his career.

What happened? One cause of Scott's difficulties was a season-long feud with Williams, who benched him for not hitting, sat him down for being overweight, and accused him of not hustling. By the end of the season, Scott was a confused, frustrated young man.

The offensive star of the 1968 Red Sox was Harrelson, who led the league with 109 RBI and hit 35 home runs. For a time, he had a chance at the Triple Crown, for anyone who was batting near .280 had a shot at posting the highest average in the league. Center fielder Reggie Smith, in just his second year, showed promise of becoming a star, but the Sox had holes in other positions. At catcher, they had 39-year-old Elston Howard, who injured his elbow and found his way into Williams' well-populated doghouse. Joe Foy had a subpar season at third, and with so many players slumping, the Sox never had much of a chance at the pennant. Although they won just six fewer games than they had in 1967, they finished 17 games behind the Tigers.

In the 1950s, a successful season in New York meant the Yankees playing either the Giants or Dodgers in a Subway Series. By 1968, New Yorkers were excited because the Mets climbed out of the basement into ninth place and the Yankees broke the .500 barrier for the first time since 1964. Yankees fans of the 1950s and early 1960s would have been devastated by an 83–79 record, but a last-place finish in 1966 and ninth place the following year had lowered expectations.

The Yankees were no longer the Bronx Bombers; their .214 batting average was by far the worst in the league. But they had a little power, which enabled them to surpass four teams in runs scored, and they had good pitching. Their 2.79 ERA was fifth in the league, and the top three starters, Mel Stottlemyre, "Rookie of the Year" Stan Bahnsen, and lefty Fritz Peterson, combined for a 50–35 record with a 2.36 ERA.

One of the beautiful things about baseball is that, during the course of 162 games, even the worst teams will have shining moments, and for brief periods, mediocre clubs will look like World Series champs. The Yankees had such a stretch during late August, when they played the American League champion Tigers in what was scheduled to be a four-game series. The second game of Friday night's doubleheader, however, lasted 19 innings and was terminated by the league curfew with the score tied 3–3. That necessitated a second doubleheader on Sunday, meaning that, including the 19-inning affair, the two teams would play the equivalent of six games in three days.

Today, with pitch counts and innings limits, there is no way a manager could nurse a pitching staff through such an ordeal, especially since, in 1968, they didn't make daily roster changes to bring up fresh arms. A ten-man staff had to somehow cover 55 innings in a three-day period.

The Yankees got two complete games from their starters, and in the 19-inning affair, reliever Lindy McDaniel threw seven perfect innings. When Yankees starter Steve Barber was knocked out early in Sunday's first game, manager Ralph Houk decided he didn't want to waste one of his relievers. He sent outfielder Rocky Colavito in to pitch.

Colavito, a New York native, was playing the final season of his illustrious career in his home town, and was a fan favorite. When he came in to pitch, the crowd erupted, for Houk had turned what appeared to be a tedious game into an exciting event.

Colavito pitched 2⅔ scoreless innings while the Yankees made a remarkable comeback. He was the winning pitcher, then hit a home run as the Yankees won the nightcap. The second-game win was New York's 12th in 15 games. The Yankees couldn't keep up that kind of pace, but by the end of the year they were still four games over .500.

In their first season in Oakland, the Athletics won 20 more games than they had in 1967. During their 13 seasons in Kansas City, the Athletics averaged 64 wins a year, with a high of 74 in 1966. Manager Bob Kennedy, in his first year at the helm, brought his club home with an 82–80 mark—no Athletics team had won more games since the 1948 club managed by Connie Mack. Charley Finley rewarded Kennedy for his fine performance by firing him at the end of the season.

No manager works a miracle without talented players, and the youth movement the Athletics began in Kansas City came to fruition in California.

"[T]his young, talented ball club," said *Sports Illustrated*, "is growing up quite fast in spite of Charles Finley."[24] "The move to Oakland had a lot to do with our attitude," said pitcher Lew Krausse. "We all liked Kansas City well enough, but if we'd stayed there the bad stuff would have been hovering over our heads."[25]

The Athletics were a young club, with an average age of just 23. Many of the youngsters would form the nucleus of the Oakland dynasty of 1971–1975, but in 1968 not many people knew who they were. A couple of weeks into the season, explaining the disappointingly small crowds in Oakland, *Sports Illustrated* said, "There are few recognizable names on the club aside from coach Joe DiMaggio, base stealing champ Campy Campaneris, and those of the two young pitchers, Catfish Hunter and Blue Moon Odom, whose names attract more attention than their pitching."[26]

A less sophisticated observer, a Chicago cab driver, told Oakland writer Ron Bergman, "You know what's wrong with this here Oakland team? There ain't a one of them you'd recognize if he walked on the street right at you."[27] And that was a team that included Reggie Jackson.

Within a few years, the Oakland players would be very recognizable. Odom, Campaneris, and outfielder Rick Monday were named to the 1968 All-Star team, the first time the franchise had that many on the squad since it was in Philadelphia. During the Kansas City years, the only reason an Athletic was named to the team in some years was the requirement that each club have at least one representative.

One of Oakland's problems in 1968 was a lack of power. "The balls sure carry out of here," said Orioles manager Hank Bauer after watching four of them sail over the outfield wall in the Oakland home opener,[28] but the ball didn't carry that often for the 1968 A's. Jackson hit 29 homers, but he was the only one in double figures. In July, Finley hired 69-year-old, retired locomotive engineer Barney Stuart and gave him a large engine bell to ring every time the A's hit a home run, but Stuart didn't get a lot of action.

One reason the ball didn't carry was because of the weather. "It was awfully cold at night," said Oakland outfielder Jim Gosger, "almost like San Francisco. Most of the time the wind was blowing in over the mountains, especially at night. In the daytime, the ball jumped pretty good, but not at night. I only remember one time when I didn't have my long underwear on. It was cold."[29] The Athletics did have speed, as Campaneris led the league with 62 steals and the team led the AL with 147.

On June 28, the Athletics moved into third place, a lofty position that elicited a variety of reactions. Angels manager Bill Rigney described the Oakland club as "garbage collectors"[30] and couldn't imagine how they were above his club in the standings. Odom predicted a World Series appearance. "We've got a young ball club," he said, "and we'll be in there a lot sooner than most folks might think."[31]

The A's did make it to a World Series four years later, but they did so without Kennedy and much of the staff. Life under Finley was never easy, and in 1968 the turmoil began at the end of May when Vice President Bill Cutler either quit or was fired. Cutler said he was fired, but Finley said that he offered Cutler another job, which he refused. On that basis, Finley challenged a claim for unemployment compensation by Cutler, who had 11 children to support.

Toward the end of the season, farm director Art Parrick, director of scouting Ray Swallow, and Southern California scouting supervisor Bob Zuk resigned. Equipment manager Al Zych left with the hope of getting a job with the new expansion club in Kansas City.

Finley replaced Kennedy with Hank Bauer, who'd managed his team in 1961 and 1962. Bauer had quit at the end of the latter season, thinking Finley was going to fire him and wanting to beat him to the punch. When he rehired Bauer, Finley said that he hadn't intended to fire him in 1962 and that his leaving had been a big misunderstanding. He predicted a pennant in 1969.

Happiness is a factor of expectations, and while the Yankees and Athletics were feeling good about themselves for breaking the .500 mark, the Twins, who finished just one rung beneath them, were greatly disappointed. They went from pennant contenders who were eliminated on the final day of the 1967 season to a seventh-place, sub-.500 team that was eliminated shortly after the campaign began.

The 1968 Twins had four hitters (Tony Oliva, Rod Carew, Ted Uhlaender and Cesar Tovar) who batted more than .270, which in 1968 constituted a Murderers' Row, and in August they had the top three hitters in the league, but they lost slugger Harmon Killebrew for nearly half the season after he pulled a hamstring stretching for a throw in the All-Star Game.

Minnesota was weak at catcher and shortstop. During the previous winter, the club had acquired veteran Dodgers receiver John Roseboro as part of the trade in which they surrendered Versalles. Roseboro had been a valuable Dodger ever since the club had moved to Los Angeles, but he was about to turn 35, and the Dodgers thought his career was on the downward slope.

They were right. Roseboro was getting along in years, and he also had difficulty adjusting to the Twins' culture, which under owner Calvin Griffith was much less welcoming to racial minorities than the more multi-cultural atmosphere that prevailed with the Dodgers. Roseboro hit just .216, and it took a strong second half to get his average that high. He had streaks of 0–29, 0–18, and 1–25, and was hitting just .144 in mid–May.

Part of the gamble of the Versalles trade was that Roseboro would be a solid catcher. The other caveat was that Versalles could be replaced at shortstop by Jackie Hernandez, a 27-year-old Cuban with a strong arm and a weak bat. In 1966, he had appeared in 58 Angels games and managed just one hit (he batted only 23 times). "He doesn't get many hits," said Griffith when Hernandez won the Twins' starting job, "but he makes them count."[32]

When the season started, Hernandez proved Griffith correct in the first part of his assertion. He didn't get many hits. He also made a lot of errors, 25 in 79 games. In July, Hernandez was sent to Denver and replaced by Ron Clark, Rick Renick, and Cesar Tovar, who played everywhere. One reason a player plays everywhere is that he is not particularly outstanding anywhere, which was the case with Tovar. None of the three replacements was anywhere near the standard of Versalles at his best but, in fairness, neither was Versalles in 1968.

The Twins won their first six games of the season but gradually fell off the pace and into the second division. Injuries were a contributing factor, as during July, in addition to Killebrew, the Twins lost Carew, Oliva, top reliever Al Worthington, and starter Dave Boswell, essentially ending any chance of contesting for the pennant. They finished seventh with a record of 79–83.

The Angels were a deep disappointment to their fans, owner Gene Autry and, perhaps most of all, to manager Bill Rigney. The team had finished strong in 1967, playing a spoiler's role in the frantic pennant race's final week. From last place and 12 games under .500 on June 1, the Angels had rallied to finish just 7½ games out of first. "This is the best and deepest Angel squad we've ever had," Rigney said just before the start of spring training in 1968.[33] It was the first time he harbored realistic hopes of winning the pennant. Although his surprising 1962 club had finished third, it was a miraculous performance with a weak team. Rigney believed his 1968 team could win on merit.

By the end of May 1968, the dream was gone. The Angels were near the bottom of the American League standings and playing like they were going to drop even further. "This is my eighth year with the Angels," Rigney said, "and I've never seen things this bad. I've never seen a team look so awful."[34] By the end of the year, the Angels had the worst record in their history. They had the lowest team batting average, scored the fewest runs, and hit the fewest home runs, and their batters struck out more than any Angels team before them.

The problems were myriad, the greatest being, as with every team, a lack of hitting. Shortstop Jim Fregosi, called by *Baseball Digest* "the Angels' indispensible man,"[35] got off to an impressive start, but went into a season-long slump and hit just .244 with nine homers and 49 RBI. California had little power (83 homers) and not much speed (62 stolen bases). First baseman Don Mincher was beaned by Sam McDowell the first week of the season and suffered from headaches all summer. He went from 25 home runs to 13. Third baseman Paul Schaal was also hit in the head and missed an extended period of time. Nineteen-year-old Aurelio Rodriguez, called up to replace him, went on the shelf with an emergency appendectomy.

The Angels' defense was shoddy, making 140 errors, compared to 111 the previous year. The third base position, devastated by injury, went from 17 errors to 35. The pitching also collapsed, particularly the bullpen, which went from a combined total of 67 wins and saves in 1967 to 49 in 1968. Minnie Rojas, who'd been the AL "Fireman of the Year" in 1967, had arm trouble and was ineffective. Well-traveled veteran lefty George Brunet led the starters with 13 wins, but he also lost 17 games. Rickey Clark, 12–11 as a 1967 rookie, lost his first eight decisions and finished 1–11. The brightest spot in a dismal season was the arrival of 23-year-old Andy Messersmith, who looked sensational in the bullpen and was promoted to the starting rotation. He pitched 9⅔ consecutive innings of hitless relief over one stretch—a no-hitter in pieces—and displayed an outstanding curve ball. Overall, in 81⅓ innings, he was 4–2 with a 2.22 ERA.

After the sorry campaign was over, however, most of the Angels, including Rigney, did not attribute the club's failure to a lack of pitching, hitting, or fielding. It was a crisis of spirit that had doomed the Angels. "We had a breakdown of the closeness and the spirit that always has been associated with Angel teams," Rigney concluded.[36] Later he added, "Somewhere we lost it and I'll be darned if I know where."[37] Rickey Clark agreed. "There just wasn't any spirit," he said, "and I don't know why."[38] Maybe the eighth-place finish had something to do with it.

The White Sox, like the Twins, were 1967 contenders who opened the 1968 season looking as though they would be eliminated by Memorial Day. For a while, it seemed as though they might never win a game, losing their first ten before finally defeating the Twins on April 26. One of the reasons for the club's slow start was its .193 team batting average during the first 12 games (11 of which were losses), with just seven home runs, the lowest total in the league. The White Sox scored only 11 runs in their first nine games.

According to Oakland's Jim Gosger, part of the problem was self-induced. "They used frozen balls," he said. "Some of them got mixed in with our balls once during batting practice. They would put them in the refrigerator and they were like rocks. And they'd water the field right in front of the plate and grew the grass high and thick. They had some fast guys like Don Buford at the top of the lineup and they'd bang the ball into the dirt and run."[39]

It was hard to win with a run a game, especially since the vaunted Chicago pitching staff also had early-season problems. The White Sox, who'd led the AL in earned run average in 1967, had the second-worst mark in the circuit after 12 games. Joe Horlen and Gary Peters, who'd placed first and second, respectively, in individual ERA the previous year, were pounded in their early starts.

Horlen, who'd posted a 19–7 record the previous year, lost his first five decisions. He'd had a little soreness in his shoulder the final month of the

1967 season, but thought his arm was just tired from 258 innings of work. When Horlen reported to Sarasota the following spring, however, there was little strength in his arm, and by the time the season started, he experienced sharp pain each time he threw.

And if poor hitting and bad pitching weren't enough to lose games, Chicago's fielding wasn't very good either. The seventh consecutive loss occurred when the Sox misjudged two fly balls in the tenth inning. Pete Ward, one of the few White Sox players who could swing the bat, had defensive deficiencies the Sox alternately tried to hide at first base, third base, and the outfield. Ward committed six errors in the first nine games.

The City of Chicago had perhaps the two most disliked managers in the major leagues in Leo Durocher and Eddie Stanky, who was Durocher's protégé and had been one of his favorite players. Durocher could be clever, he dressed nattily, and he had some charm and pizzazz, but Stanky was just an irritant. He had been a player of modest talent who made it to the big leagues on sheer effort after eight seasons in the minors. His intensity had made him a major leaguer, but a manager couldn't will his team to victory. When things went poorly for the White Sox, he got testy, and things couldn't be going worse than they were in April of 1968. Stanky reacted predictably, blasting fans for booing his team and comparing them unfavorably to theater-goers, who would never think of booing actors. Of course, they might boo actors who performed as poorly as Stanky's crew did in April.

After consecutive loss number seven, Stanky ignored the writers, went into the trainer's room, and pretended he was sleeping. Finally, nearly an hour later, he emerged to face a phalanx of impatient men facing deadlines. If they'd planned to be hard on the White Sox manager before, cooling their heels for an hour didn't improve their mood. "He has deep loathing for virtually all of [the writers]," wrote legendary Chicago columnist Jerome Holtzman. "They don't know baseball. Only he does. Who are they with their questions?"[40] When Stanky did talk to the press, he snarled and snapped and insisted he wasn't going to quit. Owner Arthur Allyn was equally adamant that he wasn't going to fire Stanky.

No major league team can keep losing 11 of every 12 games, and the White Sox eventually began to play better. After his initial difficulties, Horlen began to pitch well, running off a streak of 37 scoreless innings in May. By the end of the year, he had improved his record to 12–14 and lowered his ERA to a very impressive 2.37.

Peters, the other Chicago ace, never regained his form. He suffered a groin injury in May, kept trying to return too soon and, favoring his groin, injured his elbow. He was out of action for a month and a half and finished 4–13, a precipitous decline from his 16–11 mark in 1967.

A third White Sox starter, lefty Tommy John, started the season with seven straight wins, followed by five consecutive losses, then three more wins. On August 22, he sustained torn ligaments in his left shoulder following a brawl with the Tigers' Dick McAuliffe, ending his season. The severity of the injury was such that it was thought his career might be over, which in fact it was 21 years later.

With all of the problems in the White Sox's starting rotation, which posted only 20 complete games, by far the fewest in the major leagues, it was fortunate that they had an outstanding bullpen, led by knuckleballers Hoyt Wilhelm and Wilbur Wood. Wilhelm, who turned 46 on July 26, made his 907th major league appearance the following day, breaking Cy Young's record for most games pitched in a career. He retired the Athletics in order on six pitches in his one inning, and said later he was shooting for 1,000 appearances, a mark he reached with the Atlanta Braves two years later. Wilhelm appeared to be as sharp as ever in 1968, posting a 1.73 ERA and 12 saves in 72 games.

Right-hander Bob Locker made 70 appearances out of the Chicago pen, but the most active White Sox reliever, and the busiest in major league history, was left-handed knuckleball artist Wilbur Wood, winner of *The Sporting News* "Fireman of the Year Award". On September 21, Wood broke the American League record with his 83rd appearance, and three days later claimed the major league mark with his 85th, surpassing the record Cubs' submariner Ted Abernathy set three years earlier. By the time the season was over, he'd been in 88 games.

Since 1968, pitchers have equaled or surpassed Wood's mark 18 times, but of those, only Mike Marshall pitched more innings. In 1998, Detroit's Sean Runyan pitched in 88 games, but threw just 50⅓ innings. Wood not only pitched frequently in 1968, he threw 159 innings, even starting twice. Thirty-eight times he pitched two or more innings, and 11 times three or more in relief. In mid–August, Wood pitched five days in a row and threw four shutout innings on the fifth day.

In addition to their starters not finishing games, the White Sox excelled in losing the close ones, and with a weak-hitting team, there are a lot of close ones. The Chicago offense was so feeble that in one game Stanky batted pitcher Gary Peters, a good hitter, in the sixth position in the lineup. The White Sox's final average of .228 was sixth in the league, but they scored just 463 runs, dead last and 35 runs below the ninth-place Angels. One day, after the Tigers scored a run against the White Sox in the first inning, Jim Murray wrote, "This put the game out of reach of the Chicago Banjoists 1–0."[41] Scoring only 2.86 runs per game, it was difficult to win unless the club played very tight ball, but only the Twins made more errors. On September 3, the White Sox set an all-time record by losing their 39th one-run decision of the year, and by the end of the season they'd lost 44, including nine by the score of 1–0.

The White Sox's ninth-place finish was their worst ever and their 67 wins the lowest total since 1950. Needless to say, despite Stanky's stubbornness and Allyn's protestations that he would stand by his beleaguered manager, the feisty pilot did not survive the season. "I was in ninth place when I left," he said. "Very few managers can remain when they're in ninth place unless they can tell a lot of jokes. And I can't tell a lot of jokes."[42] On July 12, Stanky was fired, despite the fact that Allyn was obligated to pay him through the 1971 season. Al Lopez, who led the Go-Go Sox to the 1959 pennant, was called out of the retirement he'd begun more than two years earlier.

Lopez seemed less than eager to be back in harness but said he would finish the season. On his first day on the job, the Sox swept a doubleheader from the Senators, but even Lopez couldn't heal Horlen's shoulder, Peters' elbow, John's shoulder, or the hitters' ailing bats.

The new manager was the opposite of the intense Stanky and was known in those times of differing semantics as the "Gay Caballero". The tension that had paralyzed the Chicago club was released. The locker room was made more accessible to reporters, Stanky's system of petty fines was rescinded, and the players were allowed to wear that radical article of clothing, the turtleneck, on airplanes and in hotel lobbies.

While the White Sox were an artistic failure on the field, the experiment of playing nine games in Milwaukee was a financial success. The club wanted to show the Milwaukee fans what White Sox baseball was like, and they did, losing eight of the nine games, being shut out four times, and scoring just 16 runs overall. But while the

Reliever Wilbur Wood set a major league record by appearing in 88 games in 1968. He later became a starter and won more than 20 games each season from 1971–74, with a high of 377 innings pitched in 1972, the most by any AL pitcher since Ed Walsh threw 393 innings in 1912

Sox averaged just 7,439 fans per game in Chicago, they attracted an average of 29,366 in Milwaukee. In the final game, with former Braves hero Eddie Mathews playing for the visiting Tigers, the crowd was over 42,000. Buoyed by their 1968 success, the White Sox announced a three-year plan to play in the Wisconsin city.

The final rung on the American League ladder was occupied by the Senators, 37½ games back with a 65–96 mark. Under former skipper Gil Hodges, the Nats had steadily improved from 58 wins and tenth place in 1963 to 76 wins and sixth place in 1967. The team regressed under new manager Jim Lemon; the only excitement in the nation's capital was provided by slugger Frank Howard, who led the league with 44 homers and finished second to Ken Harrelson with 106 RBI. Over a period of six games from May 12–18, Howard hit ten home runs, the most ever hit during a six-game span. Two of the shots, both off Sam McDowell, were monstrous, traveling an estimated 455 and 480 feet, respectively.

The Senators had little to back Howard on offense, as highly touted first baseman Mike Epstein was a bust. Epstein started the 1968 season slowly, but Lemon said he would be his first baseman for 162 games. When Epstein's average sank to .076, Lemon decided that, even in this inoffensive age, he could not have a first baseman who couldn't hit half his weight, and he sent Epstein to Buffalo. The husky slugger soon returned to Washington and hit better but finished the season at just .234, with 13 homers and only 33 RBI. As disappointing as the RBI total was, only Howard and two other Senators had more.

Even with Howard's fabulous production, the Senators finished ninth in team batting average and next to last in run production. The pitching was even worse, as the club finished a distant last in ERA, surrendering 50 more runs than ninth-place California. Veteran Cuban pitcher Camilo Pascual (13–12) and young Joe Coleman (12–16) were the only reliable starters, and the bullpen was never the same after ace reliever Darold Knowles was snatched away to active military duty in July.

As with every season, one team was happy at the end and the rest looked to next year with varying degrees of optimism. The Tigers hadn't found a way not to win, and many of their competitors found ways to lose. Detroit had some good power hitters well-suited to their stadium, and they had Denny McLain, with just enough pitching behind him.

McLain's arm was shot by the time the World Series came along, but Mickey Lolich won three games and the Tigers rallied from a 3–1 deficit to defeat the Cardinals. It had been 23 years since the Tigers had appeared in a World Series, and it would be 16 before they were in another. But in 1968, for a city torn by racial violence and a shrinking manufacturing base, it was a prideful moment. "My town," Detroit columnist Joe Falls wrote at the end of the season, "as you know, had the worst riot in our nation's history in the summer of 1967.... But then something started happening in the middle of 1968. You could pull up to a light at the corner of Clairmount and 12th, which was the hub of last year's riot, and the guy in the next car would have his radio turned up [listening to the Tiger game]. It was a year when an entire community, an entire city, was caught up in a wild, wonderful frenzy."[43]

11

It Will Be a Miracle If the Montreal Ball Park Is Ready in Time

Like nearly everything baseball did in the 1960s, the 1969 expansion was handled in a disorganized, embarrassing manner. Everyone knew more expansion was coming at some point. There was increasing political pressure to do so, and the immediate economic benefit to the existing clubs was too great to ignore. Each club's share of the franchise fees would be more than the annual profit of most clubs. In 1967, the Orioles lost $57,000. The following year they showed a profit of $551,000, totally attributable to proceeds of $738,000 from the sale of players in the expansion draft.

The first hint that expansion was imminent was an announcement by the American League in the fall of 1967 that it intended to broach the issue at a special meeting to be held in Chicago on October 18. In addition to the financial incentive of adding two new teams, the league had a further reason to move quickly, for Charles O. Finley, owner of the Athletics, had again precipitated a crisis.

Finley had been trying to move the Athletics for several years. He made exploratory visits to Oakland in 1962 and 1963, learned that a new stadium was a strong possibility, and talked with Horace Stoneham of the Giants about the possibility of playing in Candlestick Park until the new facility was complete. When the Oakland-Alameda County Coliseum opened in 1966, Finley attended the first Oakland Raiders game.

After every other American League owner voted against allowing Finley to move to Louisville in 1964, he courted Dallas-Fort Worth and Seattle without success. At the October 18, 1967, meeting, Finley was going to ask the league to allow him to move his team to Oakland. Although Oakland had a population of only 361,000 (1970 census) versus Kansas City's 507,000, the grass was greener in the West primarily due to a radio and television contract that boosted the Athletics' annual income from $75,000 to $1.3 million. Finley engaged the consulting firm of Booz, Allen, and Hamilton to present his tale of the financial woe that plagued him in Missouri and the pot of gold that awaited him in California. Meanwhile, Missouri politicians planned to argue that with its recently approved stadium bond issue, Kansas City presented at least as great a financial opportunity as that offered by Oakland.

In order to assuage the people and politicians of Kansas City, American League owners combined Finley's application with a proposal that provided new franchises for Seattle and Kansas City. The first vote on the package resulted in a 6–4 vote in favor, one short of the two-thirds margin needed for passage. The teams in opposition were reported to be the Yankees, Orioles, Indians, and Senators. The Yankees changed their vote on the second ballot, giving Finley permission to relocate and giving Seattle and Kansas City new teams that would begin operations no later than 1971. That date presented a problem, however, for it meant that Kansas City would be without major league baseball for up to three years. "In one muddle-headed disaster," Bowie Kuhn wrote many years later, "the league left the excellent Kansas City area and doomed the Bay Area to mediocrity by putting a second club there—all to accommodate their arch villain, Charley Finley!"[1]

The decision brought an impassioned outburst from Missouri senator Stuart Symington, who had first criticized Finley when he tried to move to Louisville in 1964. Few politicians can resist a public forum and a popular issue, and with an attractive piñata like Charley Finley, Symington swung his stick with gusto. He called Finley "one of the most disreputable characters ever to enter the American sports scene," said Oakland was "the luckiest city since Hiroshima,"[2] and stomped out of the meeting. Kansas City mayor Ilus Davis prepared to seek an injunction to prevent the Athletics from leaving. Although teams had moved several times prior to 1965, each had been from a city with two major league clubs. The moves of the Braves in 1965 and the Athletics in 1968 were the first that left a city bereft of major league ball.

American League President Joe Cronin, who thought he had placated the Missourians with a new franchise and the prospect of ridding themselves of the odious Finley, panicked. He reconvened the session and, in a stormy meeting with Symington, Davis, and their colleagues, agreed, contingent upon approval by the National League and the commissioner, to name the Kansas City owners by March 1, 1968, and put the new club on the field for the 1969 season.

Cronin had avoided a lawsuit and calmed the Kansas City delegation, but by promising to put clubs in Kansas City and Seattle by 1969 he angered the National League, which had also been considering Seattle as a potential expansion city. NL President Warren Giles blasted the American League for its precipitous action and said his league might consider putting its own team in Seattle. Buzzie Bavasi, general manager of the Dodgers, said he would like to operate a Seattle club in either league.

Less than two years later, baseball learned that Seattle couldn't even support one club, let alone two, and it is hard to believe the NL seriously considered putting a second team there. Dick Young thought that the National League was trying to get the American League to take Dallas-Fort Worth and give Seattle to them.

Cronin had acted quickly to head off the Kansas City faction, and the entire process seemed premature and hasty. Two franchises had been granted without identifying the ownership entities in either city. A group from Seattle was given a last-minute invitation to the October 18 meeting, and Lamar Hunt, owner of the Kansas City Chiefs football team, received less than 24 hours notice to appear on behalf of Dallas-Fort Worth.

The National League weighed its options. One was to fight over Seattle, which the senior circuit considered the most desirable potential new location. Going to Dallas was another alternative. Whatever course the league chose, it would not be decided upon by Warren Giles. As always, the owners would make the decision, and there were a number of personal agendas that muddied the waters. Astros owner Roy Hofheinz was dead set against competition in Dallas-Fort Worth. The Braves had left Milwaukee for Atlanta just two years earlier, and there was a rumor that they would not vote for a new club in Milwaukee unless the city reimbursed them for the approximately $1,000,000 in legal fees they incurred in effecting their escape. San Diego was considered suspect because of a meager television market, but Walter O'Malley was miffed that the Angels had left Dodger Stadium for Anaheim and was hoping that adding a new team in San Diego would squeeze the Angels' market. He also talked about putting a team in Japan. Buffalo and Toronto were other possibilities.

C. Arnholdt Smith, long-time operator of the San Diego Padres of the Pacific Coast League, sprang into action. He spent $30,000 on a slick brochure titled *San Diego NOW* that touted the demographic attributes of the southern California city. The greatest objection to San Diego was the fact that, unlike regional teams in Minnesota and Kansas City, it had to draw exclusively from its metropolitan area. It was hemmed in by Mexico to the south, the ocean to the west, desert to the east, and Los Angeles with its Dodgers and Angels to the north.

Buffalo began talking about a new stadium and shifted its campaign, led by former Reds executive Bill DeWitt, into high gear. In March, the Erie County Legislature voted 18–1 to approve a resolution of intent to construct a new stadium. A delegation from Buffalo journeyed to Vero Beach, training site of the Dodgers, to enlist O'Malley's support.

As the major league winter meetings approached, Giles was coy, not indicating whether his league would expand immediately to keep pace with the American League or wait. When the executives convened in Mexico City, the National League voted to add two teams not later than 1971. The American League officially awarded the Seattle franchise to a group led by Max and Dewey Soriano, the latter being the president of the Pacific Coast League. Bill Daley, a Cleveland businessman and former chairman of the board of the Cleveland Indians, was the chief financial backer. Daley was 76 years old, and his role was to supply the money while the Sorianos ran the team. His only connection to Seattle was that he had once considered moving the Indians there.

Seattle was a city with a long-standing inferiority complex that had acquired civic confidence in 1962 when it hosted the World's Fair, a spectacular exhibition featuring the iconic Space Needle. The city had a long history in minor league baseball, principally in the Pacific Coast League, and despite having failed twice with public referendums to finance a new stadium, prevailed on the third try when voters backed a domed stadium. Seattle is known for its rain, and a domed stadium was considered essential if the city were to have major league ball.

By the end of February, it appeared that San Diego was a front-runner for one of the National League franchises, and with Seattle definitely in the American League camp, it appeared the National League was going to put its second new entry in Dallas, Milwaukee, or Buffalo. But then, from nowhere, a new contender appeared. For the first time, people began to mention Montreal as a possibility. It was an intriguing thought, for a franchise in Montreal would be the first outside the United States.

As usual, individual owners ventured their opinions piecemeal. O'Malley continued to talk about Japan. Gussie Busch stated in late March 1968 that he was in favor of expansion in 1969, but feared he was a minority of one. Under the constitution of the National League, however, a minority of one was omnipotent, for unanimous approval was required for expansion. At the same time, Bob Carpenter of the Phillies said he was determined that new teams would not begin play in 1969. He worried about diluted talent, especially with major leaguers subject to military call-up, and urged caution. The Astros also wanted to wait until after 1969.

Near the end of his term, Commissioner Frick had suggested that expansion teams be given a two-year lead time before beginning play. But, as usual, no one listened to Frick. On April 19, 1968, after a five-hour meeting in Chicago, the National League announced that it would expand the following year, the same time as the American League. Representatives from San Diego, Montreal, Milwaukee, Dallas, and Buffalo made presentations and submitted the names of potential investors. San Diego and Buffalo were considered the front-runners, with both cities promising domed stadiums if they were selected.

Montreal's chances were hindered by unfavorable weather, the lack of a suitable playing site, and the perception that it was primarily a hockey and football city. The heavy debt load accumulated from Expo 67 and from the recent construction of the city's subway system seemed to preclude any massive expenditure for a new stadium. Montreal's Triple-A team had failed in 1960, and the city had no high-profile investors. The principal champions of a Montreal franchise were the city's politicians.

Just six days after the NL meeting, the two leagues met jointly and, astoundingly, spoke of working together. The American League said it would wait until its counterpart had selected its two new members before deciding upon its divisional lineup and a schedule for 1969.

On May 27, the National League made its decision. Dallas, opposed by Hofheinz, was out. The wounds inflicted by the lawsuit when the Braves left Milwaukee were too raw, and Milwaukee, too, was eliminated. Montreal, the long-shot, was surprisingly in, leaving Buffalo and San Diego competing for the final spot. Montreal had been a dark horse throughout the process but, as the other contenders were eliminated, found itself without enemies, which in the required unanimous selection process was an immeasurable advantage.

Buffalo had two things Montreal didn't have—enthusiastic money men and plans for a new stadium. They also pointed to the opportunity to draw from the Canadian market and the estimated 10 million visitors who came to Niagara Falls each year. However, while they waited for the new stadium to be built, a Buffalo team would have to play in decrepit War Memorial Stadium, affectionately known as "The Rock Pile" and located in a riot-torn urban area that made attendance at night games highly adventurous.

After the locker room was broken into on several occasions in 1968, Buffalo's International League Bisons began bringing their uniforms and equipment back to the hotel after each game. Attendance was just 105,000 in 1967, and the team split its 1968 home games between the Rock Pile and Niagara Falls. It was a grim picture, providing evidence that sometimes it was better not to have a minor league team, so that prospective expansion clubs could dream on a blank slate.

On the first ballot, Buffalo had nine votes, with just San Francisco in opposition. Eventually, however, the Giants had their way and Buffalo's support evaporated. After ten hours and somewhere between 16 and 18 secret ballots, Giles announced that San Diego and Montreal would be the newest members of the National League and would begin play in 1969.

The losers did not take defeat gracefully. Dallas unleashed a blast at Hofheinz and the NL for allowing the Houston owner to blackball their application. Politicians from New York, Wisconsin, and Texas appealed to Commissioner Eckert on behalf of Buffalo, Milwaukee, and Dallas. As always when politicians were angry, they threatened to revisit baseball's unique exemption from antitrust laws.

The backers of the Buffalo application were perhaps the most upset, for the city had a deep-seated inferiority complex and was very sensitive to slights. People poked fun at Buffalo's weather, its ethnic, blue collar population, and its gray industrial skyline. When the All-American Football Conference merged with the NFL in 1949, Buffalo, which was one of only three profitable franchises, was ignored by the NFL in favor of Baltimore. The city had recently applied for admission to the National Hockey League and been rejected.

The champions of the application to the National League were brothers Seymour H. Knox III and Northrup "Norty" Knox, who were as cultured and polished as their names suggested. The latter was the former captain of the U.S. polo team, and the family founded the well-known Al-bright-Knox Art Gallery in Buffalo.

The Knox brothers had been the leaders of the failed bid for an NHL franchise in 1965. They were convinced that their application was thwarted by James Norris, owner of the Toronto Maple Leafs, who had a sour taste for the city since experiencing business reverses there and also didn't want Buffalo's televised games beamed anywhere near his market.

Most of the erstwhile hockey investors became enthusiastic backers of a baseball franchise when the major leagues announced they were expanding. They delegated attorney Robert Swados to prepare a comprehensive proposal to document the city's case, and he made a very strong argument. He thought the owners had been impressed, and after he made his presentation, Swados worked on his acceptance speech. After all, the Buffalo group had $12.5 million in the bank to cover the $10 million franchise fee and $2.5 million for operating expenses. Erie County had appropriated $50 million to build a domed stadium. Yet the league selected the ill-prepared and undercapitalized Montreal group, which had only the assurance of Mayor Jean Drapeau that he would somehow get a stadium built by 1971 or 1972. "I think they just got tired," said Swados. "They had a long day and they finally picked a city they could all agree on, whether it was the best city or not."[3]

Although both leagues, unlike the mismatched expansion of 1961–1962, had finally agreed to expand in the same year, there were significant differences. The entry fee for the American League clubs was $5.5 million each, while that of the new National League entries was almost double that amount.[4] The American League planned to have two six-team divisions and play 156 regular season games, followed by a best-of-five series between the division champions. The composition of the divisions was undecided, for it appeared that if the split were made on a geographic basis, the Western half of the league would be weaker, and the established Minnesota and Chicago clubs objected to losing games with the better Eastern clubs. Chicago owner John Allyn threatened to file a lawsuit if he was forced into the Western Division.

The National League planned to operate as one undivided 12-team circuit and maintain the 162-game schedule. Giles claimed that his circuit was committed to continuing the "tradition" of an undivided league. "Every time I read that 'tradition' malarkey," wrote Dick Young, "I wonder where the tradition was when the Giants and Dodgers moved out of New York and when the Braves moved out of Milwaukee and Boston."[5]

One of the objectors to a divisional setup was the Mets, who stood to lose six home games against the Dodgers and Giants, which traditionally meant total attendance of 300,000 or so. Chairman of the Board M. Donald Grant estimated that reducing the Giants and Dodgers dates would cost the Mets about $250,000 per year. He was not opposed to divisions, he said, just to divisions split on an east-west basis. He suggested revising the structure each year based upon the prior season's standings.

The maintenance of a unified National League meant that, while the American League would have a playoff, the National would not. "For sheer perverseness, self-damage and ineffective greediness," wrote Leonard Koppett, "the National League's rejection last week of a two-division setup can hardly be matched in baseball history." Koppett was particularly hard on the Mets, who he accused of being greedy, shortsighted, and incorrect. "Willie Mays won't last forever," he wrote. "When he retires, the special appeal of the Giants will wither away, as the special appeal of the Dodgers already has since Sandy Koufax's retirement."[6]

The Dodgers and Giants had been the top draws in New York for each of the Mets' first five years. In 1967, the first year the Dodgers played without Koufax, the Dodgers slipped to fourth, behind the Giants, Braves, and Cardinals. "The Mets are making clear," Koppett continued, "they lack faith in the interest of their customers in Met success, and hope to continue to ride piggyback on the attractiveness of visiting teams."[7]

The idea of each league operating in such a divergent manner did not appear to be in the best interest of baseball, and Commissioner Eckert pledged to get together with the two leagues to work out a compromise. On June 26, baseball's executive council recommended that each league split into two divisions with 162-game schedules, a finding endorsed with great relief by the commissioner. Finally, on July 10, at a meeting during the All-Star break, the recommendation was accepted and baseball found equilibrium once more.

It had all worked out in the end, but the clumsy process had been embarrassingly acted out in public. Had both leagues, on July 10, 1968, announced they were expanding into 12-team leagues with a total of four divisions, which is what they eventually decided, there would have been no controversy. The two leagues played out their differences and internecine squabbles in public,

creating the perception, which was absolutely correct, that baseball was rud-
derless.

After all the confusion, major league baseball had agreed to add four
teams. Kansas City was the most solid of the group, with a wealthy, energetic
owner and use of Municipal Stadium, which had been home to the Athletics.
Seattle had experienced management but needed to renovate old Sick's Stadium. San Diego had a going concern in its Pacific Coast League club. Montreal had a franchise.

Seattle probably had the best fight song, titled "Go, Go, You Pilots":

> Go, Go You Pilots!
> You proud Seattle team.
> Go, Go You Pilots!
> Go out and build a dream.
> You brought the majors to the
> Evergreen Northwest.
> Now Go, Go You Pilots!
> You're going to be the best.
> Welcome the Yankees
> With pinstripe suits and all.
> Red Sox and Royals
> From April 'till the Fall.
> American Leaguers
> You've got what's known as class.
> So, welcome to Seattle
> It's going to be a gas.
> Go, Go, Go, Go, Go, Go, Go, Go
> Now Go, Go You Pilots!
> You're going to be the best.
> White Sox and Tigers
> The Angels and the A's.
> See them at the ballpark
> On those good ol' summer days.
> Orioles and Senators
> The Indians and Twins
> Our Pilots ask no favors
> As they battle you for wins.
> So Go, Go You Pilots!
> You proud Seattle team.
> Go, Go You Pilots!
> It's time to shout and scream.
> We're with you Pilots
> You're big league all the way.
> So Go, Go You Pilots!
> Go, Go You Pilots!
> Go, Go You Pilots!
> When the umpire hollers, "play!"[8]

Kansas City didn't have a snappy song, but it would prove to be the strongest of the new franchises and the first to build a competitive team. Perhaps the biggest reason for the success of the Kansas City Royals was owner Ewing Kauffman. Kauffman had not been previously involved in baseball, but he was one of the new breed of successful businessmen who wanted a toy, one that would enhance the reputation of his city. Unlike many of his type, however, Kauffman knew what he didn't know. "I intend to get the best men I can find for the job," he said, "and let them run it."[9]

Kauffman was the first local owner of a Kansas City major league baseball team, and he was determined that the city would not lose it again. He gave assurances to the American League and the city that the Royals would remain in Kansas City during his lifetime, and his estate plan was drafted to ensure that the Royals would remain in place after his passing.

Kauffman was a classic American success story; in 1967, he was given the Horatio Alger Award. He was born on a farm about 60 miles from Kansas City, attended college for two years, was an unsuccessful life insurance salesman, and then enlisted in the Navy in 1942. Following the war, he answered an ad for a pharmaceutical salesman. If he couldn't make money protecting people in the event of their death, perhaps he could make a living keeping them alive. Kauffman loved his new job and was quickly promoted. Since he was soon earning more than the president of the company, however, his commission rate was reduced, and he quit. With $4,500 in savings, Kauffman decided to start his own company.

He began manufacturing pharmaceuticals in his basement in 1950, earning $1,100 his first year. By the time he acquired the Royals, he was making $2,000,000 a year, and his stake in Marion Laboratories was supposedly worth $60 million.

Initially working by himself, Kauffman developed two drugs and went on the road selling them to doctors. If he got an order, he went back home, packaged the order, and mailed it. As the business grew, Kauffman began hiring people, mostly people like himself, men from farms and small towns with modest backgrounds who had worked their way through college. He believed that hard work and skill led to success, and he rewarded those who showed the work ethic he prized. Kauffman instituted a stock ownership plan for his employees and a generous retirement plan. When a reporter for *The Sporting News* came to interview him in January 1968, he pointed out proudly that the company's janitor had $80,000 in stock and $160,000 in his retirement plan.

Thanks to the political pressure the city placed upon the American League, Kansas City was almost assured of a franchise, and there were several applicants, most of whom planned to raise capital by selling stock to the public. Kauffman was the only bidder who was capable of financing the transaction

168   Baseball on the Brink

himself, and when he showed up at the Mexico City meeting with two letters of credit totaling $10 million, the decision to award him the franchise was an easy one. "The actual selection," Kauffman said later, "took exactly ten seconds."[10] Perhaps the reason the process was so rapid was that Charley Finley, claiming other commitments and his wife's upcoming operation, did not attend.

"Probably the best thing the Royals had going for them," said Bob Wirz, the club's first public relations director,

> was that Charley Finley was gone. He was not well-liked because of the quality of his teams and the shenanigans with the animals he brought in—the mule mascot and the zoo on the hill in right field. People were so happy to have him gone and have someone like Ewing Kauffman owning the team. I don't think Ewing was that well known when he bought the team, but people knew he was a *local* businessman. That was vitally important after the experience with Finley. He also had a great reputation for building Marion Laboratories, starting by bottling pills in his basement.[11]

Kauffman had said he would let his baseball people run the team, but many busybody owners, including George Steinbrenner, said the same thing when they arrived on the baseball scene. For most, however, their self-confidence and ego overcame their good intentions, and they become convinced that the skills that enabled them to succeed in other businesses were transferable to baseball. Kauffman, however, was true to his word. He hired Cedric Tallis as executive vice president and Lou Gorman as farm director and let them build a team without interference.

The one project that captivated Kauffman was his baseball academy, a revolutionary concept that he began in 1970. "Ewing was a brilliant man," said Wirz. "Whenever he got involved in something, he wanted to learn all about it. He really learned a lot about baseball, and that was why he started the Academy down in Sarasota."[12]

The theory behind the academy was that if the Royals recruited men with great athletic ability but limited baseball experience, skilled coaches could mold a few of them into major league players. The experiment presaged the Caribbean academies now conducted by most major league teams, for in addition to teaching baseball skills, the players attended college courses, where they learned both academic and life skills.

At the time the academy opened, under the overall direction of Syd Thrift, then a scout and later a renowned executive, scouting and player development were much less scientific than they are today. Most scouting was based on visual observation, and training techniques had changed little in the past 50 years. Kauffman's unfamiliarity with baseball was an advantage in the sense that rather than being wedded to traditional methods, he began analyzing player development from a fresh perspective. He was astonished to learn that teams didn't test players' eyesight, merely noting whether they wore glasses. Believing that depth perception was one of the keys to playing baseball, particularly batting, Kauffman hired an eye doctor who developed a test for depth perception. The doctor discovered that depth perception was the key to hitting in night games and that there were methods that could improve it.

Batting coach Charley Lau began experimenting with video, using a machine that weighed 200 pounds and had to be brought to the field on a dolly. The Royals brought in track stars, gymnasts, and baseball stars like Ted Williams to talk about different aspects of the game. They used scientific measurements to determine things like taking the optimal lead, rather than relying on instinct and guesswork.

The academy produced 14 major leaguers, including Frank White and U.L. Washington, who formed the double play combination for the 1980 American League championship team, and infielder Ron Washington, who later managed the Texas Rangers to the World Series. "I don't think Frank White would have ever played a day of professional baseball," said Wirz, "had it not been for the Academy."[13] White concurred. "I wouldn't have played baseball at all, I know that," he said. "I think I'd be working at Hallmark or something."[14] "Without the Academy," said Ron Washington, "I'd be back home in Louisiana working in the fields."[15]

Despite its successes, baseball traditionalists looked upon the Academy with disdain. "[M]ost of the men working inside baseball," wrote a reporter years later, "viewed the Academy in one of three ways: they ignored it (thinking it was a waste of time), resented it (seeing it as an insult to their tradition), or feared it (what if it actually worked?)"[16] "It became a bit of a tug and pull," said Wirz, "between the player development people who wanted to go the traditional routes while Kauffman and Syd Thrift believed in a lot of cutting edge technologies."[17]

In 1974, Kauffman was convinced to close the Academy and save the $500,000 annual expense. "I think in hindsight," said Wirz, "they might have given up on the Academy too soon."[18] "You know," Kauffman told scout Art Stewart about a year before his death, "the biggest mistake I made in baseball was letting them talk me into closing the Academy."[19]

American League owners were confident Kauffman would succeed in Kansas City. He had integrity, a track record of success, and the financial wherewithal to cover any losses. Prospects were not as rosy in Montreal. "Lots of baseball fans were surprised," reported *Sports Illustrated,* "that Montreal received one of the two new National League franchises, but the city itself is apparently flabbergasted."[20] By early July, flabbergast had turned to impatience with Mayor Jean Drapeau. Drapeau, a 52-year-old, dapper, dynamic man with a bald head and neat little mustache, had unlimited self-confidence and had assured everyone that a new stadium would be approved and constructed.[21]

Few people have influenced a city to the degree that Jean Drapeau shaped Montreal during the second half of the 20th century. He served as mayor from 1954 through 1957 and from 1960 through 1986, and under his leadership, Montreal constructed a subway system, produced Expo 67, acquired a major league baseball team, and hosted the 1976 Olympics.

Drapeau, however, had a tendency to shoot from the hip, trusting that things would somehow fall into place. He had bet his reputation on the success of Expo 67 and won, but the Olympics were a gamble that didn't pay off. "The Olympics can no more lose money," he boasted, "than a man can have a baby."[22] When expenses, initially budgeted at $310 million, exceeded $1.3 billion, leaving the city with a debt that took decades to eliminate, a political cartoon showed Drapeau placing a call to a prominent Montreal physician who performed abortions.

The baseball enterprise succeeded the successful Expo and preceded the disastrous Olympics, and Drapeau's reputation for pulling rabbits out of hats led the baseball investors to make a commitment based upon his promise that a new stadium would be completed by 1972.

"Teams do not really move to cities anymore," wrote Frank Deford in *Sports Illustrated.* "They move to stadiums, and Montreal, which does not have to concern itself with messy referendums that involve voters, as do cities in the U.S., got the franchise primarily because Mayor Jean Drapeau, an effervescent little La Guardian dynamo, was able by himself to absolutely promise the league that Montreal would construct a magnificent domed stadium by 1971."[23]

By July, the Montreal investors had grown tired of hearing Drapeau tell everyone that the stadium would eventually be built but that the time was not right to push approval of the financing. They were impatient with locals who said Montreal could not afford to spend at the major league level. They'd not hired a single employee and said that if no decision on the stadium was forthcoming by July 15, they were out. Whiskey magnate Charles Bronfman,[24] the lead investor, said he had stepped forward out of civic duty, not because of an overwhelming desire to own a baseball team. "Who needs it?" he said.[25]

Clearly, Drapeau needed Bronfman more than Bronfman needed a baseball team. Bronfman was wealthy but, unlike Ewing Kauffman, he was not a self-made man. Charles's grandfather, Yechiel Bronfman, had emigrated to Canada from Russia and established a liquor business, from which his son Samuel founded Distillers Corporation, Ltd. in 1924. Four years later, Samuel merged his firm with Joseph E. Seagram and Sons and named the combined operation Distillers Corporation-Seagram's Ltd.

After graduating from McGill University, Charles joined the family business in 1951. By the mid–1960s, Seagram's had expanded into oil and gas, and

Charles was accumulating wealth that would eventually make him a billionaire. He was clearly the deep pocket Drapeau needed to convince the National League that a cold Canadian city could establish a viable major league franchise.

One of the weaknesses of the Montreal investment group was that none were baseball men, most were not even fans, and all appeared to be wealthy businessmen impressed in the cause of civic duty. One got the feeling they had volunteered under the assumption that Montreal had no chance of being awarded a franchise, which would allow them to satisfy their civic obligation without having to perform in the end. When someone asked Warren Giles to identify the backers for the franchise, he replied, "I don't know their names."[26]

"The franchise was gathered in such remarkable style," said Bronfman, "that it was here well ahead of the organizational groundwork. Three days before the franchise was granted, I wasn't even in, and none of the sponsors had even had a formal meeting."[27] Much to the chagrin of the investors, the $8 million investment they were expecting to make had grown to $12–13 million.

The National League, which should have been very concerned, was not. "What is happening among the backers of the team and the city over the stadium," said Pirates owner John Galbreath, a member of the league's expansion committee, "is no concern of the league's. It is strictly a club matter and we have no part in it. The problems are their own, not ours."[28] But if Montreal didn't have a place to play when the St. Louis Cardinals arrived for the opening game the following April, it would be very much a league concern.

The two people most excited about bringing major league baseball to Montreal were Drapeau and his assistant, Gerry Snyder. When the amateur draft took place in June, it was Snyder who made the selections, assisted by one of the investors, a legal advisor, and information provided by other major league teams.[29] When asked if any of the three Montreal representatives had any experience in sports, Snyder volunteered that investor John Newman had played college and minor league football.[30]

Bronfman indicated that he intended to hire veteran baseball executive John McHale, then an assistant to Commissioner Eckert, to run his operation, but McHale would not come aboard until the stadium issue was resolved. "We have no company now," said investor Claude Levesque. "Who is going to employ anyone?"[31]

Not only was the new stadium not even on the drawing board, renovations to the Autostade, where the new club expected to play until the dome was complete, had not begun. Dick Young described the Autostade as being located in "the dankest, coldest, windiest part of the city." "Another Candlestick?" he wondered.[32]

In its July 20 issue, *The Sporting News* cast serious doubt on the ability of Montreal to place a team on the field for the 1969 season. It stated that the city was greatly surprised it had been selected and questioned the diligence with which the National League had vetted the prospective franchisees and their resources. "If the Montreal effort does collapse," said *TSN*, "and we're not saying it will—the NL will be a little bit embarrassed, as well it should be."[33]

In mid–July, Drapeau's representative explained to the National League that the city could not vote on a new stadium without detailed cost estimates, which would not be available for several months. He assured the league that a stadium would be built and that recommendations would be made to the city council as soon as possible after May 1, 1969. He also talked about the possibility of putting a roof over the Autostade. It was no more than had been said before, but the league, grasping at that thin, unsubstantial straw, convinced Bronfman to move forward.

Shortly after Bronfman re-affirmed his commitment, three of his partners, Levesque, Robert Irsay (later the despised owner of the Baltimore Colts who moved the club to Indianapolis) and Marv Bourgie, withdrew from the syndicate. Irsay claimed that Giles had asked him to take over the operation because Bronfman was backing out, which brought an angry denial from the latter. "We don't need Mr. Irsay or the likes of Mr. Irsay," he fumed, and said he didn't even know Irsay.[34]

On August 7, amidst rumors that the club might be moved to Milwaukee or Buffalo, Giles went to Montreal to meet with the remaining investors and the city council. He was told that putting a roof on the Autostade was unfeasible, and plans to use it on a temporary basis were impractical. Nothing had been accomplished since the National League had granted the city a franchise, and Giles envisioned the horrific possibility that he might have to go back to the cities his league had rejected and offer them a team at this late date. In addition to the embarrassment, trying to replace Montreal with either Dallas or Milwaukee would re-open the battles with Hofheinz and the Atlanta ownership. Montreal's greatest asset was its inoffensiveness, but a team without a stadium was very offensive.

On August 7, Drapeau met with Giles and admitted that he had neither the commitment to build a domed stadium nor a temporary facility. But Montreal's mayor was not about to give up and pleaded for one more day. And on that day he delivered. As *The Sporting News* reported, "Mayor Jean Drapeau appeared with a life preserver just as Montreal was about to go down for the third time."[35]

Drapeau took Giles to the northeast section of the city and showed him a facility called Jarry Park, more centrally located that the Autostade. There was a local all-star game taking place, and Drapeau's appearance elicited cheers from the crowd, both for the mayor and for the new team. The park could be expanded, Drapeau assured Giles, to seat 30,000 by Opening Day. The city would pay the first $3,000,000 of renovation expenses if the team would pay anything over that amount. Giles, eager to support any option that would salvage the floundering franchise, thought it was a great idea.

Bronfman had been hesitant to put up the first installment of the franchise fee, but a few hours after Giles gave his blessing to Jarry Park, he proclaimed, "We're going to play ball."[36] He made the initial payment of $1.2 million on August 14, a day before the deadline. "This is a great day for the city of Montreal and a great day for the National League," said a greatly relieved Giles as he held the check aloft.[37] McHale, who'd attended all the meetings, apparently was ready to play ball as well and came aboard to give the franchise professional management. He hired Jim Fanning, head of the Major League Baseball Scouting Bureau, as general manager. The club began to sell tickets and, as reporter Ted Blackman noted, was "ready to move toward sixth place in the N.L's Eastern Division."[38]

To reach even sixth place, the new team needed a manager, players, a completed ballpark, and a nickname. In mid–September, McHale hired 43-year-old Gene Mauch, dismissed by the Phillies earlier in the year, as his manager. Mauch had played for Montreal briefly as a Dodgers farmhand in the 1940s. He was excited to be employed again, pleased to have the opportunity to build a team from the ground up, and delighted to manage a team that did not include Richie Allen.

McHale signed his first player, 21-year-old, left-handed pitcher David Hartman, and began to prepare for the expansion draft in October, from which he would get the majority of his talent. On September 16, bulldozers moved onto the playing surface of Jarry Park and began to prepare the ground for the laying of new sod. In mid–November, there was an official ground-breaking, and Snyder tossed a pitch to McHale in the snow-covered area near home plate. It was 20 degrees, windy, and a foot of snow lay on the ground, but everyone recalled that last April 14 (the scheduled Opening Day for 1969), Montreal registered a record 83 degrees.

Last, but not least, the team acquired a name. The early favorite was *Voyageurs,* which satisfied the bilingual requirement, but the final choice was Expos, after the exhibit which had given Drapeau his reputation as a creator of great events.

As if the first months in the life of the new Expos weren't difficult enough, McHale and Fanning faced two obstacles unique in the annals of major league baseball. First, the Canadian dollar was worth about eight percent less than the U.S. dollar. Player salaries would be paid in U.S. currency, good for the players but an additional cost to the owners.

The second difficulty was language. In Montreal, people spoke French *or* English rather than French *and* English. Montreal was not truly a bilingual city; it was two monolingual populations residing in the same city. Although three-quarters of all Canadians considered English their primary language, about 82 percent of Montreal's population spoke French, as did about 80 percent of the residents of the Province of Quebec. All promotional materials, including scorecards, yearbooks, and ticket information, had to be produced in two languages. Messages on the scoreboard would be displayed in both English and French. There would be two broadcast teams and two broadcast networks, which would double the production expense without increasing revenue.

There were other complications. In order to facilitate travel, McHale needed to get a special waiver of the Montreal airport's ban on overnight takeoffs and landings. More importantly, the city had a prohibition against selling liquor at any sporting event other than racing. The Expos were able to obtain a permit that allowed them to sell beer at concession stands, but the city would not allow roaming vendors.

In October, the Expos selected 30 players from the ten established National League teams. They picked well-known veterans like shortstop Maury Wills and first baseman Donn Clendenon of the Pirates and pitchers Larry Jackson of the Phillies and Jim "Mudcat" Grant of the Dodgers, as well as a number of unknown youngsters.

In early March, just a month before the start of the 1969 season, the Expos were still without a broadcast contract, either in English or French. English stations claimed the market was too small, and production costs associated with broadcasting major league baseball too high, to justify the level of rights fees paid to other major league teams. Finally, midway through spring training, the Expos were able to secure a contract with The Canadian Broadcasting Corporation to televise 21 games, from which the club expected to realize $300,000. By late March, the Expos completed their network by signing up an eight-station French-language radio network.

Meanwhile, workmen fought the clock and struggled through a bitter winter trying to get Jarry Park ready for April 14. In early January, reports from Montreal indicated that although the field was beneath four feet of snow, work was eight days ahead of schedule. "You must accept the club's word that the stadium construction is ahead of schedule," *The Sporting News* reported in late January, "because there is no visible evidence of a ballpark at Jarry except for two concrete dugouts protruding from the snow-covered pasture."[39]

On January 20, the Expos made an installment payment of $6 million to the league, which distributed $600,000 to each of the ten holdover clubs. The remaining $3 million was to be paid over a three-year period.

By early February, there were 56 inches of snow covering the playing field, but Lou Martin, overseeing the construction for the ballclub, said the park would be finished by April 1, despite the fact that steel needed for the erection of the grandstands arrived three weeks late, after it was shipped to the wrong customer. Once the steel arrived, crews began working 18–20 hours per day to assemble the prefabricated stands. "While the fixtures aren't the best in baseball," *The Sporting News* noted, "they meet major league standards."[40] "It will be a miracle if the Montreal ball park is ready in time," added Dick Young.[41] He speculated that the Expos might open the season on the road or, ironically, play their early games in Milwaukee, which had been jilted twice by the National League.

The Expos, however, were determined to open the season in Jarry Park. "It'll be ready," John McHale said.[42] By April 1, the snow had yielded to frost and McHale was more cautious. "They've given us no indication it won't be ready," he said.[43] Martin said the only thing that could prevent completion was rough weather, a phenomenon that occurred with great frequency in Montreal in early April.

National League schedule makers wisely put Montreal on the road for Opening Day, and on Tuesday, April 8, the new club made its debut in New York by beating the Mets, 11–10, in a game that featured three Montreal home runs, including one by pitcher Dan McGinn. The Expos were victorious in their first opener while the Mets, who began operations in 1962, remained winless in opening games.

Six days later, the first major league game on Canadian soil took place in nearly-completed Jarry Park on a sunny, 64-degree day. Just a few days earlier, it hadn't seemed possible that the park would be ready, but on April 14 the Expos and Cardinals took the field before a crowd of 29,184. The Expos won again, 8–7, and veteran outfielder Mack Jones became an instant Expos hero with a three-run homer in the first inning.

The condition of the infield was horrible, and some of the fans had to sit on chairs placed where permanent seats had yet to be installed. The catcher's area was like quicksand, and columnist Bob Addie pointed out that "It was the first time a catcher ever had to throw from a foxhole."[44] Curt Flood of the Cardinals said, "I hope I don't get killed out there."[45] "A lot of parks have soft turf in the spring," McHale said. "We accomplished a miracle, in view of the hard winter Montreal had, in getting ready at all."[46]

The Montreal fans didn't care about the mushy infield or the unfinished stands. A crowd of 5,000 welcomed the team at Dorval Airport when they arrived in the city after their exhibition season. A parade the day before the New York opener drew 150,000. A jubilant Drapeau addressed the crowd before the parade and threw out the ceremonial first ball at Shea Stadium.

Less than a year earlier, it seemed impossible that Montreal would be selected by the National League. In July, no one thought Bronfman's investors would come up with the money or that Drapeau would find a place for the new team to play. Just four days earlier, they were saying it would take a miracle to get the stadium finished in time. But on April 14, 1969, the Expos beat the defending National League champions, and despite nearly losing a couple of outfielders in the muck, the day was a rousing success. The Expos were on their way to losing 110 games and finishing 48 games behind the division-winning Mets, but they were in the major leagues.

12

Nobody in the World Can
Be Another Mickey Mantle

Since its beginnings in the mid–19th century, baseball has had heroes, men who were not only immensely talented but possessed a special, almost indescribable aura that set them apart from other good players. Like religion, sociologist Harry Edwards notes, sports has always had its saints.[1] The long line began with Jim Creighton, baseball's first great pitcher, who ensured his immortality by dying tragically in 1862 at the age of 21. The late–19th century saw the emergence of men like King Kelly and Cap Anson, whose "rough around the edges" personalities mirrored the ethos of their times. The 20th century brought a succession of legends, from Ty Cobb and Christy Mathewson, Babe Ruth and Lou Gehrig, Joe DiMaggio and Ted Williams, and then Mickey Mantle and Willie Mays. Fans rooted for them at the ballpark, they read about them in the newspapers, they saw them in newsreels and movies, and eventually they watched them on television. Even people who didn't follow baseball knew who they were.

For a hundred years, there had been men who brought their magical aura to the sport. People came to the park just to see them play—attendance went up dramatically when Sandy Koufax pitched for the Dodgers or when Mantle and the Yankees came to town—which meant more ticket sales, more hot dogs and beer sold at the park, and more products sold by baseball's advertisers. Under the salary structure that prevailed through the 1960s, star players made much more money for the owners than they were paid in salary. They were prized economic assets, and their images were carefully protected, with the willing assistance of the media. A major league beat was a coveted position, and reporters weren't about to rock the boat by exposing the personal peccadilloes of a team's star player.

Owners were not about to let the public know its heroes had feet of clay—or that famous and relatively wealthy young men had libidos equal to their baseball ability. Yankees general manager George Weiss knew all about

Mickey Mantle's active personal life, thanks to private detectives he employed to keep an eye on his players. Once, during contract negotiations, Weiss took a manila folder from his desk drawer and hinted that if Mantle didn't sign for his proposed terms, Mrs. Mantle might be made aware of the contents of the folder.

It's highly unlikely that Weiss would have followed through with his threat, and even more improbable that he would ever let the public know what mischief Mantle engaged in when the Yankees traveled. Weiss, Yankees manager Casey Stengel, the players, and reporters who covered the team knew about Mantle's escapades, and many envied him, but what happened in the locker room, the hotel room, or the hotel bar stayed there.

The American public knew Mickey Mantle as a one-dimensional, heroic figure who hit home runs, performed courageously while dogged by numerous injuries, and did things on a baseball field that no one else could. With his rugged build, blond crew cut, and aw-shucks smile, he looked like a baseball hero. Even his name, a matched pair of two-syllable words that flowed smoothly off the tongue, was perfect.

It was not until 1970 and the appearance of Jim Bouton's shocking *Ball Four* that baseball fans learned that their heroes were a little different from what they'd been led to believe. They were, disappointingly, a lot like them, with human, unheroic flaws. The publication of *Ball Four* unleashed a firestorm of angry reaction from the baseball community, both from the establishment and from Bouton's fellow players. Ironically, the more they condemned the book, the more copies were sold.

Bouton, who was still an active player when the book appeared, was asked to pay a visit to New York for a conversation with Commissioner Bowie Kuhn.[2] Although he was employed by the owners, Kuhn saw himself as a guardian of baseball's public image and didn't think that stories about ballplayers running around looking up women's skirts contributed to a positive image of the game. Bouton thought the image Kuhn sought to maintain was false and unsustainable. "I didn't smash any heroes or ruin the game for anybody," he wrote in his sequel, *I'm Glad You Didn't Take it Personally*. "You want heroes, you can have them. Heroes exist only in the mind anyway."[3]

Players' Association Executive Director Marvin Miller accompanied Bouton to the meeting with Kuhn, and Bouton reported Miller's response to the commissioner as follows: "What you're saying is that what was good about the past was that the public had this image of the player wearing a halo. But I believe fans today are different. They're a lot more sophisticated and a lot more concerned with players as human beings. I could well make a case that something which took away this phony, unrealistic view of the life of a professional player and showed that it was a great deal more down to earth could be very good for baseball. "[4] He said that as a boy he knew that Babe Ruth was a sybarite, but worshipped him anyway.

Miller was suggesting a course that was diametrically opposed to the line of reasoning prevalent in baseball for decades, and Kuhn wasn't buying. During his tenure as commissioner, Kuhn disagreed with Miller on virtually everything, and the fact that the leader of the players' union liked hedonistic players probably didn't surprise him, nor did it convince him that baring baseball players' weaknesses was in the best interests of the game. After much verbal sparring, Kuhn and Miller finally agreed that the commissioner would release a statement that he disagreed with Bouton's decision to publish the book, but would not take any disciplinary action.

I was 16 when *Ball Four* came out, and I thought it was fabulous, funny, and probably the most entertaining baseball book I'd ever read. Decades later, after I'd been writing for some time and interviewing former athletes, I re-read it and had a different opinion. I still consider it a ground-breaking, highly entertaining work, but some aspects of the book trouble me. What bothered me most was that Bouton published what his teammates had every right to believe were private conversations. Remarks that are perfectly appropriate and funny in the context of the locker room are often embarrassing when seen in print by wives, children, and parents—or, to Bowie Kuhn's concerns, by fans of our National Pastime.

Bouton defended himself against that allegation by saying that he believed most of his teammates knew he was writing a book. Seattle outfielder Jim Gosger admitted that everything in the book was true and he thought it was hilarious, but denied that Bouton's teammates were aware that he was taking notes for a book. "We never knew," he said. "I don't think anyone had an inkling of what Bouton was doing."[5]

Regardless of whether he was working undercover, Bouton claimed he had a right to publish his thoughts and observations. "Does a man have the right to write everything that's in his own head?" he asserted, citing Thomas Wolfe's *Look Homeward Angel* as an example.[6] No one questioned Bouton's legal right to publish his book; they were merely expressing their offense at what he had written. In many ways, his situation was similar to that of Wolfe, who portrayed his family in such a negative manner that they shunned him, which was exactly what was happening to Bouton.

Cincinnati Reds pitcher Jim Brosnan wrote books in diary style about the 1959 campaign (*The Long Season*) and the 1961 season (*Pennant Race*). Brosnan exposed a side of baseball not previously seen by the general public, but he was discreet, speaking of alcohol and amphetamines only briefly, referring obtusely to sex, and in most cases refraining from strong personal criticism. Still, Brosnan's books were considered edgy, and in 1964 he was given an ultimatum to either stop writing or quit baseball; he chose the latter option.

In the spring of 1960, a Brosnan article that was allegedly critical of Cardinals manager Solly Hemus and executive Bing Devine caused the Indians to prohibit infielder Johnny Temple from writing a column and the Giants doing the same to Daryl Spencer. Other clubs reiterated that a player must have his club's permission before writing anything. The press supported the clubs' position, mostly, it appeared, from fear of competition. "The attitude of the writers," said Dan Daniel, who covered the Yankees, "is that if any player has anything worthwhile to say, the information belongs to them and not a magazine which would pay the player."[7]

Brosnan was an accomplished writer and did not have an acknowledged co-author, while Bouton used veteran New York writer Leonard Shecter. Shecter was somewhat of a pariah among the New York press and was viewed warily by most players. He often violated the sanctity of the locker room and reported news that his fellow writers had chosen to ignore for the "good of the game." He made his reputation by reporting a fight between inebriated Yankees pitcher Ryne Duren and coach Ralph Houk on the train during a celebration of the 1958 pennant, an incident the other writers ignored in the interest of protecting the Yankees' image. Shecter was not interested in discretion, and with him as a collaborator, Bouton pulled no punches.

There were good guys and bad guys in *Ball Four*, including some *really* bad guys. Bouton and the intellectual companions he befriended during the season, primarily pitcher Mike Marshall and outfielder Steve Hovley, were consistently presented as the voices of mature, intelligent reason in a sea of rampant stupidity. The most stupid people were general managers, managers, and coaches. It is hardly surprising that the baseball lifers who populated the pages of *Ball Four* were not intellectually curious, well-rounded men. That, in many cases, is precisely why they remained in baseball their entire lives. Nor is it shocking that the brash, outspoken Bouton, always challenging the values of the game to which they had devoted their lives, rubbed most of them the wrong way.

Bouton criticized many of his managers and coaches for being too wedded to the traditions and values of the past. What he may not have fully understood is that, for many people, the allure of baseball is its history and its ties to a past that will never change and is thus more comforting than the uncertain present and future. Joe Schultz, Frank Crosetti, and Harry Walker, with their hackneyed and often butchered clichés and reminiscences about old players, were reflecting what many old fans wanted to see in the game. To them, the revelation that there were sex, drugs, and pettiness in the game that brought them joy was disconcerting. It was too much like their real lives.

In some cases, Bouton was simply unfair. Throughout his entire summer in Seattle, and on page after page of his book, he complained to his manager, his pitching coach, and his readers that he wasn't given sufficient opportunities to pitch. A check of the record book shows that Bouton pitched in 80 major and minor league games that year, which was close to the existing record. Granted, he didn't get to start many games, and he wasn't always pitching in key situations, but his performance was no more than adequate, and in his one start in Seattle, he couldn't get through the fourth inning.

When the first excerpts from *Ball Four* appeared in serial form in *Look* magazine in May 1970, reaction was immediate and extreme. Shortly afterward, Bouton pitched for the Astros against the Mets in Shea Stadium and was booed. After giving up three runs in a third of an inning, he left the mound to another chorus of boos, and compared the experience to walking into a wall, nose first.

Even those who hated the book acknowledged that it was engaging, well-written, and a revolutionary look at a heretofore hidden part of baseball. There were many good reviews from well-respected writers and critics, including historian David Halberstam. Surprisingly, *Sporting News* publisher C.C. Johnson Spink, generally a conservative defender of baseball's status quo, told Bouton he liked the book.

There were, however, a number of angry denunciations. Dick Young, the legendary columnist for the *New York Daily News*, panned the book and called Bouton and Shecter "social lepers" who were exacting revenge for being ostracized by the New York sports establishment.

Young began his reporting career in 1942, and during the 1950s and early 1960s was in many ways the Jim Bouton of the press box, one of the first writers to go into the locker room and report on controversial topics that were sometimes embarrassing to a team or player. By 1970, he had either grown more conservative or, as Bouton believed, was envious that Bouton had written a ground-breaking, best-selling insider book rather than him.

Bouton is a man with a not inconsiderable ego, which he referred to as the "ham" in him. He is convinced of the rightness of his opinions and often intolerant of those who disagree with him. After Young criticized him, he told the writer that the people who supported Young were dumb and those who backed Bouton were smart. "You know who's listening to you?" he said. "The hard-hat types, that's who, the dum-dums, the kind of people who write obscene letters and don't have the guts to sign their own name.... On the other hand, I'm getting a lot of really good letters, letters from businessmen who have secretaries, letters from people who care, neat, thoughtful letters, and all of them are signed. Those are the kind of people who are on my side."[8] Of course, Bowie Kuhn was not a hard-hat or a "dum-dum," and he clearly wasn't on Bouton's side.

All the publicity, both positive and negative, spurred sales of the book, much to Bouton's delight. He dedicated his second book to Dick Young and Bowie Kuhn, for all their help in drawing attention to *Ball Four*. Bouton was thrilled by the success of his book, partly for the financial rewards, but even more for the attention it brought him. Ironically, the man who challenged the public's notion of heroes wanted very much to be a hero. He'd been one in 1963 and 1964 before his arm gave out, and now he was one again. Bouton was recognized everywhere he went and, even when he was treated as a pariah, he was at least noticed.[9]

Decades after they retired, many of Bouton's former teammates still despised him for what they believed he had done to the image of the game and to men they considered their friends. Joe Pepitone resented the fact that Bouton wrote about the indiscretions of others but not his own. In many cases, players were particularly angry that he had soiled the public image of Mickey Mantle.

"I'm not too happy to speak about Jim Bouton," said a former Yankees pitcher. "He should have kept his mouth shut. The things he said about Mickey he had no business saying. I lost all respect for him and I don't even like talking about him."[10]

In 1969, the year chronicled by Bouton in *Ball Four*, the Yankees opened their season without Mantle, the first time they'd done so since 1950. On March 1, he announced his retirement from baseball because, no matter how hard he tried, he could no longer do the things he once did with ease, such as go from first to third on a single or get around on a good major league fastball. Even the designated hitter rule wouldn't have helped, for most young pitchers could throw their fastball by him, and the combination of his weak legs and diminishing reflexes sometimes made him appear helpless at the plate. His left knee was so bad that he could no longer push off batting left-handed, and he seemed to be hitting almost flat-footed. On the bases, the man who'd been perhaps the fastest in baseball when he was young ran haltingly with a severe limp.

Perhaps the most poignant aspect of the film of Mantle hitting his 500th home run in 1967 was the way he hobbled around the bases. "I feel like crying when I see the guy run," said a rookie Oakland outfielder named Reggie Jackson early in the 1968 season. "I'd almost hate to throw him out, but it's my job."[11] "I wince when I see his leg buckle under him when he runs," added Carl Yastrzemski.[12] Al Weis spoke of how deep the White Sox played Mantle when they realized he couldn't run anymore.

Mantle almost retired after the 1965 season, when his shoulder hurt so badly he couldn't throw, and in 1967 he moved to first base to ease the strain on his arm and legs. But after the 1968 season, Mantle was at the end of the line, and there were no more adjustments that could forestall the inevitable. He had just hit .237, the lowest average of his career, hit 18 home runs, and had driven in just 54 runs. The only time since his rookie year that he'd hit fewer homers was 1963, when he missed more than half the season after breaking his foot and damaging his knee crashing into the center field fence in Baltimore. Although he had the highest OPS on a weak-hitting Yankees team, Mantle was a liability in the field and on the bases. He was still a better hitter than the average major leaguer, but he no longer hit like Mickey Mantle.

Although Mantle was still the most dangerous hitter in a decidedly non-menacing Yankees lineup, that was not the main reason his fans (and the Yankees) wished he could play in 1969. Baseball was losing more than just a great player, for Mantle, in many ways, was the face of baseball in the 1950s and early 1960s, a sanitized product in baseball's last innocent era. Willie Mays and Hank Aaron were outstanding players, but the face of baseball in the 1950s had to be a white face. Blacks were too new to major league baseball to define an era. They were symbols of tolerance, integration, and of a change in the game, but they were not symbolic of the game's essence. Mantle was.

All winter, there were rumors that Mantle would retire, but he denied them. In December, Dick Young wrote a column indicating that Mantle told him he would probably quit. There was a brief labor dispute in February 1969, but when it ended and the Yankees reported to Fort Lauderdale, Mantle had still not made a formal announcement. Nor had he signed a contract. Manager Ralph Houk said that if Mantle wanted to retire, Houk would not try to talk him out of it, as he had done after the 1965 season.

On the last day of February, the Yankees said they expected Mantle to sign the following day. He flew to Florida and breakfasted with Yankees President Mike Burke, but did not sign a contract. Instead, the Yankees called a press conference at the Yankee Clipper Hotel, at which Mantle announced his retirement, effective immediately. "I can't hit anymore," he said. "There's no use trying."[13] He would not be a coach for the Yankees or be connected with them in any way, but would instead concentrate on his many business interests, principally Mickey Mantle's Country Cookin', a Southern restaurant chain. Mantle told Dr. Sidney Gaynor, the Yankees' physician, that he might as well retire too, since without Mickey around, there wouldn't be much work for him.

Mantle was almost as renowned for his injuries as he was for his great accomplishments. Stan Musial, when asked what Mantle had that no other player of his generation had, smiled ruefully and said, "Two bad legs."[14] "I saw him limp, limp, limp," said pitcher Tex Clevenger, "and then go into a ballgame with both legs taped from his ankle to his crotch, steal second and put himself into scoring position to win the game."[15] "Mickey was just super-human," said Tom Tresh. "He had so much talent that he could play through his injuries. We didn't even know how he was playing through them. What could he have done if he wasn't hurt all the time?"[16]

Or if he'd taken better care of himself. One Mets player recalled being invited to speak at a banquet in Connecticut and learning that he was the first ballplayer to be invited by the group in four years. "Their last experience," he said, "was with Mantle as a keynote speaker. He showed up drunk, passed

onbertbert4ononon

out at the head table, cut his mouth, and they had to lead him off the dais with blood running out of his mouth. The guy who was in charge of the banquet decided it just wasn't worth having another ballplayer."[17]

While most fans didn't know of Mantle's private weaknesses, his teammates did, and they still idolized him. Clete Boyer named a son after him, as did Tresh. "He even weighed 7 pounds 7 ounces," said Tresh, "and since Mickey's number is 7, it was a natural."[18]

"Mickey was my hero," said former catcher Doc Edwards. "I don't think I ever told him that when I played with him, but he was. I had the best seat in the house, right behind home plate, and I saw all of the great ones—Killebrew, Aaron, Mays—but there was only one guy, who when he came to the plate when I was sitting behind it, made me feel like home plate had been plugged in. That was Mick. The hair stood up on my arms. It stood up on my neck. It was amazing."[19]

J.C. Martin was another catcher with a choice seat. "Guys would come up to the Yankees," Martin said, "and they'd say, 'Here is another Mickey Mantle.' They said it when [Marv] Throneberry came up and they said it when [Bobby] Murcer came up. Bobby used to wear his clothes and hat like Mantle, and Throneberry did, too. Tom Tresh was another one. But, hey, nobody's another Mantle and we all knew it. Nobody in the world can be another Mickey Mantle. He was the greatest I ever saw. You'd watch the guy take batting practice, and he swung just like everybody else, but when he hit the ball, it didn't come down. *It just didn't come down.*"[20]

"I got called up in 1958," recalled pitcher Johnny James, "and we were in Detroit. I was sitting in the bullpen when Mickey hit that ball off the roof at Briggs Stadium. It was the loudest crack of the bat I'd ever heard in my life. I'd only been there a few days, and I didn't know if I should be impressed, or if he did that all the time. Everybody else in the bullpen was going nuts, so I thought maybe that wasn't something he did all the time. My greatest recollection is the sound of the ball going off that bat. It was the loudest I'd ever heard in my life."

James first saw Mantle in 1951, Mickey's first spring with the Yankees. That year the Giants, who normally trained in Phoenix, swapped with the Yankees, who trained in St. Petersburg, to give the fans in Florida and Arizona a glimpse of a different team. The fans in Phoenix had a treat, for they got major league baseball's first look at 19-year-old Mickey Mantle. James, a high school student, attended a Yankees exhibition with a few of his friends.

The game was at old Gilmore Field in Hollywood. We'd heard so much about Mantle that spring—about his great speed, his great power. The first time Mantle came up he hit a really hard single over the pitcher's head. The next batter hit a sharp line drive to left field on one hop. Usually, a runner on first would get to second. Mantle went from first to third as fast as anybody I'd ever seen in my life. They didn't come close to throwing him out. You could hear about thirteen thousand people take in their breath watching him run from first to third. Thirteen thousand people gasped at once.[21]

When he first came to the big leagues, Mantle was a shy country boy. By the 1960s, he'd become comfortable in New York, but he never forgot how lonely he'd been as a rookie and often went out of his way to make young players feel welcome. "I remember walking through the clubhouse my first day," said outfielder Archie Moore. "Mickey was sitting in the whirlpool, and he motioned me over and introduced himself—like I really needed to be introduced to know who he was."[22]

Twenty-two-year-old outfielder Tom Shopay was called up to the Yankees for the final month of the 1967 season. In just his third game, he hit a three-run homer against the Twins. "I was so happy," Shopay recalled, "that I was laughing when I crossed home plate and came into the dugout. Mantle came over to me and *he* started laughing. He said, 'I can't believe how happy you are.' I said, 'You cannot believe how I feel now.' He said, 'Yeah, I can.'" Jim Bouton was in the Yankees' bullpen and retrieved the ball, which Mantle signed for Shopay. "He signed it," Shopay said, "and underneath his name he wrote, 'nice going.' You don't forget things like that."[23]

Another story about Mantle bears repeating, even though it may be apocryphal. As a former Yankee told the tale, a number of players, including Whitey Ford, were in a bar in Detroit. A member of the traveling party, either a writer or a front office employee (the player couldn't remember) was blond, relatively young, and had a prosthetic leg. Ford walked up to two Detroiters who had been imbibing freely and pointed to him. "Do you know who that is?" he asked the men. They didn't. "That's Mickey Mantle," Ford replied. To someone who had consumed a dozen or so beers, the man could pass for Mantle. Ford brought them over to "Mickey's" table, and one of the men said that they had heard of the terrible condition of Mantle's legs. He wanted to know how bad Mickey's legs really were. The man lifted up his pant leg to reveal the prosthesis, leaving two inebriated Detroit fans with what they believed to be the scoop of the century.[24]

Now Mantle was gone, and the Yankees wouldn't be the same. "You missed his presence in the clubhouse," said catcher Jake Gibbs. "That was the number one thing. Mickey had become a friend to so many people. He had become a friend of mine. When I first came up, Mickey kind of looked after me. I didn't run with him at night, but he liked me and we became friends over the years."[25]

"He liked me," was one of the proudest statements many Yankees veterans made about their careers. To be liked by Mickey Mantle was a wonderful thing, something to treasure for a lifetime. Hal Stowe was in a number of Yankees training camps and got to know Mantle fairly well. "Even after Mantle got out of baseball," said Stowe, "he'd let me know when he was coming through Gastonia [where Stowe operated a family restaurant]. And for the short time I was up there, he treated me just as nice."[26] Stowe pitched in only one major league game, but 40 years later, despite the frustrations of his baseball career, he was able to say proudly that the great Mickey Mantle had been a friend of his.

When former Yankees are asked to recall their greatest moments, many speak of events involving Mantle rather than themselves. Pitcher Dooley Womack's biggest thrill as a Yankee was the game in which Mantle hit his 500th home run. Womack (who saved the Yankees' win) and Mantle were the last two Yankees in the locker room after the game, and Mantle thanked Womack for making the moment special. If the Yankees had lost, he said, the home run wouldn't have meant nearly as much.

"The biggest thrill I had in baseball," said former Yankees infielder Len Boehmer, "was on June 8, 1969, when Mantle retired. It was *awesome*. I've got goose bumps right now just thinking about it. I think of all the other things that happened to me, and I don't get the goose bumps. But I think of that and they just pop up immediately. It was an awesome experience."[27]

Billy Cowan joined the Yankees in 1969, the first year Mantle was not with the club. "Any time he showed up," Cowan said, "it was a different clubhouse. It was like a god walked in there."[28] "When Mickey walked into the clubhouse [in 1969]," said Shopay, "there was an air in there. When he wasn't there, there was something missing. He was the last of an era that was gone—the Phil Rizzutos and the Whitey Fords. It was as if we had to start a new era and begin all over again because it just didn't seem the same."[29]

It wouldn't be the same for the Yankees, but would it be the same for baseball when Mantle was no longer a Yankee? He wasn't even close to being the best player in the game by 1968, but he was a presence. He was even cheered for striking out, which he did frequently. Baseball had one of the more difficult years in its history in 1968, and it was not a good time for the game to lose an all-American hero.

Not only was Mantle gone, but many other stars of his generation were coming down the home stretch. Willie Mays would turn 38 in May and Hank Aaron and Roberto Clemente were in their mid–30s. New heroes were needed, but unfortunately two players who'd seemed on the verge of stardom, Tony Conigliaro and Jim Palmer, had been the victims of some very bad luck.

If the Red Sox's Human Resources Department was looking to hire a hero, Conigliaro would have been a terrific candidate. First, he was a good ballplayer, not a terrific all-around athlete like Mantle, but a solid hitter with a good power stroke perfectly suited for the inviting Fenway Park left field wall. Conigliaro was handsome and personable, and was a local boy who'd grown up in East Boston. He sang in local night clubs and, with his dark good looks, was the heart-throb of almost every young female baseball fan in Boston and of many young ladies who didn't know the pitching rubber from the third base coach. He appeared on "The Dating Game" and, like Angels pitcher Bo Belinsky, dated actress Mamie Van Doren.

Conigliaro's penchant for injury was almost as bad as Mantle's. The start of his professional career was delayed after he broke his thumb punching a man he thought was trying to move in on his high school girlfriend. In 1964, after just one season in the lowly New York-Penn League, the 19-year-old opened the season in center field in Yankee Stadium. He hit the first pitch he saw at Fenway Park for a home run and hit his 20th home run of the season in the first game of a July 26 doubleheader against the Indians, putting him within reach of the rookie record of 38. In the second game, however, Cleveland's Pedro Ramos hit Conigliaro, who was notorious for crowding the plate, and broke his arm. He missed about six weeks and finished the year with 24 homers.

In 1965, Conigliaro led the league with 32 home runs despite missing three weeks after a Wes Stock pitch broke his wrist. In spring training in 1967, a pitch from teammate John Wyatt hit him in the back and fractured his collarbone.

Five months later, Conigliaro was hit again, and this time it was much more serious. On August 17, 1967, Ted Williams told Ed Penney, a friend of Conigliaro's who was visiting his sons at Williams' baseball camp, "Tell Tony that he's crowding the plate. Tell him to back off."[30] The following evening, Penney saw Conigliaro before the game and repeated what Williams had told him. Conigliaro laughed. He'd already told his brother Billy that he was going to move even closer.

Just before he stepped to the plate that night against Angels right-hander Jack Hamilton, Tony told Coach Bobby Doerr he was looking for Hamilton to throw him an outside slider, which meant he would be leaning into the pitch more than usual.[31] Instead of the outside slider he was expecting, however, Hamilton, who had a history of wildness, threw Conigliaro a high, inside fastball. Most who saw the incident said Conigliaro froze. "I yanked my head at the last split-second," he said, "and wouldn't you know it, my batting helmet flew off just as the pitch hit me on the left side of the head—on the temple. That's all I remember."[32]

A man was once killed by a pitch in a major league game. Many have been knocked unconscious and nearly died. But there may never have been an injury as gruesome and ugly as Conigliaro's. When he was photographed in his hospital bed, the handsome face that had enchanted the women of Boston was grossly disfigured by a closed, blackened left eye. "I woke up in the hospital," he said, "and my left eye was damned near out of its socket, like maybe three inches."[33]

Less than a month later, Conigliaro went to Fenway Park and had his brother Billy pitch to him. He could barely see the ball, and although he hit a couple of pitches solidly, he was guessing where the ball was. He missed the rest of the season and the World Series.

When Conigliaro reported to Winter Haven in the spring of 1968, he had to answer two threshold questions. Would he back off the plate and perhaps lose his aggressiveness, and if he didn't, would he be able to see the ball well enough to hit major league pitching? His injured left eye was the one that, as a right-handed batter, was closest to the pitcher and the key to picking up the ball.

During his first batting practice session of the spring, Conigliaro hit a couple of balls over the fence. "Tony's going to be OK," manager Dick Williams said. "I was watching him closely and he didn't flinch a bit."[34] Afterwards, when asked about the possibility that pitchers would throw at him to intimidate him, Conigliaro said that the first time that happened he would charge the mound with his bat.

In his second game of the spring, he got a single and double and drove in a run. He started well, and for a while seemed to be his old self, but by the end of the exhibition season he had just ten hits in 62 trips to the plate for a .161 average. At one point he struck out eight times in ten at-bats. Just before opening day, Conigliaro went to Boston and visited an eye specialist.

The news wasn't good. The vision in Conigliaro's damaged eye was deteriorating, and the doctor told him he couldn't play in 1968 and would probably never be able to play again. At the age of 24, with 104 big league home runs, it appeared as though Conigliaro's career was over.

The Red Sox announced that Conigliaro would be placed on the disabled list rather than classified as voluntarily retired, so that he could collect his estimated $45,000 salary and accrue the additional year he needed to qualify for a pension. It was expected that after the year was over, owner Tom Yawkey would offer him a sinecure position as a scout, for that was the way Yawkey treated his players. In the 1940s, a Sox farmhand named Chuck Koney lost a leg when a stove exploded at his home, and he had been a Red Sox scout ever since.

During the summer of 1968, Conigliaro tried to nurture his singing career, and although he didn't have a great voice, his fame opened some doors. He sang *Secret Love* as Joe Garagiola's guest on the *Tonight Show* and performed in several Boston-area nightclubs. But Conigliaro was a baseball player, not a singer, and if he couldn't see well enough to hit, perhaps he could pitch, as he'd done at St. Mary's High School. He asked the Red Sox if he could go to the Florida Instructional League in the fall and try his luck on the mound. On August 14, almost a year to the day after he'd been hit, Conigliaro took batting practice. After swinging for an hour, he said his vision was better than it had been in months.

In October, the Red Sox made Conigliaro available in the expansion draft, but neither the Pilots nor Royals thought he was worth a $175,000 gamble. The same day the draft was taking place, he headed for Florida, where in his first start, he pitched three innings and gave up three runs. Afterwards, he said he was pleased.

Conigliaro's second start was a disaster. He gave up 11 hits and 15 runs in just 2⅓ innings. He threw 80 pitches and experienced great difficulty with his control, walking six and hitting one batter. In the course of his two disappointing outings, however, Conigliaro had discovered that while he could not pitch, he could see well enough to hit. He played the outfield after his pitching was done, got a couple of hits, and saw the ball well.

After the Instructional League season ended at Thanksgiving, he returned to Boston for an eye exam and received a good report. "I will be in right field next year," he said in early December.[35] "We're counting on him," GM Dick O'Connell said later in the month. "His left eye is so good it's truly amazing."[36]

"If Conigliaro returns to what he was before he got hurt," said Carl Yastrzemski, "we might have a dynasty in Boston."[37] "A comeback by Tony Conigliaro would be good for all baseball," added new commissioner Bowie Kuhn.[38] Conigliaro's doctors continued to issue encouraging reports, and in early December, he hit the soft tosses of Red Sox pitcher Darrell Brandon in an indoor cage at Harvard and said he saw the ball without any trouble.

Conigliaro had an active winter, visiting Vietnam on a goodwill tour, singing in nightclubs, appearing on the *Merv Griffin Show,* and hunting Asian sheep for *The American Sportsman* television show. In January, he said he could see fine when he looked out of both eyes, but when he covered the right one, the damaged left eye was about 95 percent. When he reported to Winter Haven for spring training, Conigliaro said his vision was fine and he expected to have a great season.

On March 7, Conigliaro made his first exhibition appearance, going hitless in two at-bats while drawing a walk and scoring a run. Every time Conigliaro stepped to the plate, either in batting practice or in a game, he received a thunderous ovation. Everyone was waiting to see whether he flinched on inside pitches, which he didn't. Better still, he was pulling the ball and hitting it hard. On March 27, Conigliaro hit a home run into a stiff Tampa wind against the Reds' Mel Queen, his first since August 8, 1967. He then hit homers on consecutive days.

When the Red Sox opened their season on April 8 at Baltimore, Tony Conigliaro was the right fielder, batting in the fifth position. He scored the winning run in the 12th inning of a 5–4 Boston victory. Six days later, the Red Sox opened their home season against the Orioles before the largest Opening Day crowd ever at Fenway (35,341). When Conigliaro was introduced before the game, he received such a heartfelt, welcoming ovation that it required a strenuous effort for him to fight back tears. The Sox won again, and he drove in the winning run with a fifth-inning single.

Between the Baltimore and Boston openers, the Red Sox played in Cleveland. In the 13th inning of a game on April 11, Indians manager Alvin Dark summoned Jack Hamilton to the mound, the first time Hamilton had faced Conigliaro since the fateful evening of August 18, 1967.

Afterward, both men played down the significance of the confrontation. Conigliaro said he knew the beaning was an accident, and Hamilton said that he was very sorry about what had happened and that he regarded Conigliaro as he did any other batter. For the record, Conigliaro bunted and flied out in two appearances against Hamilton, and the Red Sox won the game 2–1 in 16 innings.

The Red Sox did not create the dynasty Yastrzemski had predicted, but it was certainly not Conigliaro's fault. He played 141 games, more than he'd played in three of his four prior seasons, and batted .255 with 20 home runs and 82 RBI, winning the Hutch Award for his comeback. Baseball had one of its heroes back, in a touching, heartwarming manner that gave the game a boost it needed badly during the spring of 1969.

Orioles right hander Jim Palmer also emerged from limbo in 1969. During the 1966 World Series, the 20-year-old Palmer shut out the Dodgers in Game 2. The losing pitcher that afternoon was Sandy Koufax, making his final major league appearance. Perhaps, as the old idol left the stage, the young Palmer would take his place. Palmer was handsome like Koufax, he was intelligent like the Dodgers left-hander, and he had a personality that would land him in the Orioles' broadcast booth for years after he retired.

The only thing Palmer had in common with Koufax in 1967 and 1968 was having an arm that prevented them from pitching. Palmer pitched only 49 major league innings in 1967 and none in 1968. His problems began while pitching a one-hitter against the Yankees in May 1967, when he felt some discomfort in his shoulder. Palmer lasted only an inning in his next start and spent most of what remained of the 1967 season and all of 1968 in the minors or on the disabled list. He became so discouraged that he contemplated switching in the opposite direction as Conigliaro. Conigliaro, who could throw but couldn't see, tried to become a pitcher, while Palmer, who could see but not throw, thought about trying to come back as a position player.[39] As in the case of Conigliaro, it might have been a quixotic quest for Palmer, who in 1966, his last full season, had batted .096 with 33 strikeouts in 73 at-bats.

In the fall of 1968, Palmer was also made available in the expansion draft, but neither Kansas City nor Seattle wanted to take a chance on a sore-shouldered pitcher, even one who'd thrown a shutout in the World Series just two years earlier. Palmer went to the Florida Instructional League and then played for the Santurce Crabbers in the Puerto Rican Winter League.

In Puerto Rico, the pain miraculously disappeared. No one, including Palmer, knew why, but suddenly he could throw hard again. "It was a miracle as far as I was concerned," he said, "like getting a new toy."[40] Palmer discarded the notion of playing another position and reported to the Orioles' camp in Miami with a new lease on life and a place in the starting rotation. Although he missed some time with a back injury, Palmer finished 16–4 with a 2.34 ERA and pitched a no-hitter against Oakland.

In 1969, as Conigliaro and Palmer made their reappearance on the major league stage, a youngster named Reggie Jackson received national attention for the first time. The Kansas City Athletics made Jackson the second selection in the 1966 free agent draft, and in 1968, his first full season in the major leagues, he hit 29 home runs. Jackson had a lot of tools, for he was big and strong, had a lot of power, could run, and had a powerful throwing arm. He struck out a lot, but so did Babe Ruth and Mickey Mantle.

Jackson also wanted very much to be a star. Some talented players shun the limelight, preferring to let their performances speak for them, but no one was more eager for attention than Reginald Martinez Jackson. Prior to the mid–1960s, stars had been, for the most part, anointed by the media. There were a couple of players, like Babe Ruth and Dizzy Dean, who basked in the limelight and had a knack for the colorful quote, but for the most part the image of baseball stars was created by sportswriters. Interviews were not a staple of sports reporting, and when they were conducted, questions were usually predictable softballs. Inventive reporters were happy to make up clever quotes to supplement the drab material supplied by players.

It was considered presumptuous for a young player to seek the limelight; fame was supposed to come when the media decided he had earned it, a process that paralleled American history. In the early days of United States politics, it was considered undignified to campaign openly for political office. Candidates had to be coy and at least pretend to be coaxed into running. They didn't travel around the country seeking votes; for the most part they stayed close to home and let surrogates do their bidding. It wasn't until the 20th century that frenetic personal campaigns became part of American politics.

Prior to the 1960s, baseball players were expected to emulate the reluctance of 18th- and 19th-century candidates. When Jim Bouton and fellow rookies Joe Pepitone and Phil Linz cultivated the New York media and sought attention, even though they weren't doing all that much on the field, Yankees veterans let them know that this was not "big league" behavior, and it was certainly not the way a Yankee was expected to behave.

By the mid–1960s, television was replacing print as the medium through which many Americans got their sporting news, and the camera gave players the opportunity to generate their own charisma, rather than waiting for reporters to bestow it upon them. Players like Jackson and Denny McLain could express themselves in their own fashion, rather than relying on reporters to communicate their thoughts to the public. And they weren't modest. When asked about his strikeouts prior to the 1969 season, the 22-year-old Jackson replied, "I have light tower power, I know that. So it would be acceptable if I could cut my strikeouts down to about 115."[41]

Jackson would not fully realize his celebrity potential until he arrived in New York in 1977, but in 1969 he got his first taste of stardom by hitting home runs at a pace that challenged the single-season record of Roger Maris. There were a number of years in which some slugger ran ahead of the pace of Ruth and Maris, because both, in their record-breaking seasons, started slowly. Ruth hit a flurry of home runs in September, and Maris got hot during the summer months after hitting just one round-tripper in April.

By the end of June 1969, Jackson had 29 home runs. Maris had 27 on the same date and Ruth 25. After the offensive doldrums of 1968, it was delightful to write and talk about baseball records that didn't involve shutouts or strikeouts, and the media showered Jackson with attention. He appeared shirtless on the cover of *Sports Illustrated* to show off his rippling muscles and never disappointed reporters by failing to deliver an interesting quote.

Like most hitters who were ahead of Maris and Ruth, Jackson dropped off the pace in the second half of the season, but still finished with 47 homers and 118 runs batted in. He also struck out 142 times, well above his goal of 115, but who really cared? Home runs and strikeouts were exciting; ground balls to second base were not, and baseball needed excitement.

In baseball's search for new heroes in the late 1960s, they found a couple of old ones, icons from the era when the game had an undisputed hold on American sports fans. In the years immediately following World War II, during one of the great postwar baseball booms, Joe DiMaggio and Ted Williams were probably the two most famous athletes in America. In 1968 and 1969, both returned to baseball full-time for the first time in several years.

There were a number of strategies for increasing attendance, but the one that appeared foolproof was to move to another city. With a new stadium and a honeymoon period, every team that changed base since the Braves left Boston in 1952 experienced dramatic attendance growth—until the Athletics moved to Oakland in 1968. After years of trying to get out of Kansas City, Charley Finley relocated his Athletics to an area in which the San Francisco Giants, running unopposed, were struggling. While other teams doubled and tripled attendance in their new homes, Finley's As drew only about 100,000 more than they had in Kansas City the previous year.

Looking to make a big splash, Finley signed DiMaggio, the biggest baseball name in the Bay Area, to a two-year contract as executive vice president and advisor on personnel. His real job, however, was to be Joe DiMaggio. During spring training, he donned his familiar number 5, on the back of a very unfamiliar green and gold uniform, and worked with the A's hitters. During the season DiMaggio served as coach without portfolio in the Oakland dugout.

DiMaggio's role was mostly ceremonial, but the next year Theodore Samuel Williams was named to a much more substantive position, manager of the Washington Senators. Since retiring after the 1960 season, Williams had been a spring training hitting instructor for the Red Sox, but spent most of his time hunting and fishing and serving as a representative for Sears.

While DiMaggio was shy and often unsociable, Williams had a booming personality that matched his flamboyance on the field. Love him or hate him, people never forgot Ted Williams. Egotistical, brash, and profane, Williams alienated the Boston media, and many felt it cost him the 1941 and 1942 MVP Awards. He refused to tip his cap to the fans or to leave the dugout for "curtain calls", and despite his great accomplishments, Williams' relationship with fans and the media was testy. But baseball needed excitement, and Ted Williams had always attracted attention. The Senators, whose performance and attendance had been abysmal, had a new owner who, like Charley Finley, understood the importance of recognizable names, even if they weren't playing.

The "new" Washington Senators were born in 1961 as an expansion franchise that replaced Calvin Griffith's "old" Senators, who moved to Minneapolis following the 1960 season. The new club proved a suitable substitute for the old, maintaining the tradition of finishing at or near the bottom of the American League standings each year. In their maiden season, the new club finished 61–100, tied for ninth, and in subsequent years they finished tenth, tenth, ninth, eighth, and eighth. Under the patient leadership of Gil Hodges, however, the Senators showed gradual improvement, and in 1967 seemed on the verge of respectability, with a 76–85 mark that placed them in a 6th-place tie with Baltimore.

After the 1967 season, Hodges, who had a year remaining on his contract, left to manage the Mets. He'd been a hero when he played in Brooklyn, and the Mets had coveted him ever since Casey Stengel retired in 1965. They finally convinced the Senators to release Hodges from his obligation in return for young pitcher Bill Denehy and $100,000.

To replace Hodges, the Senators hired 40-year-old Jim Lemon, a former slugging outfielder for the "old" Senators, who guided the club back to their familiar perch in the basement with a 65–96 mark. The 1968 Washington entry was the last tenth-place club in American League history, for the following year baseball would switch to four six-team divisions. The poor performances of the Senators had a dampening effect on attendance, which bottomed out at 535,604 in 1963 and, after peaking at 770,868 in 1967, dropped precipitously to 546,661 in 1968, the lowest attendance of any major league team.

Following the death of co-owner James Johnston from cancer on December 28, 1967, his partner, James H. Lemon, Sr. (no relation to manager James R. Lemon) assumed control of the club. Johnston and Lemon were the last survivors of ten partners who, led by Elwood "Pete" Quezada, put up $300,000 each to acquire the expansion franchise in 1961.

Lemon was not that interested in running the Senators and said that in any event he didn't have the money to buy out Johnston's estate. Owning a baseball team could be fun, but it wasn't very enjoyable when your team was mired in the second division and hemorrhaging money every season. Once, Lemon visited his friend Dwight Eisenhower at Walter Reed Hospital after Eisenhower had suffered one of his series of heart attacks. "What's the matter with your ballclub?" the ex-president asked. "I listened to those broadcasts all the time and some of those games made me ill."[42] Lemon wanted to sell, but as *The Sporting News* pointed out, "The Senators do not have much to offer, except a last place club, a farm system that needs help and a comparatively new, yet inadequate, stadium."[43]

One potential buyer was Lamar Hunt, founder of the American Football League and owner of the Kansas City Chiefs. It was commonly assumed that if Hunt purchased the Washington club, he would move it to his hometown of Dallas. By early November, however, Hunt was out of the running and Lemon was negotiating with four different groups. One included comedian Bob Hope, another Stan Musial, and a third was led by general manager John Quinn of the Phillies. The fourth group, a partnership of businessmen Robert Short and Jeno Paulucci, appeared to have the inside track.

Short, 51, was a Minnesotan and a graduate of Georgetown Law School. He owned Admiral Motor Freight, Gopher Airlines, and a number of hotels, including the Leamington and Sir Francis Drake Hotels in Minneapolis. Short was very active in politics, contributing $100,000 to Hubert Humphrey's presidential campaign in 1968 and serving as Treasurer of the Democratic National Committee. He also had previous experience as a sports mogul, having bought the Minneapolis Lakers for a nominal sum, moved the team to Los Angeles, and sold it to Jack Kent Cooke for $5 million.

After a difficult negotiation, Short became the owner of the Washington Senators for $10,000,000. Even before the sale was consummated, there were rumors that the franchise would be relocated again. Short couldn't move to his home state of Minnesota, since Griffith had already placed the prior incarnation of the Senators there. He had moved the Lakers, however, and from the time he acquired the Washington franchise, baseball people suspected that wanderlust might strike him at any time, particularly if he lost money in Washington and a distant city offered him a new stadium and a few other goodies.

When he was introduced as the new owner, Short said he did not buy the club with the intention of moving it, but would consider leaving Washington "as a retreat action." "If they don't want the Senators here," he said, "if there's no radio, no box office support—then Dallas or Milwaukee or some other places do."[44] Short's immediate economic goals for the Senators were to upgrade the park, increase safety in the area, and improve the broadcast package, which he said was the worst in the major leagues.

Short couldn't survive in Washington if he couldn't improve the Senators' attendance. "I can round up a girls' team and draw 500,000," he said. "That's what attendance was last year."[45] One of the difficulties in attracting spectators was that Short wasn't going to have a very good team, and his only recognizable star was mammoth slugging outfielder Frank Howard. Later, Short would eviscerate his team in search of big names, trading promising young players for washed-up former stars like Denny McLain, but without free agency, there weren't a lot of options.[46]

While players were bound by the reserve clause, there were a number of prospective managers who were free agents, and Short's best play was to put a big name in the dugout. The hapless Mets had worked wonders with Casey Stengel just a few years earlier, drawing fans to the Polo Grounds while his Mets lost game after game. Jim Lemon had been neither charismatic nor successful, and finishing in last place in 1968 ensured that he would not be on Short's team. Both Lemon and general manager George Selkirk were fired in early February.

"When Short told me he was looking for a manager," said Senators general counsel Stan Bregman, "my suggestion was that it would be great for baseball to hire Elston Howard, but Short didn't know who the hell Howard was. He used to call the umpires referees and the manager the coach when he first came in. That was his knowledge of baseball. So we were sitting in his office and he called [Yankees President] Mike Burke and asked him about Howard. I couldn't hear what Burke was saying, but when Short hung up, he said, 'I don't think I want him.'"[47]

As baseball's first African-American manager, Howard would have drawn attention, but Short didn't think he was famous enough. The Redskins, who shared a stadium with the Senators, had recently hired Vince Lombardi to coach their team, and there was no greater star in the coaching firmament than Vince Lombardi, winner of two Super Bowls and five NFL championships in nine years.

Short needed someone with the star quality of Lombardi and started thinking about possibilities. Mickey Mantle was undecided whether he wanted to play in 1969, but Mantle didn't seem serious enough to be a manager.

Charley Finley already had Joe DiMaggio. Yogi Berra was a coach for the Mets, but Yogi had managed once and been found wanting.

There was one unemployed former baseball star whose name was magical and whose absence had enhanced his legend. Ted Williams, however, had indicated that he never wanted to manage. "I think the job of managing a ballclub," he said just before his final season as a player, "is the worst job in the big leagues. At least as far as I'm concerned. I wouldn't want it."[48] After eight years away from the game, however, Williams missed baseball. How much fishing can a man do?

"I think the only name [Short] knew in baseball," said Bregman, "was Ted Williams. Ted was always in his mind."[49] Short needed someone like Williams, but Williams didn't really need Short, for he was earning a reported $100,000 a year as a spokesman for Sears, with no pressure and lots of free time. But when Bob Short determined to do something, it usually got done.

The previous summer, Williams, with John Underwood as his ghost writer, told his own story for the first time, in a series of articles for *Sports Illustrated*.[50] He appeared, at least in Underwood's carefully chosen words, to have mellowed from the brash, argumentative man who frequently clashed with reporters and fans. Williams admitted that at times he'd acted immaturely and caused some of his own troubles, but proceeded to dig up perceived slights and engage the battle once more. The final installment presented Williams' theories on hitting, a treatise that was eventually expanded into a book. Jim Lemon had been so impressed he made copies of the article and gave it to each of his players. It didn't help them, and it didn't save Lemon.[51]

Four days before the start of spring training, following an intense, ten-day courtship, Short introduced Ted Williams as the new manager of the Washington Senators, with a five-year contract at $100,000 per season and a number of fringe benefits. The entire package was reportedly worth $1.5 million at a time when Willie Mays was earning about $100,000.

"He gave him everything in the world," said Bregman. "He gave him an option to buy 10 percent of the team. He gave him a free apartment in the Shoreham West Apartments. He let him hire whoever he wanted. Short could be a very persuasive guy, a very affable guy, a very charming guy and a very lovable guy—when he wanted people to like him."[52]

Short told Williams he had seen him play in Minneapolis when he was a boy and worn holes in his pants watching him hit.[53] Williams called Short one of the smartest men he'd ever met. Short was smart in the sense that he recognized the value of spending money and publicizing it, something most baseball owners did not do. Short appreciated the marketing benefit of a $1.5 million manager just as owner Sonny Werblin of the Jets capitalized on the publicity generated by Joe Namath's $400,000 contract.

Given Williams' well-known antipathy toward the press, the most antic-ipated moment of his new assignment was not Opening Day, but the first press conference. The questions were predictable. Was he tempted to activate himself as a pinch-hitter at the age of 50? He was not. What did he know about the Senators' players? Not much. Would he be able to deal with the press? Washington wouldn't be a problem, he said. "There was only one little town I had trouble in.[54] Don't believe all of those stories you've heard about me." Dick Young, who'd covered Williams as a player, speculated that Williams could be the first manager to throw a reporter across the Potomac.[55]

Williams' first year was a tremendous success, as the Senators had their finest season in many summers. The Presidential opener attracted a record 45,113, including new President Richard Nixon, new Commissioner Bowie Kuhn, and American League President Joe Cronin. Short, Treasurer of the Democratic National Committee, and Bregman, a Humphrey campaign man-ager, sat with Republican President Nixon and made cautious small talk. Despite all of the celebrities in the stands, the greatest ovation of the day was reserved for Theodore Samuel Williams.

True to his word, Williams got on well with the press, and he not only attracted attention, he instilled spirit into the Washington club, taught some of the players how to hit, and also how to win. He was loud and profane, but he was enthusiastic. Williams wasn't a great tactical manager, but he had coaches for that. "Williams did not have any confidence in himself as a man-ager in the beginning," said Bregman. "Short had to hire Joe Camacho to stand next to Williams so he could advise Ted on what to do next."[56] "Ted concentrated on boosting morale and improving our hitters," said pitcher Dave Baldwin, "and he was very good at both of those tasks."[57]

Williams convinced some of the Senators to stop swinging for the fences and simply make solid contact. Eddie Brinkman, a light-hitting shortstop who'd batted .187 in 1968, hit .266. Mike Epstein, the scholarly, enigmatic minor league star who couldn't decide if he wanted to be Babe Ruth or William Saroyan, went from 13 home runs to 30.

At the All-Star break, the Senators were 51–50, in fourth place in the Eastern Division. No Washington team had finished above .500 for a full season since 1952, when Williams was flying bomber missions over Korea. There'd been years they hadn't won much more than 51 games all season. In 1969, Williams brought the Senators home with an 86–76 record, the most wins a Senators club had posted since 1945. Attendance jumped from 546,661 to 918,106, the second-highest total in Washington history. Short had gotten his money's worth.

The joy was short-lived, for by 1972, Short was tired of Washington and Short and Williams were tired of each other. The Senators became the Texas Rangers, Short was hung in effigy, and not long thereafter Williams went back to hunting and fishing.

Tony Conigliaro's comeback was also brief. In 1970, he was even better than he'd been in 1969, hitting 36 homers and batting in 116 runs. Just a few days after the season ended, however, Conigliaro's world turned upside down. On October 11, his father met him at the airport and told him he'd been traded to the California Angels. Conigliaro was stunned—first, that the Red Sox would trade him, and second, because neither of the two key players the Red Sox received from the Angels, rookie second baseman Doug Griffin and pitcher Ken Tatum, seemed to be adequate compensation for one of the American League's best power hitters. What had caused Tom Yawkey, who'd paid Conigliaro's salary during the summer of 1968, to get rid of him for a rookie and an average relief pitcher?

Conigliaro was very popular in Boston, but after leading the Red Sox to the 1967 pennant by winning the Triple Crown, Carl Yastrzemski became an icon. He hawked bread, mustard, kielbasa, and numerous other commodities, and his face and name seemed to be everywhere. Yawkey liked Conigliaro, but in 1970 he had to make a choice, and he chose Yastrzemski. The problem was that Conigliaro didn't like Yaz and Yaz didn't like Conigliaro. The 1970 Boston clubhouse was not a harmonious one, with a sharp division between the adherents of Yastrzemski and outfielder Reggie Smith and those of Tony Conigliaro.

Fans who saw Yastrzemski on the national stage, in World Series and pennant race games, saw a player diving, hustling, and playing like the superstar Yaz could be when he wanted to. Those who watched him play an entire season, including cold days in April and hot, humid days in late summer when the Red Sox were out of contention, saw a different player, one who often peeled off toward the dugout halfway to first base, stood at home plate and flipped his bat in the air after hitting an infield grounder, and made half-hearted efforts in the field.

Red Sox outfielder Jim Gosger was once told by manager Billy Herman that he was making Yastrzemski look bad because of his hustle. "If Carl got a hit the first time up," Gosger said, "he was into the game. But if he didn't get a hit he wasn't. That's the way he played. Fortunately, he got a lot of hits his first time up. He was a hell of a defensive player when he wanted to be, but he was mostly offensive-minded."[58]

Conigliaro resented Yastrzemski's lack of effort, and he and some other Red Sox players thought the Boston superstar operated under a different set of rules. By the end of the 1970 season, the Red Sox were convinced that one of their star outfielders had to go, and it wasn't going to be the 1967 MVP.

Going to California was devastating, but it was Conigliaro's left eye, which had never fully recovered after his injury, that put a premature end to his career. By 1971, his vision was deteriorating, and he had developed a blind spot that prevented him from seeing certain pitches. Conigliaro hit just four home runs in 74 games with the Angels, he grew frustrated, and his behavior became increasingly erratic. In a 20-inning game during which he struck out five times in eight at-bats, he lost his temper and twice threw violent tantrums directed at plate umpire Merle Anthony. "This man belongs in an insane asylum," said California manager Lefty Phillips.[59]

After the game, Conigliaro called Angels general manager Dick Walsh and the two talked until 4 am. At 5:15 a.m., the Angels hastily called a press conference at which the outfielder announced his retirement at 26, an age when most ballplayers are just beginning their prime years, but by which point Tony C. had already begun and lost two careers.

Conigliaro attempted a third career in 1975 but retired again after just 21 games. He ran a Boston nightclub with his brother Billy, invested in real estate, did some sportscasting, and talked about an acting career. In 1982, as Billy was driving him to the airport for a flight to San Francisco for a job interview, Tony suffered a heart attack that left him in a vegetative state until his death in 1990 at the age of 45.

Jim Palmer's comeback proved lasting. Beginning in 1970, he won 20 or more games eight of the next nine years, capturing three Cy Young Awards in the process. After a 19-year career during which he won 268 games and election to the Hall of Fame, Palmer has been a Baltimore broadcaster for many years.

Reggie Jackson also had staying power, but Denny McLain, like Conigliaro, flamed out quickly. The abuse his shoulder took in 1968 damaged it for good, and although he won 24 games and a second Cy Young Award in 1969, that was his last good season. In two years, he'd pitched 661 regular season innings and 16⅔ more in the World Series with a badly injured shoulder. By 1973, he was out of professional baseball and about to embark on a post-baseball career that included two stretches in prison and a life of thumbing his nose at authority. McLain had always believed he would be forgiven his trespasses as long as was a star, but apparently he never contemplated what would happen when he was no longer winning Cy Young Awards.

In the spring of 1969, as baseball tried to come back from one of the most difficult seasons in its long history, Mickey Mantle was gone, but Ted Williams, Tony Conigliaro, and Jim Palmer were back, and new stars like Denny McLain and Reggie Jackson were making headlines. In a few years, Willie Mays would be gone, as would Williams, but by that time, Nolan Ryan had started throwing no-hitters and breaking strikeout records, and Rod Carew was winning one batting championship after another. When they retired, others, equally talented and charismatic, took their place. *Ball Four* was the first of many tell-all, gossipy sports books, but even after fans learned that professional athletes were as blemished as they were, they continued to follow them online as avidly as their parents had followed *their* heroes in the pages of *The Sporting News*.

Perhaps it was heroes who made baseball popular, or maybe it was the game of baseball, with its opportunities for drama and its thirst for idols, that provided a stage that made heroism inevitable. There would never be someone just like Mickey Mantle or Willie Mays, but there would always be another baseball hero waiting in the wings.

13

Either Miller or
Baseball Has to Go

During the first half of the 1960s, owners had become very adept at controlling expenses, the most significant of which was salaries. The reserve clause made it easier, for all they had to do was offer the players just enough to keep them from finding another profession or to prevent them from jumping if a rival league was formed.

While ticket revenue wasn't showing much growth, baseball's income from television and radio was escalating rapidly, and a $30 million contract signed in 1965 got the players thinking that they should be getting a bigger share of the pie. Had the owners been more receptive and conciliatory at that point, Marvin Miller might be remembered, if at all, as an obscure executive of the Steelworkers Union. But moderation is rarely exercised by those who hold nearly total control of a situation, and baseball owners were no exception. They took a hard line, and instead of the acquiescence they'd received in the past, they got Marvin Miller.

Before Miller arrived on the scene, the players had a union, but it wasn't militant and it lacked leadership. Few players' careers lasted as long as ten years, and most ended sooner. They therefore had less incentive to make a long-term commitment to the union than workers in traditionally unionized fields, who might spend 40 years on the job. Industrial workers were accustomed to unions and saw them as protective; most athletes did not, and many were hostile to the idea of a strong organization, for athletes have unique skills that give them the bargaining power that unskilled laborers lack. The most odious facet of baseball's labor situation was the reserve clause, but most major leaguers thought it was good for baseball. Few favored its elimination.

In the early 1960s, the only outside guidance the players received was from Robert Cannon, a full-time Wisconsin judge who was paid $15,000 per year by the Players Association to serve as its advisor. Cannon committed a limited amount of time to Association affairs and was not confrontational.[1] He dealt with what came before him and focused on minutiae, such as conditions in bullpens and dugouts, water coolers, etc. Cannon, Marvin Miller wrote later, "never met an owner he didn't like."[2]

Cannon continually reminded the players that they were the luckiest men alive to be paid to play ball and claimed that baseball had the "finest relationship between players and management in the history of the sport."[3] In 1964, testifying before Congress, Cannon said that the "thinking of the average major league ballplayer" was "we have it so good we don't know what to ask for next."[4]

Cannon's main goal was to protect what the players already had and lobby for small gains. "[He] would brag about winning reforms such as a water fountain in the bullpen," said Miller in 1969, "and having the benches painted; he concentrated on trivia."[5] Cannon was respectable, personable, and worked well with the owners, who were happy to have such an accommodating adversary. "Of course the owners liked him," said Mets pitcher Larry Miller. "He didn't do anything. He maintained the *status quo*."[6]

When Marvin Miller became the executive director of the Players' Association in 1966, he brought a militancy to the union that frightened the baseball establishment. Here he is seen (right) negotiating with management's John Gaherin (left) and mediator Curtis J. Counts in April 1972 in an attempt to end baseball's first in-season strike.

In January 1966, the Players Association decided to name a full-time Executive Director and gave the job to Cannon. A few days after he accepted the position, however, he changed his mind, for he was unwilling to give up his judge's pension and did not want to relocate to New York. He also said that some players wanted a militant and, if that were the case, he was not the man for the job.

"I wanted Cannon," said Bob Friend, the National League player representative, "but Bob really didn't want it. Jim Bunning and Robin Roberts brought Marvin Miller in, and he was very impressive. He didn't force his way in. He said, 'Fellas, I don't want a long term contract. Let's see if I can do the job and whether you want me. Then we'll sit down and talk about a contract.' That was very impressive."[7]

In the spring of 1966, Marvin Miller was just short of his 49th birthday and gave scant indication of being the man who would shake the game of baseball to the depths of its foundation. Born to a Bronx clothing salesman and a teacher, Miller earned a degree in economics from New York University and then joined the United States government as an economist. He saw active service in World War II and, after the war, became an assistant to the president of the International Association of Machinists.

In 1950, Miller was hired by the United Steelworkers of America, the nation's third-largest labor union. After ten years with the steelworkers, he was named assistant to the president, the position he held at the beginning of 1966. President Johnson had intervened in a bitter 1965 struggle, and there had been too much infighting and political bickering for Miller's taste. He was ready to move on and thought about teaching. He received offers from Harvard and the Carnegie Endowment for International Peace, and was surprised to hear from Professor George Taylor of the University of Pennsylvania regarding the Players Association post.

When George Taylor spoke, Miller listened, for Taylor was an icon in the labor industry. During World War II, he'd been chairman of the War Labor Board, one of whose members was young Marvin Miller. Taylor told Miller that Robin Roberts was looking for candidates to energize the players' union and, based upon Taylor's recommendation, Miller agreed to go for an interview.

Miller did not fit the image of the burly steel union boss. He was thin, an accomplished tennis and handball player, a distinguished looking man with gray hair and a neatly trimmed mustache.[8] Knowing his background, most people who met him were surprised at his soft-spoken, articulate manner. "Marvin is a no-nonsense guy," said one steel executive who had been on the other side of the negotiating table. "He does his homework and knows how to present his facts. He listens and he expects to be listened to. At the same time, he's a gentleman. I've never seen him lose his temper or pound the table."[9]

About the time that Miller was considering the Players Association post, Jimmy Hoffa was trying to bring professional athletes under the Teamsters Union banner. Hoffa, with his history of unsavory relationships and dealings, would have been a much easier mark for the owners. They threw a lot of mud at Miller over the years, but they never accused him of graft or corruption. Miller was a zealous ideologue, but he was an honest one, which made it more difficult for the owners to get rid of him.

Miller was also a baseball fan. A member of the Giants' organization once challenged him to name players from the Dodgers teams of the 1930s. After Miller rattled off the lineup, including the reserves and relief pitchers, the man admitted that Miller knew baseball.

While Miller didn't think much of Cannon, the latter wasn't overly fond of Miller and urged the players to reject him. In 1992, Cannon described Miller as a man "who doesn't have a kind word for anyone" and said that the Players Association shouldn't have hired someone "with a chip on his shoulder, anti-management and anti-ownership."[10]

Cannon and Miller had dramatically different goals. "It is too easy to dismiss Cannon and his tenure with [the] Association as nothing more than an interlude leading up to Marvin Miller['s] arrival in 1966," wrote Charles Korr, "a kind of Kerensky to Miller's Lenin."[11] Easy and probably true, except that Kerensky was much more radical. Cannon wanted the owners to like and respect him, while Miller cared only that they fear him. "The owners' attitude towards the executive director," he said in 1968, "and they vary—are largely irrelevant."[12] If Cannon thought management was justified in its actions, he said so, while Miller rarely admitted the legitimacy of any contrary opinion.

On March 5, 1966, a players' screening committee recommended the hiring of Miller, subject to confirmation by a vote of the players.[13] Before the ballot, Miller planned a tour of major league training camps to meet his prospective constituents, while the owners stepped up their campaign against him. Player reps for the Dodgers and Braves indicated that their clubs might vote against Miller, and Bob Rodgers, rep of the California Angels, issued the following statement: "There is no place in baseball for labor and this man has been associated with labor all his life. We have enjoyed a fine relationship with the owners over the past few years by dealing and bargaining in a friendly manner. We do not believe in forceful, labor-type negotiations."[14]

Rodgers and the rest of the Angels sent a letter to all 600 union members urging them to vote against Miller's nomination. Players' objections to Miller varied. Some didn't like his union background; others thought his proposed salary of $50,000 per year was too high, while still others believed that the person chosen for the job should have a law degree.

Miller made the Angels' camp his first stop on a tour that covered 16 sites in 16 days. Even Rodgers was impressed and said, after meeting Miller, that the Angels might change their minds. Other meetings were equally successful. The players expected Jimmy Hoffa, but what they saw was an educated, calm, dapper man, usually puffing on a cigarette, who convinced the players that he could get them better working conditions.

During a meeting with the Indians, manager Birdie Tebbetts asked, "How can the players be sure you're not a Communist?" He asked if Miller had ever been investigated by the FBI. Miller replied that he had, since he'd worked for government agencies, and asked Tebbetts if *he* had been cleared by the FBI, which of course he had not.[15]

Most players were impressed by Miller's presentation. Others simply felt that anyone the owners hated so virulently must be good for their cause. "When you looked at him," said Cardinals pitcher Tracy Stallard, "he didn't seem very strong. But when he started talking, he got stronger and you changed your mind about him. He'd been in some pretty tough places with the steelworkers. After you heard him talk a couple of times, you knew he meant business."[16]

Miller's contract was approved by a large majority, with only 34 negative votes. There have been many dramatic changes in the history of baseball, including rule revisions, the shift from the dead ball to the lively one, integration, the expansion of the major leagues, and the introduction of radio and television. But none changed the economics of the sport as dramatically as the hiring of Marvin Miller.

On July 1, 1966, Miller began his new job, at a time when the union finances were, he wrote, similar to those of a third world nation.[17] He also began his duties without the general counsel the players had intended him to have. In one of their early meetings with Miller, Robin Roberts told him that his counsel would be former Vice President Richard Nixon.

"I could scarcely think of anyone," Miller wrote, "I would have liked less to work with.... That Roberts would even mention his name showed how little the players knew about labor relations. Or about me."[18] "I sat there stunned, feeling like a rube on 'Candid Camera'.... Nixon represented everything I loathed in American political life."[19]

Miller told the players that Nixon was wrong for the job because he knew nothing about baseball, he would be an owners' man, and he would leave soon because he was planning to run for President in 1968. He insisted that the new Executive Director be permitted to choose his own counsel, and the players agreed.

Miller had insisted that, despite his industrial union background, he would not radicalize the Players Association and, true to his word, he moved cautiously at first, studying the situation and initially proposing no bold initiatives. "I'm not a union organizer," Miller said. "I'm a professional economist with a background in pension plans and mediation."[20] "The important feature about Miller," wrote Charles Korr, "was that he knew labor management law better than anyone the other side ever hired and soon he would know more about baseball than ownership did."[21]

Miller's first observations were that the minimum salary of $7,000 should be higher and the pension plan could be improved. He also hinted that the time would come when the basic premise of baseball economics, the concept that players were property to be bought and sold, would be called into question. Miller didn't intend to get to that point soon, however, and indicated that he was not going to suggest a strike, for the labor situation in baseball was different from that of industry.

The soft sell wasn't successful, as the owners were more interested in demonstrating that they were still in charge than in working collaboratively with the Players Association.[22] Miller quickly let them know that he was not Bob Cannon and that he would not accept their paternalistic attitude. "Never before," wrote Leonard Koppett, "have baseball owners been confronted by someone so well equipped to deal with them. They don't like it."[23] And thus the battle commenced.

Soon after Miller was appointed, the owners claimed that if their money, in the form of proceeds from the All-Star Game, were used to pay the expenses of Miller's office, it would be a violation of the Taft-Hartley Act. They were venturing into dangerous territory, for Miller knew a lot more about Taft-Hartley than they did. If the owners thought the Act applied to baseball, he said, they were admitting that baseball was interstate commerce and that the association was a labor group with which they would then be required to negotiate in good faith through a process governed by labor law. Miller was asked whether *he* considered the Players Association to be a labor organization. "I never thought of it until the owners brought it up," he replied.[24]

In December 1966, Miller asked the owners to consider increasing the minimum salary, which had been stuck at $7,000 since 1957, to $12,000. Inflation had cost the players $1,100 in purchasing power since 1957, and in 1966, 26.5 percent of major leaguers were earning less than $12,000.

The owners said they would make a proposal on wages the following summer, but a year after he made the overture, Miller had received only a counterproposal of a $9,000 minimum, with qualifications. During the major league meetings in late November 1967, the Players Association flew all the player reps to Mexico City for a meeting with the owners, who said they were too busy to meet and denied that a meeting had been scheduled. The players were furious, having traveled to another country only to be sent packing, and accusations flew from both camps. "Somebody's lying," said Paul Richards, general manager of the Atlanta Braves, "and I don't think it's the owners. If this guy continues this kind of tactics [sic], I guess we'll just have to get in the gutter with him."[25]

Richards, to his credit, was true to his word, as no one was more firmly wedged in the gutter during the course of the next two years. "Either Miller or baseball has to go," he said in 1969, "We need to make it the way it was when Judge Landis was commissioner. Judge Landis would have ordered the owners to ignore Miller."[26] And in 1969, Judge Landis would have found himself on the losing end of a courtroom decision.

The owners thought they had executed a power play when they refused to meet with the players, but all they had done was antagonize them, for Miller had infused a new attitude in place of the hat-in-hand approach of Cannon. On the final day of the meetings, Miller announced that a negotiating session with the owners would take place in New York beginning December 13. AL President Joe Cronin said that no meetings had been scheduled, and the players were stymied and angered once more.

When the owners continued to stall, Miller claimed that the players and owners had reached an "impasse" and asked for the intervention of the Federal Mediation and Conciliation Service. Just six days later, he announced that the owners had agreed to increase the minimum salary to $10,000. Meal money would increase to $15 per day. A formal agreement memorializing the changes was signed February 21, 1968.

Having achieved his first objective—an increase in the minimum wage, Miller turned his attention to the pension. He believed that part of the substantial increase in television revenue should be contributed to the plan, while the owners insisted that the contribution should be a fixed amount rather than a percentage of revenue. When the owners held firm, Miller spoke for the first time of a tactic he'd said he would not employ.

The word "strike" wasn't used. Players were asked to "boycott" the start of spring training and, if they had not signed for 1969, to refuse to enter into a contract until the dispute was settled. How could players sign without knowing what the 1969 benefits would be, Miller asked? A day after Miller made his request, Mickey Mantle and Willie Mays announced that they would honor the boycott. Mantle had told Yankees player representative Steve Hamilton that he intended to retire, but when Hamilton asked him to delay the announcement and lend his name to the cause, Mantle agreed. Denny McLain had already signed, but said he would not work out until the dispute was resolved. Al Kaline, Carl Yastrzemski, Willie McCovey, Tom Seaver, and other big stars pledged their support. The backing of the stars was key, for the owners pinned their hopes on the fact that no one would pass up the opportunity to sign $50–100,000 contracts in order to benefit players earning $10–15,000. On December 31, the union sent ballots to the players with the owners' pension offer, along with a recommendation for rejection. With

spring training scheduled to start in less than three weeks, the players voted
in accordance with the recommendation.

The owners were in a vulnerable position, for when Miller announced
his plans to boycott spring training, they were without a commissioner. While
everyone agreed that Eckert had to go, the owners couldn't agree on who
they wanted to put in his place. The new man needed guts, said Orioles owner
Jerry Hoffberger, one of the leaders of the revolt that toppled Eckert. "You
don't give the commissioner authority," he said. "He takes it."[27]

Hoffberger compared the situation to his own business, in which asso-
ciates often differed with him and he had to persuade them to go along. What
he didn't say, of course, was that he could fire his subordinates if he couldn't
convince them, something the commissioner of baseball could not do. The
owners, of course, had the ability to fire the commissioner, as they had just
done to Eckert.

Yankees President Mike Burke, although he claimed to have no interest
in the job, was one of the first names mentioned as Eckert's successor. Burke
had been one of the leading Young Turks, and from his creative marketing
ideas to his mod hairstyle, represented something new and dynamic, which
is exactly what many of the owners thought was lacking in baseball.

Burke had a number of supporters, as did Giants executive Chub Feeney.
Bill Veeck sarcastically endorsed Burke with the statement, "He was once
with Ringling Brothers Circus and should be able to handle those clowns
who own the ball clubs."[28] While the owners talked about a young, activist,
dynamic commissioner, Burke was a little too close to the cutting edge for
many of the older owners. Dynamic change is a concept more often embraced
in theory than reality.

Under baseball's arcane rules, it would be difficult for either Burke or
Feeney to get enough support to be elected. The leagues were fearful of being
dominated by each other, and therefore the vote of at least nine clubs from
each league was required for a measure to pass. Thus, the successful candidate
would need a minimum of 18 of 24 votes to be the next commissioner.[29]

The owners met for five hours on December 20 and another 13 the following day, through 19 inconclusive ballots. Burke couldn't raise nine votes
from the National League, and Feeney couldn't get nine in the American.
Walter O'Malley backed Feeney, controlled four National League votes, and
could thus easily block Burke.

Burke, Feeney, and other candidates were different from those that were
considered when Eckert was selected, or during the selection process for any
of the previous commissioners. Frick had been an insider, but he was a league
president and not affiliated directly with ownership. Each of the leading candidates for commissioner in December 1968 was associated with the management of a major league club. It appeared the owners were ready to abandon

the charade and admit that the commissioner was a representative of management. After all, the players now had Miller to represent them.

When the owners remained divided on Burke and Feeney, veteran executive John McHale was suggested as a compromise candidate, but he had just assumed his duties for the new Montreal team and declined with thanks. So did Bing Devine. Other candidates began to pop up. Leonard Koppett was an advocate for Stan Musial. Vince Lombardi was seriously considered. Charley Finley pushed the candidacy of Whizzer White, but Finley's endorsement was a kiss of death.

The reluctance of some candidates was understandable, for under baseball's structure, the only real power the commissioner had was that of persuasion. The league presidents had some power, but most of the authority was reserved by the owners. "I'd rather be an attendant in a gas station," said San Diego GM Buzzie Bavasi. "You wipe a windshield and they say thank you. Nobody says thank you to the commissioner of baseball."[30]

Yankees president Michael Burke was frequently mentioned as a candidate for commissioner after William Eckert was deposed. A dashing, fashionable man with a colorful background, he professed disinterest in the commissioner's job. Shortly after George Steinbrenner became the principal owner of the Yankees in 1973, Burke left the organization.

The history of baseball commissioners was a complex one, for the man occupying the office received credit or blame based more upon his situation, the state of baseball, and that of the world at large than on his actions. Fear breeds dictators, and Judge Landis, baseball's first commissioner and the only one who could accurately be referred to as a "czar," was given blanket authority at a time when the owners were scared, for the Black Sox scandal was, rather than an isolated event, merely the most notorious of several gambling incidents that had taken place. Just over a decade later, an America frightened by a severe depression gave Franklin Roosevelt and his administration power they never would have dreamed of giving Calvin Coolidge.

Landis would accept the job only if given absolute authority, and the owners gave it to him, signing a Pledge of Loyalty under which they agreed to abide by all of the commissioner's decisions. The players weren't asked to sign a similar oath, but it didn't matter. They had no right to appeal in the first place.[31]

Landis was tiny—just 5'6" and 130 pounds, small even by the standards of the early 20th century—but he had an imposing presence. He had a large shock of unruly white hair, and it is rare to find a photo of him with a smile on his face. Landis's visage gave the impression that he was unapproachable, and he was, in fact, a humorless dictator. Sometimes he used his power wisely but at other times he acted arbitrarily and unfairly, as he often had during his judicial career. For the baseball commissioner, however, there was no higher court of appeals, so even his bad decisions were never overturned. In his first four years in office, he banned 19 players from the game, and as long as he wanted them banned, they remained banned. He also used his power to virtually run American League founder and president Ban Johnson out of baseball.

Under Landis's iron rule, baseball prospered during the overheated 1920s and bottomed out with the rest of the country in the 1930s, which is probably what would have happened under just about any commissioner. Baseball remained segregated under Landis, as was most of American society. While he is generally blamed for the failure to allow blacks in the major leagues and was clearly a reactionary on racial issues, many other American institutions, including the United States military, remained segregated at the time of his death in 1944.

Perhaps the best thing that can be said about Landis's tenure is that baseball did not have any major scandals. With the specter of the Black Sox behind them, the owners regained their confidence and did not want another autocrat as Landis's successor. The candidates were all politicians, for by the 1940s government had expanded its reach, and it would behoove a large commercial enterprise such as baseball to have solid connections in Washington.

It took 12 ballots for the owners to select Albert "Happy" Candler, former U.S. senator and governor of Kentucky, as baseball's second commissioner. Chandler wanted the same power Landis had, and on the surface it appeared that he retained most of it, but there was one critical change. The renewal of Landis's contract required approval from a majority of the owners, while Chandler needed 75 percent (later changed to 75 percent in each league). In other words, Chandler might have power, but it was much easier for the owners to get rid of him if they didn't like the manner in which he used it.

The gregarious Chandler[32] was the antithesis of Landis, whom no one had ever referred to as Happy. He was also operating in a very different environment, a setting not conducive to dictatorship. In the spirit of Landis, he suspended a number of players who jumped to the Mexican League, but he was quick to compromise lest Congress intervene and re-examine baseball's anti-trust exemption, a threat that hung over each commissioner's head like the sword of Damocles.

Chandler first ran afoul of the owners in 1947 when he suspended Dodgers manager Leo Durocher for a year over Durocher's associations with reputed gamblers. Durocher was always skirting the rules, but he was popular, and the public, particularly that portion that rooted for Brooklyn, wasn't happy with Happy.

The year of Durocher's suspension also saw Chandler's finest hour, for it was the year that Jackie Robinson ended major league baseball's *de facto* policy of segregation. Chandler was not a racial progressive; he was a product of the South who, later in his life, got into serious trouble for insensitive remarks he made as a member of the University of Kentucky Board of Trustees. But the times were changing, partly due to the aftereffects of World War II and the Double Victory campaign, in which blacks fought for the dual goals of military victory and racial equality. Integration was coming whether Chandler welcomed it or not, and he was astute enough to sense the winds blowing. He was an enthusiastic supporter of Robinson, promising dire consequences for anyone who tried to prevent Robinson from playing; Landis had not supported integration in his time, but it would have been difficult for Chandler to oppose it in the late 1940s.

In the end, events proved too much for the new commissioner. While trying to act for the benefit of all, he inevitably offended some, particularly when he attempted to enforce the rules. He upset Yankees owner Del Webb when he investigated his possible gambling connections. Cardinals owner Fred Saigh thought Chandler was somehow behind his conviction for income tax evasion. He made enemies of the White Sox for fining them after they signed a high school pitcher before he graduated and alienated the entire American League by feuding with league president Will Harridge over supervision of the umpires, a dispute that arose when Chandler encouraged the arbiters to form an association.

Six years into his seven-year contract, Chandler had alienated nearly every one of his employers. Rather than wait to see whether the owners fired him at the end of his contract, Chandler asked for an extension in advance. After a few trial votes, it became apparent that he didn't have enough support, and the owners urged him to resign, which he did in June 1951.

Chandler's replacement was Ford Frick, who'd been president of the National League since 1934. Frick had been part of the baseball establishment long enough to know what the owners wanted in their commissioner—and by now he was truly *their* commissioner. When he was elected, columnist Joe Williams wrote, "Frick is a fine choice because he is a homely, pleasant, sincere American citizen who has all the simple decencies, plus a bent for baseball. He'll be commissioner for life."[33]

Eleven years later, Oliver Kuechle wrote, "Ford Frick was named commissioner of baseball in 1951 because the owners wanted no more of such heavy fisted administration as Judge Landis had given the office or even as Happy Chandler had given it in a lesser way. They wanted a non-meddling do nothing."[34] Chandler had done things and gotten in trouble. Frick did nothing and baseball got in trouble.

Everyone in baseball, including Frick, knew he had no power. Bill Veeck joked that AL President Joe Cronin followed in Frick's shadow, "if Frick were substantial enough to cast a shadow."[35] Gabe Paul described him as "an incompetent good fellow ... all he did was show up for work."[36] Perhaps Frick's biggest moment came during the 1962 World Series, which was delayed several days by rain. The commissioner got to walk around the soggy field, look important, and decide whether the game would be played. Whether he made the decision on his own or not, he was at center stage.

Frick claimed that he would have been a stronger ruler had the owners granted him more power. "Giving a man like Frick authority," wrote Veeck, "is like giving a hitter like Sandy Koufax a bigger bat. If you can't hit, you can't hit."[37] When Frick was elected to the Hall of Fame, Chandler said, "Next thing you know they'll be voting in Charlie McCarthy. He's a dummy, too, you know.... Why, he slept longer in office than.... Rip Van Winkle."[38]

Baseball had drifted under Frick, but not badly enough to offset the advantages of having a figurehead who let the owners do as they pleased. The decline of the game under Eckert made the owners realize that the concept of a non-entity as commissioner had gone too far. They needed a leader who could at least give the impression of competence.

Finally, on February 4, the owners announced the appointment of Bowie Kuhn, an attorney with Willkie, Farr and Gallagher, the New York law firm that handled the legal affairs of the National League, as pro tem commissioner. Kuhn had never been mentioned as a candidate but, unlike Eckert, he was well-known in baseball circles. A 6'5", 230-pound 42-year-old, Kuhn wore wire-rimmed glasses that seemed too small for his fleshy face. He carried himself with the stiff reserve attributed to aristocracy and was, in fact, descended from governors and senators.

Since 1950, Kuhn had been involved in numerous baseball issues and apparently managed to handle them without antagonizing any clique of owners, which made him a unanimous choice once Burke and Feeney agreed to step aside in the name of harmony. The new commissioner accepted the position on an interim basis, but indications were that satisfactory performance would result in a permanent appointment.

Kuhn was intimately familiar with nearly every one of the issues facing baseball and, for all the controversy he courted in later years, was a good compromise choice. Unlike Eckert, Kuhn knew a lot about baseball. "[B]aseball's owners," wrote William Leggett, "finally turned the game over to a fan."[39] As a teenager, Kuhn worked inside the scoreboard at Washington's Griffith Stadium for a dollar a day, and in 1987 still proudly carried a Social Security card that showed his employer to be Clark Griffith.

His own athletic skills were modest. As the tallest student at Theodore Roosevelt High School in Washington, he'd been cajoled into trying out for the basketball team by the young coach, Arnold "Red" Auerbach. When asked

Bowie Kuhn took over as commissioner in early 1969 at a time when, as he put it "baseball was on fire." He had a controversial reign and an ongoing battle with Marvin Miller, but when he left office in 1984, baseball was thriving.

why he wasn't on the team, Kuhn told Auerbach he was a lousy player. "You let me be the judge of that," Auerbach replied.[40] After a week of workouts, Auerbach concurred with Kuhn's assessment, and his active athletic career came to an end.

During his career with Wilkie, Farr, Kuhn worked on the Toolson case, in which a minor leaguer in the Yankees' system challenged the validity of baseball's anti-trust exemption, and on the Cellar hearings that questioned the same issue. He defended the interests of baseball when Milwaukee tried to prevent the Braves from leaving. During the course of his representation, he got to know and work with Commissioner Frick and both league presidents.

When Kuhn arrived for the first day in his new job, he found Eckert sitting in a nearby office. There were four years remaining on the former commissioner's contract, and the owners had made him a consultant. The loyal old soldier was prepared to fulfill his assignment, but Kuhn realized that having his predecessor a few doors down the hall wasn't a good idea. Like most people in baseball, Kuhn liked Eckert, and waited a few days before telling him that he would be paid, but needn't come to the office every day.

While the new commissioner found the old one at his side, he found Marvin Miller at his throat, threatening to ruin Kuhn's honeymoon with the first work stoppage in the history of the sport. The players had, for the most part, adhered to the boycott, and when Miller called a press conference and read a list of the names of players who said they wouldn't sign, the owners sprang into action. They launched a publicity campaign intended to show that the pension plan was the best in sports and that the players were, as always, greedy for wanting more.

The owners applied pressure by indicating that some marginal players might forever ruin their chances of playing in the major leagues if they didn't report on time. It wouldn't have anything to do with a blacklist, of course, it was simply because the manager wouldn't have enough time to evaluate them. "Miller speaks mainly for a few rabble-rousers and greedy ballplayers," Richards said.[41] "Let 'em strike. Maybe if they do, it will get the guys who don't want to play out of the game and let the fellows who appreciate the major leagues play ... so let 'em strike if they want to."[42]

"If it ever comes to a strike," wrote Dick Young, "I'm afraid the players won't have much public sympathy. The guy riding a subway strap finds it awfully hard to shed a tear for a big league player who can draw a lush pension at age 50, and is striking for more."[43] Leon Wagner replied, "We let it hang out in front of seventy thousand fans [although not in Cleveland, where Wagner had played the past few years]. If that many people turned out to watch a guy lay linoleum, then he should get a likewise pension."[44]

Miller stepped up the rhetoric from the players' side. "Labor-relations-wise," he said, "the owners have not yet reached the 19th century. This business of owning people is the worst form of slavery I've seen."[45] The owners offered a $1 million increase in pension contributions, which Miller said was illusory due to the increased number of players created by expansion and the existing unfunded liability. Under the owners' proposal, he said, there would be no increase in benefits.

Longtime executive Frank Lane said the players had better report or the owners would "kick their pants off."[46] In a more tangible move, the owners voted to establish a rule that would allow them not to pay players who became ill or were injured off the field. They would be placed on a "temporarily inactive list" and not paid for 21 days. The players reacted with predictable outrage, and the chasm between labor and management became wider than ever.

In early February, 130 players gathered in New York to proclaim their solidarity. There might not be a spring training, said Reds pitcher Jack Fisher, and there might not even be a season. There was no strike fund, however, and players would not receive any money if they didn't report.

Despite the seriousness of the situation, none of the owners had met with the players or their representatives; their negotiating had been done by John Gaherin, the owners' advisor on labor relations. Gaherin reaffirmed the position that the owners would determine the players' share of television receipts and would not be bound to a percentage distribution.

The brave front, however, was threatened by the fact that the owners were receiving pressure from the television networks. "We're not planning on paying major league prices for minor league games," a network spokesman declared.[47] So much for Paul Richards' threat.

"We all agreed," said Mets pitcher Ron Taylor, "not to sign our contracts and, if things weren't settled by spring training, not to report. As it turned out, some guys did and some guys didn't. Personally, I'd felt I'd given my word that I wasn't going to sign and there was no question what I was going to do."[48]

The players affected by the boycott were those who had been in the major leagues for as much as a day and had not been sent to the minors. Those who had been in the majors but were in the minors during the spring of 1969 faced a dilemma.

Don Nottebart was a veteran of eight major league seasons who spent 1968 with Hawaii of the Pacific Coast League and had been invited to spring training by the Yankees. "I called Steve Hamilton, the player rep," said Nottebart. "He said, 'Go ahead down. You're a fringe player. You're career's almost over. Nobody's going to hold it against you if you go to spring training.' Then I called Ralph Houk and asked him what he thought I should do. Ralph said, 'I can't tell you what to do, Don. I'm management. But if you come down, the guys aren't going to hold it against you.' So I decided to go down."[49]

The Chicago White Sox were the first team scheduled to report. On February 14, the opening day of spring drills, 21 batterymen showed up, including just two players with major league experience, pitcher Dan Osinski and catcher Russ Nixon, both veterans near the end of their careers. The rest of the players were rookies. All of the other White Sox veteran pitchers and catchers either stayed home or camped out in Florida to see what transpired. In all, 391 of the 402 players who voted to stay out of camp followed through.[50]

Only a handful of players checked in to the Yankees' camp in Fort Lauderdale, including Nottebart and a rookie catcher named "Thurmond" Munson.[51] No members of the 1968 club reported. "I wouldn't play if there was a strike," said Elston Howard, starting his first season as a Yankees coach. "If I played during a strike, none of the players would have any respect for me."[52]

President Mike Burke filled in at the Yankees' practice and took some grounders with the rookies. Across the state, in St. Petersburg, Bowie Kuhn stuck a plastic helmet atop his large head and took batting practice with the Mets. There had been little talk of replacement players, but if that avenue was chosen, apparently the new commissioner was ready and willing.

The Mets' front was less solid than that displayed by the Yankees, as pitchers Nolan Ryan and Danny Frisella, and catcher Jerry Grote, who'd attended the New York meeting and pledged not to sign, agreed to terms and reported on the first day of camp. "If it had been any one of the other 23 teams in baseball," Grote said, "I wouldn't have signed. But this team has treated me well."[53] Pitcher Bob Hendley, trying to come back after elbow surgery, arrived a day later, as did Tug McGraw and Cal Koonce.

Other Mets were in Florida working out on their own. Jerry Koosman reported unsigned and said, "Don't tell anybody I'm here."[54] Tom Seaver was in town and said he felt he owed the club something because of the fine manner in which they'd treated him. He didn't want to see baseball become unionized, but also felt he owed the players something. Seaver had a date in his mind by which he felt obligated to report, but would not divulge it. He said he would not strike.

In the meantime, Seaver worked out with Koosman, Bud Harrelson, Taylor, and Al Jackson. "We don't talk about the strike," Jackson said. "We don't want to influence each other. We just want to get ready to play."[55] Taylor was more poetic, quoting Emerson. "On the debris of our despair," he said, "we build character."[56] Koosman had a more practical observation. "It has everything that the big camp has," he observed, "except money."[57] Koosman had earned $12,000 for winning 19 games as a rookie, and Seaver, for his second straight year of 16 wins, made $25,000.

As the days went on, players began to trickle into camp, and the Mets trickled in faster than any other team. By February 22, GM Johnny Murphy had 13 players under contract and said that 30 of the 40 roster players would be in uniform within a week. The players lowered their pension request, but the owners, feeling their oats as more players reported, refused it. Joe Cronin said his league would start the season on time "no matter what."[58]

The solid wall was beginning to crack, and as more players arrived in camp, the union's bargaining position eroded. At that point, Bowie Kuhn decided to take a more active role. He told the owners they would need to moderate their stance and get Miller back to the bargaining table.

On the 25th, an agreement was reached, and the boycott was over. The principal gain for the players was the reduction of the vesting period for the pension plan from five years to four. The owners also agreed to increase their annual contribution to the plan from $4.1 million to $5.45 million.[59]

In his first 30 days on the job, Bowie Kuhn had a victory, for he'd resolved the issue without a full-fledged strike. But Marvin Miller had a victory as well. While the "boycott" had broken down eventually, it still represented the strongest stand a group of players had ever made against management. It would not be the last.

Epilogue:
Baseball Was on Fire When
I Became Commissioner

Baseball needed excitement in 1969 and they got it. Whether it was a shorter mound or a taller commissioner, or the fact that batters simply remembered how to hit, both leagues produced more offense than they had in 1968, as seen below:

	1968 (20 teams)	1969 (24 teams)
NL Batting Average	.243	.250
NL Runs Scored	5,577	7,960
NL Home Runs	891	1,470
NL Runs Scored per Team	558	658
NL Home Runs per Team	89	123
AL Batting Average	.230	.246
AL Runs Scored	5,532	7,690
AL Home Runs	1,104	1,649
AL Runs Scored per Team	553	663
AL Home Runs per Team	110	137

Another factor leading to an increase in offense was the thinned pitching staffs of an expansion year. Two of the new parks, Jarry in Montreal and Sick's in Seattle, were cozy and conducive to home run production.[1] And, as always when there was an increase in offense, there was speculation that the owners had employed self-help by juicing up the ball.

It was not just more run production that brought excitement to baseball in 1969. Nor was it the re-appearance of Tony Conigliaro or the emergence of Reggie Jackson as a young slugger. It certainly wasn't the addition of two more pennant races, for none of the four came down to the wire. The Championship

Series in each league resulted in a three-game sweep, and the World Series was over in five games.

In any other season, the lack of suspense might have led to a decline in interest, but 1969 was the year that the hapless New York Mets went from ninth place to winning the World Series. The symbol of comic ineptitude since their inception, the Mets would have been an endearing story anywhere, but in America's largest city, the Mets were very big news. Not only did they win the pennant, they came from far behind in a heartening battle of good versus evil, as the young over-achievers of even-keeled Mets manager Gil Hodges made an amazing stretch run to overtake a collapsing, dissension-riddled Cubs team managed by the villainous Leo Durocher.

The Mets drew 2,175,573 fans to their home games, an increase of almost 400,000 from 1968, and National League attendance, which had declined from 15 million in 1966 to less than 12 million in 1968, returned to the 15 million level in 1969. The two expansion clubs accounted for about 1.7 million, leaving the net increase at roughly 1.5 million. It wasn't fabulous, but at least the trend was going in the right direction.

Politicians had pressed the major leagues to expand by claiming that several U.S. cities were dying for a franchise. Attendance of the new teams didn't support that claim, for at their home openers, San Diego and Seattle, which had been waiting for years for a big league club, drew just 23,370 and 14,993, respectively. For the season, San Diego averaged just over 6,000 fans per game and Seattle a little more than 8,000. Montreal, which looked like it might never get off the starting line, paced the four expansion franchises by drawing more than 1.2 million. The new Kansas City Royals drew about 900,000, roughly 175,000 more than watched Charley Finley's club during their final year in Kansas City and about 125,000 more than they drew in Oakland in 1969.

Among the many fans who flocked to major league ballparks in 1969, one of the most frequent visitors was Bowie Kuhn. He attended seven openers and saw 13 games during the first 17 days of the season. Before the year was over, he'd attended 70 games. Kuhn also initiated the concept of making the annual All-Star contest an event rather than just a game. He hosted a reception attended by President Nixon, and even though the game was rained out and had to be played the following afternoon, he had begun a tradition that spread to football and basketball.

Although Kuhn had achieved labor peace during his first 30 days in office, 1969 marked the beginning of a long, antagonistic relationship between Marvin Miller and Bowie Kuhn. Each man wrote his memoirs, and neither had much good to say about the other. Miller's book appeared seven years after Kuhn's and he therefore got in the last shot, which was far more vicious than the blows Kuhn delivered to Miller in his book.

Miller usually got the best of Kuhn, particularly in the mid–1970s with the advent of free agency. One of the fragile underpinnings of the union movement during its early days was its limited value to ballplayers at the top of the wage scale. Miller's first efforts were directed toward raising the minimum salary, increasing meal money, and boosting pension benefits. The pension plan provided a fixed monthly payment based upon years of service and did not take salary into account. Players earning more than $50,000 a year were less likely to be dependent on their pension, for they had more money to save and invest, plus endorsement income and the opportunity to set themselves up for remunerative post-baseball careers. For the most part, their support of the union was one of fraternity and solidarity rather than self-interest. They stood to lose more income than fringe players if they went on strike, and most things the union was fighting for had little direct benefit to them. Yet their support was critical, for if players like Mickey Mantle and Willie Mays didn't back the union, its chances of success declined dramatically.

Once Miller finally tackled free agency, he no longer had to worry about the support of the superstars. While some rookies and fringe players saw their salaries increase from $7,000 to $10,000 in 1969, Reggie Jackson saw his salary soar from $200,000 to $525,000 when he became a free agent after the 1976 season. Once Miller could satisfy the self-interest of all members of his union, Kuhn's position finally became what it really had been all along, the head of the owners' union. He was slow to admit it and always portrayed himself as operating at a level above Miller, fighting for the overall interest of baseball, but he was in fact his direct adversary and always seemed to come out second-best.

Kuhn was in a difficult position. "Whenever something important came down," said Bob Wirz, who handled public relations for the commissioner's office,

> Bowie, with his legal background and his sense of fairness, would go out of his way to touch base with everyone—the league presidents, the Executive Council—and he might issue a position paper or statement to all the clubs before he'd respond to the media. In the meantime, the Players Association would be firing all their cannons from their office and they'd beat us to a pulp. They were out there first, and they'd get the first round of headlines. We were always in a reactive mode, and as a public relations person, that's an extremely difficult position to be in.[2]

Miller had the players solidly behind him, while Kuhn had a fragile coalition of owners, a collection of egos often operating at cross-purposes.

Kuhn was heavily criticized and often received negative press, which Wirz feels was unjust. "When Bowie took over as commissioner in '69," he said, "baseball was said to be slow, boring, and maybe dying."[3] "It is not dishonest to say," Kuhn wrote, "that baseball was on fire when I became commissioner in 1969."[4]

"When he left in '84," Wirz continued, "it was anything but that. Attendance was at record highs, TV ratings were very good, and the positives were just pouring out of baseball. If you're going to criticize the guy at the top for things that happened on his watch, you also have to give him credit for a lot of good things that happened on his watch."[5]

One of Kuhn's problems with the press was that in virtually every difficult decision he made, he had to rule against the interest of one or more teams. Local media tends to be loyal to their club, and when one of Kuhn's decisions had a negative impact on any team, he was generally toasted in that media market. The commissioner has no home team and therefore didn't have his own organ to support him.

Wirz has another theory as to Kuhn's difficulty with the media. "Bowie was so much taller [6'5"] than the average person," Wirz said. "He towered over people, and in those days he combed his hair straight back and he had those clear plastic glasses. Everyone knew he had an Ivy League education and was a lawyer, and I think that worked against him with the media. They couldn't relate to a lawyer. They couldn't relate to his size. They couldn't relate to the Ivy League or to his appearance."[6] The media often portrayed Kuhn as stiff, cold, and aloof but, said Wirz, who worked with him for ten years, "he was the warmest human being, the most genuine human being you could meet."[7]

Kuhn was very sensitive to his public image, and to being portrayed as a privileged elitist. "I imagine it will surprise some people to know," he wrote in his autobiography, "that my father was an immigrant, hardly the right ancestral background for the Ivy League—Wall Street 'stuffed shirt' many people take me for."[8] He might have mentioned that his mother was also from an immigrant family, but her kin arrived in America a bit earlier—in 1634, and her ancestors included five governors and two U.S. senators—as well as a distant relative named Jim Bowie. And Kuhn was, after all, from the Ivy League and Wall Street.

Marvin Miller didn't find much to like about Bowie Kuhn. If Kuhn twisted the truth somewhat to make his tenure look better, Miller came out with all guns blazing. There is no gray in Marvin Miller's world. Those who supported him were good and those who opposed him were evil. "It might sound self-serving," he wrote, "but *dedicated* (italics in original) union men didn't dwell on maximizing their income; their aim was to protect the workers' rights, perhaps even to correct some of society's ills."[9]

He didn't like some of his successors and he clearly didn't like player agents, even though they were employed by his constituents. He saw everything through his own prism, claiming that George Steinbrenner was banished from baseball in 1990 primarily because the other owners didn't like his free-spending ways and that Bart Giamatti unfairly persecuted Pete Rose for his gambling activities.

Miller referred to Kuhn's autobiography as "error-riddled" and said the former commissioner couldn't even predict the past after it happened.[10] He said he was neither impressed nor intimidated by Kuhn's height, and his only praise was sarcastic. "Kuhn must be singled out," Miller wrote, "as the most important contributor to the success of the Players Association. His moves consistently backfired; his attempts at leadership created divisions. His inability to distinguish between reality and his prejudices, his lack of concern for the rights of the players, sections of the press, and even the stray, unpopular owner—all combined to make Kuhn a vital ingredient in the growth and strength of the union. To paraphrase Voltaire on God, if Bowie Kuhn had never existed, we would have had to invent him."[11]

Still, Miller was consistently uncharitable to the man who had done so much to help his cause.[12] After condemning Kuhn's attempts to reach out to him on several occasions, which he believed was for the sole purpose of "picking his brain," Miller concluded, "There was scant possibility of reciprocity in that department."[13] His final thrust concerned Kuhn's post-baseball career, when he commented on Kuhn's pending testimony before a grand jury. "I sincerely hope he will be given due process," Miller wrote, "in a court proceeding unlike any he ever conducted as commissioner."[14]

Again, in fairness to Kuhn, it must be noted that he was constrained by his environment. The role of commissioner had evolved over time and, with the exception of Eckert, the performance of the men who held the office was a reflection of their times. It is no accident that most of America's most revered presidents either served in time of war or earned their reputations during wartime, for they are given greater power and the nation tends to unite behind them in a common cause. The owners united behind Landis, sometimes reluctantly, and gave him almost unlimited power, for they believed that the survival of major league baseball was at stake. None of his successors was in a similar situation, and even though baseball was in deep trouble in early 1969, Kuhn's power was very constrained.

As a lawyer, Kuhn understood that the game had to change, and prior to 1976, he tried to interest the owners in a proactive strategy toward free agency, which he knew was coming whether the owners liked it or not. The owners weren't interested and, when an arbitrator's decision went against them, they were placed in a defensive mode once more.

The last man who tried to serve as a commissioner responsible to both owners and players was Fay Vincent. It proved impossible, and Vincent resigned under pressure in 1992. "To do the job without angering an owner is impossible," he said. "I can't make all 28 of my bosses happy."[15] Making both the owners and the players happy would have been beyond impossible.

Vincent was succeeded by Bud Selig, who explicitly acknowledged what everyone had known for decades: the commissioner did not govern baseball;

he was the head of the owners' "union", the man who would lead them in negotiations against the players' union.

Labor confrontations created two lengthy strikes and a salary structure the players of the 1960s could not have imagined. There was a doping scandal in the early 21st century. Baseball was supposed to be dying in 1968, and strikes, multi-million dollars salaries, and scandals were the types of things most observers thought would kill it. But they didn't. Miller and Kuhn battled fiercely, but perhaps the most important point was that there were things in baseball worth fighting over. In 1968 it appeared that there might not be anything left of baseball by the mid–1970s, but the game had prospered, perhaps in spite of those entrusted with running it.

Total attendance, which was 23 million in 1968, topped the 30 million mark in 1973 and, five years later, buoyed by the addition of two more teams, broke 40 million, about 75 percent above 1968 levels. The owners had always claimed they would be bankrupted if salaries went up or the reserve clause was invalidated. Yet, as salaries skyrocketed and, following the 1976 season, players were allowed to become free agents, the value of baseball franchises soared. In 2010, the Texas Rangers, which Bob Short had purchased for $10 million in 1969, sold for $593 million.

Baseball had been starved for offense in 1968, but in 1998 Mark McGwire obliterated Roger Maris's record by hitting 70 home runs, with Sammy Sosa not far behind at 66. In the 119 major league seasons prior to 1990, there had been 19 instances in which a player exceeded 50 home runs in a season. In the 1990s there were 12, and in the 21st century men have hit more than 50 homers 14 times. Pitchers were throwing harder than ever, but hitters had adjusted.

Although many of the sluggers were later found to have been cheating, fans loved the excitement of the home run, and no one was seriously talking about the imminent death of baseball. While it was no longer the dominant sport in America, more fans were going to baseball games than ever before, and they were paying higher ticket prices.

Baseball, which had been on the brink in 1968, was thriving by the 21st century. The challenge from football was stronger than it was 50 years ago, but apparently there was room for both sports, and many more, on the American scene. The owners had once feared radio and television, but even with cable broadcasts sending a glut of sporting events into American homes, fans came out to see the game in person, for baseball had become a full-scale entertainment event, with music, dancing, games, and scoreboards that made the Astrodome board seem tame. Baseball was no longer on the brink.

Chapter Notes

Introduction

1. Ryczek, 1.

Chapter 1

1. *The Sporting News*, December 21, 1968.
2. *Ibid.*
3. *Sports Illustrated*, December 16, 1968.
4. SABR Bioproject essay by Brian McKenna (sabr.org/bioproj/person/4691515d).
5. *New York Times*, November 18, 1965.
6. http://sabr.org/bioproj/person/46915 15d. Some thought that Eckert had been confused with former Secretary of the Air Force Eugene Zuckert, and that the owners had perhaps inadvertently selected the wrong man. Ironically, after Eckert died in 1971, he was buried in Arlington Cemetery, not far from the Unknown Soldier.
7. Undated article from the *New York Times* in the Eckert file at the Giamatti Research Center.
8. *Sports Illustrated*, December 19, 1960.
9. *Sports Illustrated*, April 4, 1966.
10. *Ibid.*
11. Dick Young wrote, "I can just see it now … a baseball writer is on his way down to breakfast. He encounters Eckert in the elevator. He says, 'Good morning, commissioner.' Eckert fishes in his pocket and pulls out a file card. He looks at it and replies, 'Good morning'" (*The Sporting News*, May 1, 1971).
12. Eckert once told executive John McHale that the Yankees had been sold, when in fact the information had come from a routine by comedians Bob and Ray (Holtzman, 123).
13. Kuhn, 30.

14. Unidentified article of January 2, 1969, from Eckert file at the Giamatti Research Center.
15. *The Sporting News*, December 21, 1968.
16. *Sports Illustrated*, April 4, 1966.
17. Wendel, 135.
18. Wendel, 208.

Chapter 2

1. *Sports Illustrated*, September 9, 1963.
2. *The Sporting News*, February 6, 1965.
3. Independent in nearly all things, the American and National leagues counted attendance in different ways. Some American League clubs reported the total number of tickets sold, while others and the entire National League reported the actual turnstile count. Thus one would expect the American League totals to be slightly higher than those reported in the National League.
4. Feldmann, 166.
5. *The Sporting News* October 21, 1967.
6. *The Sporting News* October 28, 1967.
7. Amazingly, the Red Sox sold only 400 season tickets in 1967, with the remaining seats sold on a "walk-up" basis. By comparison, the Dodgers sold 15,000 season tickets. The first thing the Red Sox did after the record attendance of 1967 was raise ticket prices.
8. 1970 Census.
9. *The Sporting News*, November 18, 1967.
10. Veeck, 22.
11. *New York Times*, December 15, 1968.
12. *Saturday Evening Post*, September 7, 1968.
13. Edwards, 270.

14. Unidentified article by Til Ferdenzi, February 5, 1966, in Eckert file at Giamatti Research Center.

15. *The Sporting News*, June 8, 1968.

16. *Ibid.*

17. *Ibid.*

18. *The Sporting News*, July 13, 1968.

19. Reproduced in *The Sporting News*, July 20, 1968.

20. *The Sporting News*, October 5, 1968.

21. *The Sporting News*, January 18, 1969.

Chapter 3

1. *The Sporting News*, March 30, 1968. Ironically, the Heavenly Valley ski area, where Lonborg was injured, was operated by Hugh Killebrew who, according to *Baseball Digest*, was a cousin of Harmon Killebrew (*Baseball Digest*, June 1968, 96).

2. *Baseball Digest*, September 1968, 9.

3. *Baseball Digest*, March 1968, 20.

4. *Washington Star*, February 25, 1968.

5. Cepeda was the first National Leaguer to be selected MVP unanimously.

6. Comedian Milton Berle quipped that in 1965 Versalles had been the AL MVP, and in 1968 he was the shortstop for the Dodgers, which was like going from being the president of General Motors to opening a Honda agency (*Baseball Digest*, May, 1968, 89).

7. Maloney managed to lose one of those no-hitters, 1–0 to the Mets in 11 innings.

8. *The Sporting News*, February 24, 1968.

9. *Baseball Digest*, June 1968, 38.

10. *The Sporting News*, March 23, 1968.

11. *The Sporting News*, March 16, 1968.

12. http://www.baseballprospectus.com/article.php?articleid=8374.

13. *The Sporting News*, February 24, 1968.

14. *Ibid.*

15. *The Sporting News*, March 16, 1968.

16. *The Sporting News*, April 13, 1968.

Chapter 4

1. Feldmann, 25.

2. *Time Magazine*, September 13, 1968.

3. Interview with Don Cardwell, June 7, 2004.

4. *The Sporting News*, June 1, 1968.

5. *The Sporting News*, June 8, 1968.

6. Baldwin, 169.

7. Angell, 183.

8. *The Sporting News*, June 8, 1968.

9. *The Sporting News*, September 14, 1968.

10. *The Sporting News*, June 1, 1968.

11. Feldmann, 251. While managers struggled to find ways to generate some offense, former slugger and Washington skipper Jim Lemon showed that he could still swing the bat. Late in the 1968 season, a rat sprinted into the Senator dugout, sending the players dashing for cover. Lemon calmly grabbed a bat, took a swing, and got good wood on the rat, sending it into the afterlife with a direct hit. It was one of the Senators' best performances with a bat all year.

12. *New York Times*, June 7, 1968.

13. *The Sporting News*, June 29, 1968.

14. *New York Times*, May 26, 1968.

15. Undated article from McLain file at the Giamatti Research Center.

16. *Sports Illustrated*, July 29, 1968.

17. Wendel, 56.

18. *The Sporting News*, February 10, 1968.

19. Wendel, 178. McLain believed he had a partially-torn rotator cuff starting in 1965. In 1977, he received a settlement of $31,500 from a workman's compensation claim for the damage done to his shoulder (McLain, 217).

20. *The Sporting News*, December 18, 1965. Dave Baldwin roomed with McLain in Iowa in 1973 and recalled that McLain was obsessed with the Watergate hearings, insisting that if the burglars had done it right, they could have gotten away with it (Baldwin, 302).

21. *Time Magazine*, September 13, 1968.

22. McLain frequently said that he didn't like baseball all that much, and preferred playing the organ. He predicted he'd be out of baseball by the time he was 30, and he was correct, although he didn't leave by his own choice.

23. McLain said he received $15,000 a year to promote Pepsi.

24. *Sports Illustrated*, July 29, 1968.

25. McLain, 83.

26. McLain, 85.

27. McLain, 89.

28. *The Sporting News*, April 2, 1966.

29. McLain, 90.

30. In some sources, McLain said he was afraid of needles and hardly ever had a cortisone shot, while in others he said he had them regularly.

31. McLain, 100.
32. McLain, 101.
33. *The Sporting News*, October 21, 1967.
34. Wendel, 126.
35. Drysdale, 142.
36. *Los Angeles Times*, June 30, 2005.
37. *Ibid.*
38. Interview with Jim Gosger, January 10, 2009.
39. *The Sporting News*, March 30, 1968.
40. *The Sporting News*, July 6, 1968.
41. *The Sporting News*, September 28, 1968.
42. *The Sporting News*, February 24, 1968. Hunter proved prophetic, for it was when Finley failed to fund a required annuity payment that the pitcher became a free agent and signed a lucrative contract with the Yankees.
43. Five years later, Reese again played a role in history, as Nolan Ryan's 383rd strikeout victim, the one by which Ryan broke Sandy Koufax's single season record.
44. Three weeks earlier, Perry had narrowly missed a no-hitter against the Cubs, yielding just a seventh inning single to Glenn Beckert.

Chapter 5

1. *The Sporting News*, January 5, 1963.
2. Veeck, 61.
3. Miller, 370. A classic example was Finley's support of the designated hitter and designated pinch runner, one an idea that was accepted and the other one that was properly ignored.
4. A second ball girl, Debbi Sivyer, wasn't as famous as Miss USA, but later became the founder of Mrs. Fields' Cookies.
5. Harrelson, 137.
6. *Sports Illustrated*, July 14, 1965.
7. Supposedly, the monkeys were given cough syrup and sleeping pills to keep them calm (Michelson, 98–9).
8. When Harry Caray became an Oakland broadcaster in 1970, Finley tried to get him to change his trademark expression "Holy Cow" to "Holy Mule." Caray refused.
9. Interview with Bill Bryan, June 19, 2002.
10. Ray, 133.
11. The club hired Virginia Pace to explain the game to women.
12. The land for the Astrodome was acquired from Smith and Hofheinz.
13. Edwards, 262. The Astrodome was re-

ferred to as the Eighth Wonder of the World. When Houston Oiler owner Bud Adams saw Hofheinz's proposal for his team's lease, he called it the Ninth Wonder of the World.
14. There were rumors that the Astros manipulated the air conditioning system so the breeze would blow out when the home team was batting and in when the opponents were at the plate. An engineering consultant was engaged to study the problem and determined that was not the case.
15. Hofheinz also initiated a scheduling change that would eventually become almost universal. In 1965, the Astros had 81 home dates without a single doubleheader. That year, 19 percent of all NL games and 28 percent of AL games were part of doubleheaders.
16. Piersall, 43.
17. *New York Times*, May 31, 1960.
18. *New York Times*, June 18, 1960.
19. *New York Times*, June 19, 1960.
20. *New York Times*, July 24, 1960.
21. Allen, 28.
22. Allen, 69.
23. *New York Newsday*, September 7, 1962.
24. *The Sporting News*, October 26, 1963.
25. *The Sporting News*, February 29, 1964.
26. *The Sporting News*, August 8, 1964.
27. *The Sporting News* pointed out that Dyer still trailed Cincinnati's Earl Lawson in being punched by players. Lawson had been on the receiving end of haymakers from the Reds' Johnny Temple and Vada Pinson on different occasions (*The Sporting News*, September 5, 1964).
28. *The Sporting News*, January 29, 1966.
29. Unidentified article of August 11, 1964 in the Leon Wagner file at the Giamatti Research Center.
30. *The Post and Times-Star* (Cincinnati) March 17, 1969.
31. Unidentified article by Joe Donnelly in the Wagner file at the Giamatti Research Center.
32. *Sports Illustrated*, August 18, 1969.
33. Unidentified article by Regis McAuley dated June 21, 1969 in the Wagner file at the Giamatti Research Center.
34. *The Post and Times-Star* (Cincinnati) March 17, 1969.
35. Unidentified article by Russell Schneider in the Wagner file at the Giamatti Research Center.

36. *Los Angeles Times*, January 25, 2004.

37. Harrelson claimed he was wearing turtlenecks in 1959.

38. Interview with Bill Denehy, June 12, 2003.

39. *Sports Illustrated*, September 2, 1968.

40. Pitcher Dave Baldwin roomed with Harrelson briefly in Washington and noted that he was in the room most evenings well before curfew. "From what I saw," he wrote, "I suspect that Hawk wasn't the man-about-town of the spicy Harrelson legend. Sometimes a tale is just a tale" (Baldwin, 245).

41. The first person to wear a Nehru jacket at a baseball game was Jawaharal Nehru, who attended one of the 1960 World Series games in New York.

42. Apparently, Woolf was overly optimistic, since he later told Harrelson he couldn't live without his baseball salary.

43. Harrelson, 3.

44. Finley threatened to blackmail Aker by exposing his marital infidelity, but Aker foiled the plan by telling Finley his wife already knew (Michelson, 113). Ford Frick was often chided for shirking authority by claiming that important issues were "a league matter," but AL president Joe Cronin did him one better by declaring the Kansas City dispute to be a "club matter" in which he had no intention of getting involved.

45. The Kansas City episode is covered in *Sports Illustrated*, August 14, 1967, and Harrelson, 179–92.

46. Harrelson, 203.

47. In a symbolic changing of the guard, Harrelson dated Tony Conigliaro's ex-girlfriend, Julie Markakis.

48. Harrelson, 224.

49. Harrelson, 226.

50. Harrelson, 208.

51. *Sports Illustrated*, July 14, 1969.

52. *Sports Illustrated*, July 21, 1969.

53. *The Sporting News*, May 17, 1969.

54. *Sports Illustrated*, May 5, 1969.

55. *The Sporting News*, May 17, 1969.

56. When August Busch bought the St. Louis Cardinals in 1953, he wanted to change the name of Sportsman's Park to Budweiser Park but was prohibited from doing so by the National League. Now, of course, the vast majority of major league parks are sponsored by and named for corporations.

Chapter 6

1. Information in this section from interview with Rich Beck October 16, 2002.

2. Baldwin, 111.

3. Interview with Jerry Hinsley, August 20, 2002.

4. Interview with Bill Denehy, June 12, 2003.

5. *Sarasota Herald-Tribune*, March 3, 1970.

6. *Hartford Courant*, February 20, 1966.

7. Clendenon, 61.

8. *New York Times*, March 2, 1969.

9. Interview with John Ellis, November 8, 2005.

10. One baseball casualty of the Vietnam War was Eddie Gonzalez, who served as the White Sox batboy in 1962. Gonzalez was killed in action near Saigon in January 1968 (*Baseball Digest*, April 1968).

11. *Washington Star*, March 8, 1968. Ironically, Martin returned to Asia to have his greatest years, playing in the Japanese Pacific Coast League from 1974 to 1979 and hitting 189 home runs in six seasons.

12. *NINE*, Volume 22, Number 1 (Fall 2013), 123.

13. *New York Times*, January 27, 1968.

14. *New York Times*, April 4, 1968.

15. When Holtzman was called up, his manager, Leo Durocher, said, "Our guy took a step forward—not backward," in contrast with Muhammad Ali (Feldmann, 87).

16. Wendel, 11.

17. Interview with Steve Whitaker, June 2003.

18. *Ibid.*

Chapter 7

1. McLain, 68.

2. McLain, 69.

3. Wendel, 11–12.

4. Wendel, 80.

5. Gilbert et al., 24.

6. Interview with Stan Bregman, December 29, 2008.

7. Baldwin, 257.

8. *The Sporting News*, April 20, 1968.

9. *Ibid.*

10. Flood, 37.

11. Baldwin, 221.

12. *Baseball Digest*, May 1968, 94.

13. Miller, James, 125.

14. Harry Dalton Collection.

15. Edwards, 210.

16. For information on Ashford, see Mark Armour's entry in SABR Bioproject: http://sabr.org/bioproj/person/40af3222.

17. kareemabduljabbar.com.blog/2008/05.

18. www.isreview.org/issues/61/feat-zim.shtml.

19. *The Sporting News*, May 18, 1968.

20. Ironically, when Mexico City was selected to host the games, the city with the second most votes was Detroit.

21. *The Sporting News*, November 9, 1968.

22. Wendel, ix.

23. Edwards, 123.

24. Email from Dave Baldwin, January 13, 2016.

25. Baldwin, 158.

26. Flood, 28–9.

27. Interview with Jim Gosger, January 10, 2009.

28. Wendel, 109–110.

29. *The Sporting News*, June 22, 1968.

30. *Baltimore Sun*, November 28, 1999.

31. Pappas's personal life was also controversial. In his autobiography, he admitted to many incidents of infidelity, including an escapade that involved a Playboy bunny. His wife Carol became an alcoholic, possibly, Pappas admitted, because of his tendency to wander from the marital fold. In 1982, Mrs. Pappas disappeared while returning from running errands. Five years later, she was found at the bottom of a pond. It was presumed that she was drinking, became disoriented, and took a very wrong turn.

32. *The Sporting News*, June 22, 1968.

33. Wendel, 46.

34. *The Sporting News*, June 22, 1968.

35. *Ibid.*

36. *Ibid.*

37. *Ibid.*

38. *Ibid.*

39. *Ibid.*

40. *Ibid.*

41. *The Sporting News*, June 29, 1968.

42. *Ibid.*

43. *Ibid.*

44. *Ibid.*

45. Pappas had also alienated Reds management by lodging a protest that the club had violated the Basic Agreement by failing to provide first class seats for players on team flights.

Chapter 8

1. *The Sporting News*, March 9, 1960.

2. *New York Times*, February 8, 1966.

3. *New York Daily News*, March 3, 1960.

4. *New York Times*, July 12, 1962.

5. *The Sporting News*, September 12, 1956.

6. Bavasi played a joke on pitcher Johnny Podres, who'd earned $20,000 for the 1959 World Champions, by sending him a 1960 contract for $12,500. Podres eventually signed for $25,000.

7. Drysdale, 140.

8. *New York Times*, April 1, 1966.

9. *Sports Illustrated*, April 4, 1966.

10. Interview with Joe Grzenda, December 19, 2002.

11. Interview with Bob Taylor, December 3, 2003.

12. Interview with John DeMerit, November 21, 2000.

13. Interview with Bob Taylor, December 3, 2003.

14. Ironically, while Drysdale was making a landmark stand for labor, his Van Nuys restaurant was being picketed by members of the Hotel, Motel and Restaurant Employees' Union.

15. Drysdale, 127.

16. *New York Times*, March 27, 1966.

17. *New York Times*, March 24, 1966.

18. Drysdale, 130.

19. *New York Times*, March 8, 1969.

20. Interview with Bob Friend, May 28, 2002.

21. *The Sporting News*, August 9, 1961.

22. Interview with Billy Cowan, June 16, 2003.

23. Interview with Clem Labine, August 10, 2000.

24. Interview with Ed Bressoud, June 1, 2002.

25. Interview with Herb Moford, October 30, 2000.

26. Interview with Don Bosch, January 14, 2003.

27. *The Sporting News*, March 16, 1960.

28. *The Sporting News*, December 2, 1959.

29. Interview with Danny McDevitt, January 3, 2001.

30. *The Sporting News*, January 8, 1966.
31. *Ibid.*
32. Quoted in *New York Times*, February 9, 1969.
33. *The Sporting News*, May 17, 1969.
34. *The Sporting News*, June 3, 1959.
35. It is interesting to note that, while newspaper workers frequently went on strike, the press was adamantly against the unionization of the players.
36. *New York Times*, February 5, 1966.

Chapter 9

1. *The Sporting News*, April 27, 1968.
2. *The Sporting News*, April 13, 1968.
3. Dark was not the first Giant manager to disparage minority players. Bill Rigney, who managed the club from 1956 through 1960, joked that pitcher Sam Jones was "the only one of them who really wants to play" (*Newsday*, March 15, 1960).
4. Flood, 86.
5. Flood, 90. Ironically, considering his later challenge of the reserve clause, Flood received the 1966 J.G. Taylor Spink Award as the St. Louis Baseball Man of the Year in 1966.
6. *Los Angeles Examiner*, August 30, 1967.
7. *Pittsburgh Press*, March 9, 1961.
8. Unidentified article in Cepeda file at Giamatti Research Center.
9. The two incidents involving Hoerner are recounted in Feldmann, 123–24 and 152–53.
10. In 1965, Attorney Marvin Lewis sued Cepeda for legal fees incurred in the *Look* suit.
11. Maris had a chance to end his career in a blaze of glory. In Game Five of the 1968 Series, he pinch hit in the top of the ninth inning with the Cardinals holding a 3–1 lead in games but trailing 5–3 with two outs and two men on base. A home run would have given them a lead that, if they held in the ninth, would have won the Series, Unfortunately, Maris struck out.
12. *The Sporting News*, March 16, 1968.
13. *The Sporting News*, January 27, 1968.
14. Flood, 97.
15. *The Sporting News*, January 27, 1968.
16. *Baseball Digest*, August 1968, 29.
17. *The Sporting News*, April 20, 1968.
18. In 1969, when the Reds acquired Leon Wagner, who really *was* funny, Lawson had a field day. "Daddy Wags Keeps Reds in Stitches" was the headline over an article that included the observation "He has been in camp only a couple of days and he already has Red manager Dave Bristol splitting his sides with laughter" (*Post and Times Star*, March 3, 1969).
19. *The Sporting News*, May 6, 1969.
20. *The Sporting News*, May 25, 1968.
21. The American League Comeback Player of the Year was Ken Harrelson, who was as voluble as Johnson was reticent.
22. A 1966 scouting report by Harry Craft said of Stargell, later a lumbering first baseman of massive proportions, "runs real good."
23. In 1966, Clendenon hit 28 home runs, 25 of which came on the road.
24. *The Sporting News*, May 18, 1968.
25. *The Sporting News*, January 13, 1968.
26. *The Sporting News*, June 15, 1968.
27. *The Sporting News*, July 6, 1968.
28. *The Sporting News*, June 29, 1968.
29. *The Sporting News*, October 19, 1968.
30. Interim manager George Myatt won his only game.
31. Davis's nickname was a take-off on a song named "Land of a Thousand Dances" that was released in 1965.
32. *The Sporting News*, May 10, 1968.
33. "If Roger Maris or Mickey Mantle hit 10 or 12 home runs in Chavez Ravine this season [1962]," said Angel outfielder Leon Wagner, whose team shared the stadium with the Dodgers, "I'm going to say they are greater than Babe Ruth. I'm telling you, man, it's terrible here on the hitters" (*Los Angeles Times*, May 10, 1962).
34. The start was Dahl's only major league appearance, and he was killed in 1965 at the age of 19 in an automobile crash while playing in the minor leagues.
35. *The Sporting News*, June 22,1968.
36. *The Sporting News*, June 29, 1968.

Chapter 10

1. Undated article in McLain file at the Giamatti Research Center.
2. *The Sporting News*, August 10, 1968.
3. McLain, 92.
4. Freehan reached first 24 times after being hit by a pitch, the highest total in the American League since 1911.

5. *The Sporting News,* January 27, 1968.
6. *The Sporting News,* March 2,1968.
7. *Washington Star,* February 20, 1968.
8. *The News American,* July 18, 1968.
9. *Baltimore Evening Sun,* July 11, 1968.
10. *Sports Collectors' Digest,* August 9, 1996.
11. *Baltimore Sun,* March 10, 1996.
12. Dalton denied that he asked Bauer to resign.
13. *Baltimore Sun,* July 12, 1968.
14. Miller, James, 130.
15. *Baltimore Sun,* July 15, 1968.
16. *Baltimore Sun,* March 10, 1996.
17. *Baseball Digest,* June 1968, 30.
18. Interview with Jim Gosger, January 10, 2009.
19. *The Sporting News,* May 18, 1968.
20. *The Sporting News,* May 25, 1968.
21. Strangely, in December 1966 Culp and Ellsworth had been traded for each other.
22. *The Sporting News,* January 13, 1968.
23. *The Sporting News,* March 30, 1968.
24. *Sports Illustrated,* July 15, 1968.
25. *Ibid.*
26. *Sports Illustrated,* April 29, 1968.
27. *The Sporting News,* August 17, 1968.
28. *The Sporting News,* May 4, 1968.
29. Interview with Jim Gosger, January 10, 2009.
30. *The Sporting News,* July 20, 1968.
31. *Ibid.*
32. *The Sporting News,* April 20, 1968.
33. *The Sporting News,* February 17, 1968.
34. *The Sporting News,* June 15, 1968.
35. *Baseball Digest,* April, 1968, 22.
36. *The Sporting News,* October 19, 1968.
37. *The Sporting News,* January 18, 1969.
38. *The Sporting News,* January 11, 1969.
39. Interview with Jim Gosger, January 10, 2009.
40. *The Sporting News,* May 4, 1968.
41. *The Sporting News,* October 5, 1968.
42. *Sports Illustrated,* August 19, 1968.
43. Wendel, 198.

Chapter 11

1. Kuhn, 55.
2. Michelson, 138–9.
3. *The Sporting News,* June 8, 1968.
4. *The Sporting News,* June 15, 1968.
5. *The Sporting News,* June 8, 1968.
6. *New York Times,* June 2, 1968.
7. *Ibid.*
8. http://www.baseball-fever.com/show thread.php?36615-Go-Go-You-Pilots!.
9. *The Sporting News,* January 27, 1968.
10. *Ibid.*
11. Interview with Bob Wirz, February 4, 2009.
12. *Ibid.*
13. *Ibid.*
14. *Kansas City Star,* August 2, 2014.
15. *Ibid.*
16. *Ibid.*
17. *Ibid.*
18. Interview with Bob Wirz, February 4, 2009.
19. *Kansas City Star,* August 2, 2014.
20. *Sports Illustrated,* July 1, 1968.
21. A brief biography of Drapeau can be found in http://www.thecanadiancyclope dia.ca/en/article/jean-drapeau/.
22. *New York Times,* August 14, 1999.
23. *Sports Illustrated,* August 12, 1968.
24. A good portrait of Charles Bronfman can be found at http://www.thecanadiancy clopedia.ca/en/article/charles-bronfman/.
25. *The Sporting News,* July 13, 1968.
26. *The Sporting News,* June 10, 1968.
27. *The Sporting News,* July 1, 1968.
28. *Sports Illustrated,* July 1, 1968.
29. Unsurprisingly, not a single Montreal draftee made it to the majors.
30. *The Sporting News,* June 22, 1968.
31. *Ibid.*
32. *The Sporting News,* August 3, 1968.
33. *The Sporting News,* July 20, 1968.
34. *Sports Illustrated,* July 1, 1968.
35. *The Sporting News,* August 31, 1968.
36. *The Sporting News,* August 24, 1968.
37. *The Sporting News,* August 31, 1968.
38. *Ibid.*
39. *The Sporting News,* January 25, 1969.
40. *The Sporting News,* February 15, 1969.
41. *The Sporting News,* March 1, 1969.
42. *The Sporting News,* March 15, 1969.
43. *The Sporting News,* April 12, 1969.
44. *The Sporting News,* May 3, 1969.
45. *The Sporting News,* April 26, 1969.
46. *The Sporting News,* May 3, 1969.

Chapter 12

1. Edwards, 261.
2. Bouton, 70–84.

3. Bouton, 138.

4. Bouton paraphrased Miller, and ridiculed Kuhn, whose comments he recounted as, "grumble, grumble, grumble."

5. Interview with Jim Gosger, January 10, 2009.

6. Bouton, 93.

7. *The Sporting News*, March 23, 1960.

8. Bouton, 89. This was the era before liberals had become enamored of the working class.

9. The publicity from the book enabled Bouton to land a job as an ABC sportscaster. He had difficulty covering the Yankees, who he said had instructed their players not to talk to him. The only two players who agreed to be interviewed were pitchers Mike McCormick and Mike Kekich, whom Bouton described as "Fritz Peterson's roommate."

10. Interview with Bud Daley, September, 2001.

11. *Hartford Courant*, May 12, 1968.

12. *Ibid.*

13. *New York Times*, March 2, 1969.

14. *New York Times*, March 3, 1969.

15. Interview with Tex Clevenger, October 2, 2001.

16. Interview with Tom Tresh, June 17, 2003.

17. Interview with Larry Miller, September 28, 2002.

18. Interview with Tom Tresh, June 17, 2003.

19. Interview with Doc Edwards, January 4, 2002.

20. Interview with J.C. Martin, February 18, 2003.

21. Interview with Johnny James, January 24, 2001.

22. Interview with Archie Moore, July 29, 2002.

23. Interview with Tom Shopay, August 5, 2003.

24. Interview with Len Boehmer, February 9, 2004.

25. Interview with Jake Gibbs, November 18, 2003.

26. Interview with Hal Stowe, May 14, 2002.

27. Interview with Len Boehmer, February 9, 2004.

28. Interview with Billy Cowan, June 16, 2003.

29. Interview with Tom Shopay, August 5, 2003.

30. Conigliaro biography in the SABR Bioproject by Bill Nowlin, http://sabr.org/bioproj/person/52ad9113.

31. The scene in which Conigliaro was hit is described in Cataneo, 105–113.

32. *Washington Star*, February 22, 1968.

33. *Ibid.*

34. *The Sporting News*, March 16, 1968.

35. *The Sporting News*, December 14, 1968.

36. *The Sporting News*, January 4, 1969.

37. *The Sporting News*, March 22, 1969.

38. *The Sporting News*, March 29, 1969.

39. Palmer biography in the SABR Bioproject by Mark Armour, http://sabr.org/bioproj/person/3c239cfa.

40. Eisenberg, 199.

41. *Sports Illustrated*, April 14, 1969.

42. *The Sporting News*, October 19, 1968.

43. *The Sporting News*, November 23, 1968.

44. *The Sporting News*, January 18, 1969.

45. *The Sporting News*, January 18, 1969.

46. In 1971, about the same time he signed Curt Flood, Short indicated he might have an interest in Jim Bouton, then out of baseball, although Bouton did not think Short was serious (Bouton, 230).

47. Interview with Stan Bregman, December 29, 2008. Although Short declined to make Howard major league baseball's first African-American manager, he signed veteran black catcher John Roseboro in 1970 and told him he was an insurance policy in case Williams decided he didn't want to manage anymore (Rosengren, 160–1).

48. *New York Times*, April 20, 1960.

49. Interview with Stan Bregman, December 29, 2008.

50. *Sports Illustrated*, June 10, 17, and 24, 1968.

51. *Sports Illustrated*, March 17, 1969.

52. Interview with Stan Bregman, December 29, 2008.

53. Since Short and Williams were the same age, Williams was clearly not a very discerning flatteree.

54. *Sports Illustrated*, February 24, 1969.

55. *The Sporting News*, March 15, 1969.

56. Interview with Stan Bregman, December 29, 2008.

57. Email from Dave Baldwin, January 13, 2016.

58. Interview with Jim Gosger, January 10, 2009.

59. *The Sporting News*, July 31, 1971.

Chapter 13

1. Cannon's father represented Black Sox Joe Jackson, Happy Felsch, and Swede Risberg when they sued the Chicago White Sox for back salaries following the scandal.

2. Miller, 6.

3. Miller, 6–7.

4. Miller, James, 142.

5. *The Sporting News*, February 15, 1969.

6. Interview with Larry Miller, September 24, 2002.

7. Interview with Bob Friend, May 28, 2002.

8. Robin Roberts suggested that Miller shave his mustache, since ballplayers didn't wear them, and being clean-shaven would help him appeal to the players (Miller, 40–41).

9. *The Sporting News*, May 28, 1966.

10. Quoted in Korr, 14.

11. Korr, 14.

12. Korr, 37.

13. Robin Roberts submitted the initial list of candidates to Commissioner Eckert for screening, with the comment, "If there is anyone on the list you think we should not choose because he might be bad for the game, then he won't be chosen" (Korr, 34). As he did so many times during his tenure, Eckert let this golden opportunity slip from his grasp.

14. *The Sporting News*, March 26, 1966.

15. Miller, 52.

16. Interview with Tracy Stallard, September 27, 2002.

17. Miller, 143.

18. Miller, 3–4.

19. Miller, 9. Months later, Roberts urged Miller to consider Nixon again, saying he was still interested in the job. Miller agreed to meet the former Vice President, and the two men had a rambling, inconclusive conversation during which the job of counsel was not discussed.

20. *The Sporting News*, March 6, 1966.

21. Korr, 35.

22. Walter O'Malley told Miller he was glad to hear from labor leader David McDonald that Miller was not a socialist (Miller, 75).

23. *New York Times*, June 6, 1966.

24. *New York Times*, June 7, 1966.

25. *The Sporting News*, December 16, 1967.

26. *The Sporting News*, May 24, 1969.

27. *The Sporting News*, January 18, 1969.

28. *New York Times*, December 15, 1968.

29. Some players, including Hall of Famer Bob Feller, thought that since the commissioner theoretically represented all of baseball's constituencies, the players should have a role in selecting him.

30. *The Sporting News*, January 4, 1969.

31. Article I, Section 6 of the agreement stated that if the owners couldn't agree on a new commissioner, either league had the right to petition the President of the United States to appoint a man to the position.

32. "Happy was a very good commissioner," said long time executive Gabe Paul, "but he talked a lot" (Holtzman, 44).

33. Unidentified clipping of September 22, 1951, in the Frick file at the Giamatti Research Center.

34. *Milwaukee Journal*, July 9, 1962.

35. Veeck, 89.

36. Holtzman, 98.

37. Veeck, 326.

38. *The Sporting News*, February 21, 1970.

39. While visiting the Phillies camp during his first spring in office, Kuhn asked if anyone had questions. Someone said he'd heard Kuhn was quite a fan and asked if he knew what team Phillies coach Billy DeMars had played for. Without hesitating, Kuhn delivered the correct answer—the St. Louis Browns, for whom DeMars played all of 80 games.

40. *New York Times*, February 6, 1969.

41. *The Sporting News*, February 15, 1969.

42. *The Sporting News*, January 25, 1969.

43. *The Sporting News*, March 1, 1969.

44. Miller, 166.

45. *The Sporting News*, February 15, 1969.

46. Miller, James p, 148.

47. *The New York Times*, February 5, 1969.

48. Interview with Ron Taylor, June 11, 2004.

49. Interview with Don Nottebart, March 2, 2004.

50. Miller, James, 147.

51. Miller claimed Munson was unaware of the strike, and the Yankee catcher later became a strong supporter of the union.

52. *New York Times*, February 18, 1969.

53. *New York Times*, February 21, 1969.
54. *New York Times*, February 20, 1969.
55. *New York Times*, February 25, 1969.
56. *New York Times*, February 24, 1969.
57. *New York Times*, February 25, 1969.
58. *New York Times*, February 23, 1969.
59. $6.5 million per Miller's account.

Epilogue

1. There were 160 home runs in Montreal and 167 in Seattle.
2. Interview with Bob Wirz, February 4, 2009.
3. *Ibid.*
4. Kuhn, 3.
5. Interview with Bob Wirz, February 4, 2009.
6. One person who wasn't intimidated by Kuhn's persona was irrepressible pitcher Moe Drabowsky, who gave Kuhn a hotfoot (an old baseball gag that involved lighting someone's shoelaces on fire) following the 1970 World Series (Adelman, 36).
7. Interview with Bob Wirz, February 4, 2009.
8. Kuhn, 12.
9. Miller, 279.
10. Miller, 85.
11. Miller, 91.
12. Miller didn't have many good things to say about the owners, either. "For one thing," he wrote, "they weren't very bright, and the people they selected to carry on baseball's operations were, with a rare exception or two, not all that bright, either" (Miller, 91).
13. Miller, 111.
14. Miller, 130.
15. Holtzman, 4.

Bibliography

Periodicals

Baseball Digest
NINE
Saturday Evening Post
Sports Collectors Digest

Sports Illustrated
The Sporting News
Time Magazine

Newspapers

Baltimore Sun
Chicago Tribune
Hartford Courant
Los Angeles Examiner
Los Angeles Times
Milwaukee Journal
New York Daily News

New York Newsday
New York Times
The News American
Pittsburgh Press
The Post and Times-Star (Cincinnati)
Sarasota Herald-Tribune
Washington Star

Books

Adelman, Tom. *Black and Blue, Sandy Koufax, the Robinson Boys and the World Series.* New York: Little, Brown, 2006.

Allen, Maury, with Bo Belinsky. *Bo—Pitching and Wooing.* New York: Dial Press, 1973.

Angell, Roger. *The Summer Game.* New York: Viking, 1972.

Baldwin, Dave. *Snake Jazz.* Bloomington, IN: Xlibris, 2007.

Bouton, Jim. *Ball Four.* New York: World Publishing, 1970.

_____. *I'm Glad You Didn't Take It Personally.* New York: Dell, 1971.

Brosnan, Jim. *The Long Season.* New York: Harper & Row, 1975.

_____. *Pennant Race.* New York: Harper & Row, 1962.

Cataneo, David. *Tony C: The Triumph and Tragedy of Tony Conigliaro.* Nashville: Rutledge Hill, 1997.

Clendenon, Donn. *Miracle in New York.* Sioux Falls, SD: Penmarch, 1999.

D'Antonio, Michael. *Forever Blue: The True Story of Walter O'Malley, Baseball's Most Controversial Owner and the Dodgers of Brooklyn and Los Angeles.* New York: Riverhead Books, 2009.

Drysdale, Don, with Bob Verdi. *Once a Bum, Always a Dodger.* New York: St. Martin's Press, 1990.

Edwards, Harry. *Sociology of Sport*. Homewood, IL: Dorsey Press, 1973.

Eisenberg, John. *From 33rd Street to Camden Yards: An Oral History of the Baltimore Orioles*. New York: Contemporary, 2001.

Feldmann, Doug. *El Birdos: The 1967 and 1968 St. Louis Cardinals*. Jefferson, NC: McFarland, 2007.

Flood, Curt, with Richard Carter. *The Way It Is*. New York: Trident, 1970.

Gilbert, Ben, and the Staff of the *Washington Post*. *Ten Blocks from the White House: Anatomy of the Washington Riots of 1968*. New York: Praeger, 1968.

Harrelson, Ken, with Al Hirshberg. *Hawk*. New York: Viking, 1969.

Holtzman, Jerome. *The Commissioners: Baseball's Midlife Crisis*. New York: Total Sports, 1998.

Korr, Charles P. "From Judge Cannon to Marvin Miller: From Players' Group to Players' Union." In *Diamond Mines: Baseball and Labor*, edited by Paul D. Staudohar, 1–20. Syracuse, NY: Syracuse University Press, 2000.

Kuhn, Bowie. *Hardball: The Education of a Baseball Commissioner*. New York: Times Books, 1987.

Lowenfish, Lee. *The Imperfect Diamond: A History of Baseball's Labor Wars*. Lincoln: University of Nebraska Press, 2010.

Maraniss, David. *Clemente: The Passion and Grace of Baseball's Last Hero*. New York: Simon & Schuster, 2006.

McLain, Denny, with Eli Zaret. *I Told You I Wasn't Perfect*. Chicago: Triumph, 2007.

Michelson, Herbert. *Charley O: Charles Oscar Finley vs. the Baseball Establishment*. Indianapolis: Bobbs-Merrill, 1975.

Miller, James Edward. *The Baseball Business: Pursuing Pennants and Profits in Baltimore*. Chapel Hill: University of North Carolina Press, 1990.

Miller, Marvin. *A Whole Different Ball Game: The Sport and Business of Baseball*. New York: Birch Lane Press, 1991.

Piersall, Jimmy, with Richard Whittingham. *The Truth Hurts*. Chicago: Contemporary, 1984.

Ray, Edgar W. *The Grand Huckster: Houston's Judge Roy Hofheinz, Genius of the Astrodome*. Memphis: Memphis State University Press, 1980.

Rosengren, John. *The Fight of Their Lives*. Guilford, CT: Lyons Press, 2014.

Ryczek, William J. *The Yankees in the Early '60s*. Jefferson, NC: McFarland, 2008.

Veeck, Bill, with Ed Linn. *The Hustler's Handbook*. New York: G.P. Putnam's Sons, 1965.

Wendel, Tim. *Summer of '68: The Season That Changed Baseball, and America, Forever*. Boston: Da Capo Press, 2012.

Archival Materials

Harry Dalton Collection, Giamatti Resaerch Center, National Baseball Hall of Fame, Cooperstown, New York.

Player Files, Giamatti Research Center, National Baseball Hall of Fame

Orlando Cepeda

William Eckert

Ford Frick

Denny McLain

Leon Wagner

Interviews

Dave Baldwin

Rich Beck

Len Boehmer

Don Bosch

Stan Bregman
Ed Bressoud
Bill Bryan
Don Cardwell
Tex Clevenger
Billy Cowan
Bud Daley
Bill Denehy
Doc Edwards
John Ellis
Bob Friend
Jake Gibbs
Jim Gosger
Joe Grzenda
Johnny James

Clem Labine
J.C. Martin
Danny McDevitt
Larry Miller
Herb Moford
Archie Moore
Don Nottebart
Tom Shopay
Tracy Stallard
Hal Stowe
Bob Taylor
Ron Taylor
Tom Tresh
Steve Whitaker
Bob Wirz

Websites

Baseball-Reference.com
kareemabduljabbar.com.blog
retrosheet.org
sabr.org/bioproject

http://www.thedeadballera.com
www.isreview.org
www.baseballprospectus.com

Index